Contemporary Indian Drama in English

Contemporary Indian Drama in English

Trends and Issues

Edited by

Jaydip Sarkar

2013

Delta Book World

New Delhi - 110 002

First Published in 2013
ISBN 978-81-926244-0-2

Published by

Delta Book World
G-4, Prahlad House
4832/24, Ansari Road
New Delhi - 110 002 (India)

Tel.: 011-2328 8140, 2324 5799 * Fax: 011-2328 8140
E-mail: deltabookworld@gmail.com * kaveribooks@gmail.com
Website: www.kaveribooks.com

PRINTED IN INDIA

Preface

With a tradition almost as old as the colonial contact, Indian Drama in English has always maintained an uneasy relationship with the very root of the Indian tradition of folk and the classical dramatic literature in the vernaculars that is thousands of years old. Though the body has the thinnest generic build up inside the astounding output of Indian Writing in English today, it has generated the most contemplative issues and debates of contemporary relevance, if compared to fiction and poetry.

The collection of scholarly studies included in the present volume explores the contemporary Indian playwrights in English, to arrive at diverse revealing insights for the purpose of the undergraduate and postgraduate students as well as research scholars of English literature. Moreover, it will also be a pleasure reading to not only the academicians but all those who take interest in literature and criticism.

I express my thanks to all the contributors who readily responded to my request by contributing critical papers for the book. I also record my sincere gratitude to Mr. Anindya Bhattacharya and Mr. Shirshendu Mondal of University BT and

Evening College, and Mr. Rakesh Goel of Delta Book World for all their assistance in ensuring the successful completion of this project.

Jaydip Sarkar

Contents

1 Indian Drama in English: An Overview from Historical & Socio-political Perspectives

Jaydip Sarkar

India has the longest and the richest tradition of Drama. Its origin can be traced back to the Vedic Period, and as a manifestation of our national sensibility, it came into existence as such a means of exploring and communicating the Truth that it was popularly named as the "fifth Veda". Bharata's *Natyashastra* in Sanskrit is the most pioneering work on ancient Indian dance and drama. It is a detailed treatise that deals with all aspects of the classical Indian concept of drama including dance, music, poetics and general aesthetics. Bharta describes drama as mimicry of the actions and conduct of the people that uses the eight basic emotions of love, joy, anger, sadness, pride, fear, aversion and wonder:

> The combination called *Natya* is a mixture of rasa, bhavas, abhinayas, dharmics, vrittis, provrittis, siddhis, avaras, instruments, song and theatre-house. (Gupt 86)

According to legend when the world passed from golden age to silver age, people started getting addicted to sensual pleasure, and at that moment, Lord Indra requested God Brahma:

> Please give us something which would not only teach us but be pleasing both to eyes and ears. (Rangacharya1)

And it was God Brahma who gave the pious idea of *Natya Veda*. He combined the essence of *Natya Veda* out of the four Vedas: dance from the *Rig Veda*, song from the *Sama Veda*, mimicry from *Yajur Veda* and passion from *Athar Veda*. Vishwakarma was the celestial architect who built a stage in Indian heaven and Bharata was the actual manager.

Sanskrit drama flourished in its glory till the fifteenth century but thereafter Indian drama almost came to an end due to certain invasion on India, and it is only after the British came in India, the crippled Indian drama regained its strength. The western impact really awakened "the dormant, critical impulse in the country to bring Indians face to face with new forms of life and literature, and to open the way for a fruitful cross fertilization of ideas and forms of expression." (Iyengar 4)

Krishna Mohan Banerjee's *The Persecuted* in 1837, was the first play written by an Indian in English. It was less a play and more a dramatized debate of the conflict between orthodox Hindu customs and the new ideas introduced by Western education. The real journey of Indian English Drama begins with Michael Madhusudan Dutt's *Is This Called Civilization* which appeared in 1871.

Rabindranath Tagore and Sri Aurobindo, the two great sage-poets of India, are the first notable Indian dramatists in English. Tagore's experience in theatre began at age sixteen, when he played the leading role in his brother Jyotirindranath's adaptation of Molière's *Le Bourgeois Gentilhomme*. At age twenty, he wrote his first drama-opera– *Valmiki Pratibha* (*The Genius of Valmiki*) –which describes how the bandit Valmiki reforms his ethos, is blessed by Saraswati, and composes the *Râmâyana*. Through it, Tagore vigorously explores a wide range of dramatic styles and emotions, including usage of revamped *kirtans* and adaptation of traditional English and Irish folk melodies as drinking songs. Another notable play, *Dak Ghar* (*The Post Office*), describes how a child – striving to escape his stuffy confines – ultimately "fall[s] asleep" (which suggests his physical death). A story with worldwide appeal (it received rave reviews in Europe), *Dak Ghar* dealt with death as, in Tagore's words, "spiritual freedom" from "the world of hoarded wealth and certified creeds". His other works – emphasi zing fusion of lyrical flow and emotional rhythm tightly focused on a core idea were unlike previous Bengali dramas. His works sought to articulate, in Tagore's words, "the play of feeling and not of action". In 1890 he wrote *Visarjan* (*Sacrifice*), regarded as his finest drama. The Bengali-language originals included intricate subplots and extended monologues. Later, his dramas probed more philosophical and allegorical themes; one such play is Tagore's *Chandalika* (*Untouchable Girl*), which was modeled on an ancient Buddhist legend describing how Ananda – the Gautama Buddha's disciple–asks water of an Adivasi (untouchable) girl. Tagore's other plays include *Chitrangada*, *Raja*, and *Mayar Khela*.

Red Oleanders (*Raktakarabi*) is one of the more than sixty plays, dance dramas and dramatic sketches by Asia's first Nobel Laureate Rabindranath Tagore. The play, written in 1923-24, was begun during a visit to Shillong, and inspired by the image of a red oleander plant crushed by pieces of discarded iron that Tagore had come across while walking. A short time later, an oleander branch with a single red flower protruded through the debris, as if, he noted, "created from the blood of its cruelly pierced breast." The first English version of the play was done by Tagore himself (with perhaps some assistance from Kshitish Chandra Sen) and published by Macmillan, London, in 1925. But the reviews that followed were less than enthusiastic with criticism of obscurantism. Tagore argued that the play's theme involving unscrupulous capitalism, environmental exploitation and the importance of human relationships was not an obscure one. "It is not for me to discuss the literary qualities of this book, which being a mere translation, can have no pretension to a permanent place as literature in a language not the author's own," he wrote, "but I think, in justice to myself, I should make it clear that it has a definite meaning which can legitimately claim literary expression"(Chakraborty 7). In 1987, Ananda Lal published a translation of three plays by Tagore, including *Red Oleanders*, which was a welcome addition to making Tagore's works accessible in English.

Sri Aurobindo wrote five complete blank verse plays. Besides his six incomplete plays Sri Aurobindo wrote five complete blank verse plays. His complete plays are *Perseus the Deliverer*, *Vasavadutta*, *Radoguna*, *The Viziers of Bassora* and *Eric* and each of these plays is written in five acts. The notable feature of Sri Aurobindo's plays is that they depict different cultures and countries in different epochs, ringing with variety of characters, moods and sentiments.

Another playwright who has made significant contribution in the growth of Indian English drama is Harindranath Chattopadhay. There are seven verse plays to his credit published under the title of *Poems and Plays* (1927) and all the seven plays are based on the lives of Indian saints. His Five Plays (1929) are written in prose. The next great name is A.S.P. Ayyar who wrote six plays. *In the Clutch of the Devil* (1926) is his first play and the last one is *The Trial of Science for the Murder of Humanity*. P. A. Krishnaswamy is also a name in the history of Indian English drama whose fame rests chiefly on his unusual verse play *The Flute of Krishna*. Another dramatic voice on the Indian literary scene that demands attention is that of T.P. Kailasam. He wrote both in English and Kannada. Though Kailasam is regarded as the father of modern Kannada drama, his genius finds its full expression in his English plays such as *The Burden* (1933), *Fulfilment* (1933), *The Purpose* (1944), *Karna* (1964) and *Keechaka* (1949). Bharati Sarabhai is the modern woman playwright during the colonial era of Indian English drama. She has written two plays *The Well of the People* (1943) and *Two Women* with some considerable measure of success. Of these two plays, the former is symbolic, poetic and is besides a significant contribution to the Gandhian social order, while the letter is realistic, written in prose and probes the private world of a sensitive individual. J.M. Lobo Prabhu is the last great name in pre-Independence Indian English drama. He has written over a dozen plays but only *Mother of New India: A Play of India Village in three Acts* (1944) and *Death Abdicates* (1945) appear before Independence.

Playwrights writing during the 1960s, with more success than the earlier ones, the primary reason being that they were writing plays to be acted, were Nissim Ezekiel with his *Nalini* and *Sleepwalkers;* Gieve Patel with his *Princes* and *Savaksa;* and Pratap Sharma with his *A Touch of Brightness* and *The Professor has a Warcry.* It was at the end of this decade, in 1968, that the Theatre Group, Bombay, announced the award of the Sultan Padamsee Award for Indian plays in English. This award was won by Gurcharan Das's *Larins Sahib* and this group produced it in Bombay in 1969. Gieve Patel's *Princes* and Dina Mehta's *Myth-makers* also competed for this award. Cyrus Mistry's *Doongaji House* won the second Sultan Padamsee award, in 1978. This play dealt with the declining fortunes of a Parsi family living in the Parsi heartland – Bombay. Dina Mehta is also an award-winning playwright – her play *Brides Are Not for Burning* won an international award from the BBC in 1979.

Contemporary Indian drama, deviating from classical and European models, is experimental and innovative in terms of thematic and technical qualities. It is not an off spring of any specific tradition and it has laid the foundation of a distinctive tradition in the history of world drama by reinvestigating history, legend, myth, religion and folk lore with context to contemporary socio-political issues. Among the major dramatists who have given a distinctive shape to this enormous mass of creative material are Vijay Tendulkar, Girish Karnad, Habib Tanvir, Indira Parthasarathy, Badal Sircar, Asif Currimbhoy, Mahasweta Devi and Mahesh Dattani.

Tendulkar focuses on middle class life in India and show the isolated individual's confrontation with adverse circumstances and hostile surroundings. He strongly believes that ideas are firmly entrenched in our psyche at an early age and'our attitude has a lot to do with what we internalize in our early formative years" (Shoma Choudhary: 65). Tendulakar plays like *Sakharam Binder, Ghashiram Kotwal, Silence! The court is in Session* focus on love, sex, marriage and moral values prevalent in Indian society. He makes ample use of irony, satire, pathos and mock element. Vijay Tendulakar has received many prestigious awards like Kamladevi, Chattopadhaya award, Sangeet Natak Akadmi award, and Kalidas Samman award. He abolished the traditional form of drama of three acts of plays and created new models to bridge the gap between modern and traditional theatre There is now an awareness that the traditional form need to be utilized to revitalize Indian English Theatre. As Girish Karnad rightly points out:

> The past is never totally lost; it coexists with the present as a flow. A rich variety of theatre form still exists, with a continuous history stretching over centuries. (Karnad 11)

This new phase of Indian theatrical development happily coincides with the personal development of Girish Karnad as a dramatist. His contribution goes beyond theatre: he has directed feature films, documentaries, and television serials. He represented India in foregin lands as an emissary of art & culture. He has experimented with the fusion of the traditional and modern dramatic forms and content. The purpose of using traditional forms is to achieve a rare insight into the contemporary reality because Karnad believes that complexities of post colonialism are inherited from that the colonial and precolonial times. Precolonial, colonial and post colonial experiences in literature can not be compartmentalised in true sense. They are not divorced from each other. His play *Tuglaq* was a reflection of the changing times- the narrowing of the great divide between the rulers and ruled. Karnad reminds us of T.P. Kailasam and Rangacharya who go back to myths and legends to show absurdity of modern life with all its elemental passions and man's eternal struggle to achieve perfection. The theatre of Badal Sircar, was once described by Rustom Bharucha "as the most rigorously non commercial political theatre in India". (Bharuch 127)

Badal Sircar depicts the existential attitude of modern man in the present times. Dismayed by the paucity of good Bengali drama, he began writing plays in the 1950s. He soon found he had flair for comedy and for catching the cadence, wit, and everyday speech of middle-class Calcuttans. His early comedies have a flavour unique in Bengali literature. Badal Sircar wrote his first serious play, *Evam Indrajit*, in 1963. Its publication and premiere in 1965 attracted wide notice for its striking originality and themes of absurdist meaninglessness, identity crisis, and social conformity. It is perhaps the one contemporary Bengali drama most translated into other Indian languages.

While working in Nigeria, Sircar authored in quick succession several plays which secured his reputation. Some of the names that can be mentioned are *Baki itihas* or 'Remaining History' in 1965, *Pralap* i.e. 'Delirium' in 1966, *Tringsha shatabdi* i.e. Thirtieth Century' in 1966, and *Pagla ghora* or 'Mad Horse' in 1967. All of these were premiered by Bohurupee, followed by *Shesh nei* i.e. 'There's No End' in 1969. His concern was the pointlessness of existence, compounded by a sense of associative guilt and responsibility in disturbed persons. These persons belong to the urban middle class in a world of increasing violence and inhumanity. Badal Sircar's part in theatre was not confined to playwriting. He grew more interested in production, and formed his group Satabdi in 1967 which led him to conceptualize what he called anganmancha or Third Theatre. At first he directed his earlier plays on proscenium stages. But some changes happened after *Sagina Mahato* in 1970 that he dramatized from Gaurkishor Ghosh's novel and *Abu Hosain*, which was adapted from Girish Ghosh's play. He brought changes in style and new technique germinating his new ideas. He finally abandoned the proscenium and produced the revolutionary 'Spartacus' in 1972 in an almost bare room with spectators sitting all around. His street theatre has shown how an effective theatre is possible without the peripheral necessities like theatre hall rental, advertisements, expensive lights and sounds, sets and props and other paraphernalia. He continued with *Michhil* i.e. Procession, *Bhoma* in 1976, *Basi khabar* i.e. Stale News in 1979 and also many other plays. He has been awarded the Padma Shri in 1972, Sangeet Natak Akademi Award in 1968 and the Sangeet Natak Akademi Fellowship, Ratna Sadsya, in 1997.

Mahasweta Devi (born in1926 in Dacca, now in Bangladesh) is an Indian writer who has dedicated herself for the upliftment of the marginalized. Born into a middle-class Bengali family, Mahasweta Devi earned her M.A. in English at Shantiniketan, a renowned experimental University. In 1964, she began teaching at Bijaygarh College in Jadavpur; an Indian college for working class women, while simultaneously working as a journalist and creative writer. She is noted for her works related to the study of the rural tribal communities of West Bengal, women and dalits. She is also an activist who is dedicated to the struggle of tribal people in Bihar, Madhya Pradesh and Chhattisgarh. In her elaborate Bengali fiction, she often depicts the brutal opression of tribal peoples and the untouchables by potent, authoritarian high-caste landlords, lenders, and venal government officials. She was given the Lila Award, 1978; Saratchandra Memorial Award; Amrita Bazar Award, 1967; Tarasankar Memorial Award, 1977; Bibhuti Bhushan Smriti Samsad Award, 1990; Sahitya Akademi Award, 1979; Jnanpith Award, 1996; Magasaysay Award for literature, 1997. National civilian honours conferred on her are Padma Shri, 1986, Deshikottama, 1999 and Padma Vibhushan, the second highest civilian award from the Government of India in the year

2006.Regarding the source of her inspiration, she writes: "I have always believed that the real history is made by ordinary people. I constantly come across the reappearance, in various forms, of folklore, ballads, myths and legends, carried by ordinary people across generations.... The reason and inspiration for my writing are those people who are exploited and used, and yet do not accept defeat. For me, the endless source of ingredients for writing is in these amazingly, noble, suffering human beings. Why should I look for my raw material elsewhere, once I have started knowing them? Sometimes it seems to me that my writing is really their doing."

Mahasweta Devi's renowned works are Hajar *Churashir Ma (Mother of 1084), Aranyer Adhikar (The Occupation of the Forest), Agnigarbha (Womb of Fire), Choti Munda evam Tar Tir (Choti Munda and His Arrow), Breast-Giver* and many others. Samik Bandyopadhyay has translated five of her plays that include *Mother of 1984, Water, Bayen, Aajir* and *Urvashi and Johnny.*

Recently the country has given us some brilliant playwrights like Manjula Padmanabhan and Mahesh Dattani. Manjula Padmanabhan was the first Indian to earn international fame with her *Harvest*, a futuristic play that deals with the exploitation of human body in 21st century. Padmanabhan projects a dehumanized, tefrrifying world in which mothers sell their sons for the price of rice. But her plays are intellectual and not suited for stage while Dattani is taken to be a true successor of Girish Karnad and responsible for the revolutionary progression of English drama, as a drama teaches, as a stage director, as a sociologist explaining various complexities of society. He emerges as a compelling playwright who projects the postcolonial dichotomy at various levels. He keeps women at the centre of his dramatic world and may be called avant-garde feminist. He was greatly influenced by Tennessee Williams, Arthur Miller and Giyratti playwright Madhurye. At one phase he says:

> The playwright Madhurye influenced me a great deal in his portrayal of middle class Giyrati hypocrisises. (Subramamyam 13-14)

Dattani's play *Tara* gives us a glimpse into the modern society which claims to be liberal andadvanced into thought and action. It speaks about male chauvinism prevalent in the present society and brings about the stark reality of the woman playing second fiddle to man. Homosexuality is the another significant subject matter chosen by Dattani. In 'Bravely fought the Queen' Dattani highlights the absurdity of the situation in which woman is trapped by birth. The questions that haunt Dattani are: (a) Is homosexuality assertion of individuality? (b) Is it guided by some conviction? (c) Does it lead to some meaningful goal (d) What is the utility of marriage to such people (e) Is it quest for some exclusive identity. 'Seven Steps Round the Fire', the most popular day, dwells on the theme of eunuchs, their identity, their constitution and their connotation. In 'Where there is a Will' Dattani Portrays complicated modern urban family where the old patriarchal code finds a formidable foe inthe feminist ideas. His 'Do the Needful' exposes the fact that the institute of marriage today has lost its sanctity and is nothing but a compromise to promote Personal needs. His plays fulfill the Postcolonial condition of writing. His cry of dichotomy is present in most of his plays. He says "Change does not happen overnight, we grow liberal after not because we want to, but have to". (Datta 157)

Dattani quees his success to the fact that he had a theatre company which produced his plays. His theatre group Playpen was formed in 1984. Dattani is Indian's first playwright to be awarded the Sahitya Akadani award. He wants to use theatre as a powerful medium to bring about the social change. He has an array of themes to offer us his plays and issues he chooses to project are the most topical but also the most controversial. A deep study of his plays lead us to an interesting study of stagecraft in Indian theatre using innovations introduced by Mahesh Dattani. The earlier stage was a simple platform erected for the purpose in a palace or temple courtyard to serve as backdrop. The stage setting of Mahesh Dattani is even more complex. There are multilevel sets so that whole interior of the house is visible to the audience. Jhon Mckae, Italian Director says: "Mahesh Dattani is always adventurous in his way of using the theatrical space at his disposal: multiple levels, breaking the bounds of Proscenium, wondrously inventive use of lighting to give height, breadth and depth". (Mckae 45) He feels art of expressing the views through some powerful images, symbols stage direction and other means. But he never tried to preach, his purpose is chiefly aesthetic. According to him:

> Theatre is a reflection of what you observe. To do anything more would be to become didactic and then it ceases to be theatre. (http:// www.anitanarinetpayes/profils-md)

His plays are a refreshing treat for readers as his performances are to his spectators with the innovative theatrical techniques.

But what distresses most is that Indian English Theatre is yet to gain a sizeable number of audience. It is still not able to keep pace with the world of poetry and fiction. KR Srinivas Iyengar is highly depressed at the dismal sight of the birth and progress of Indian Drama in English:

> Modern Indian dramatic writing in English in neither rich in quantity, now on the whole of quality enterprising Indians have for nearly a century occasionally attempted drama in English but seldom for actual production. (Iyengar 226)

As M.K. Naik puts it, A play, in order to communicate fully and become a living dramatic experience, needs a real theatre and a live audience. It is precisely the lack of these essentials that has hamstrung Indian drama in English all along.

Another major reason is that English as a second language is not suitable medium of expression for two Indians doing conversations. The language barrier prevents the lower classes from coming to the Indian English Theatre.

It is only when we accept these two things that we can really have a theatre movement which is completely linked to the development of cultural social and individual identity. Only then we can achieve harmony through the language of theatre which must necessarily be filled with a sense of rootedness revealing a true Indian sensibility.

Bibliography

Bajaj, Yogita and Sangita Mehta, "Emerging Trends in Indian English Drama", *Researchers' World*: Vol. I, Issue I: Oct, 2010.

Bharuch, Rustam, *Rehearsals of Revolution: The Political Theatre of Bengal*, Honolulni: University of Hawai Press, 1993.

Chakraborty, Kaustav, *Indian English Drama*, New Delhi: PHI: 2011.

Choudhary, Shoma and Gita Rajan, ed., *Vijay Tendulkar*, New Delhi: Katha, 2001.

Dutt, Vandana, "The Dramatic Art of Mahesh Dattani", *Journal of Commonwealth Review*, Vol. XIII, No.2.

Gupt, Bharat, *Dramatic concepts: Greek and Indian, A study of poetics and Natyashastr*, New Delhi: D.K. Printworld, 1994.

http:// www.anitanarinetpayes/profils-md.htm.

Iyengar, K.R.S., *Indian Writing in English*, New Delhi: Slerling, 1985.

Karnad, Girish, "Introduction", *Three Plays*, New Delhi: Oxford University Press, 1994.

Kumar, Prema Nand, "*Indian Writing in English: Threechee Indian Literature*, Vol.XIII, No.4, Dec, 1970.

Mckae, John, " *A note on the play" on a Muggy night in Mumbai* in *collected Plays*: Mahesh Dattani ,New Delhi: Penguin India, 2000.

Rangacharya, Adya, *The Natyashastra, Eng. Trans: with critical notes*, New Delhi: Munshiram Manoharlal, 1996.

Sircar, Badal, *Changing Language of Theatre at the present time*, New Delhi: ICCR, 1982.

Subramanyam, Lakshmi (ed), Miffled Voices: *Women in Modern Indian Theatre*, New Delhi: Shakti: 2002.

Venkattareddy, K. and Dhawan, R.K., *Flowering of Indian Drama*, New Delhi: Prestige, 2004.

2

Crusader Against Hegemonies: A Brief Study of Badal Sircar

Pinaki Roy

Attempts to trace the origin of general Indian literature would unanimously begin from Sanskrit drama in prose and verse. As Anjana Dev *et al.* point out, Indian drama began approximately in 1st century B.C. (*Indian Literature* xiii), and like the ancient Greek and Roman plays, predated every other genre of Indian literature. However, during the colonial rule, Indian literary genres gradually changed from being mere mediums of entertainment and instruction to instruments for intellectual opposition to the English rule. The Indian literary scene changed into its reactionary phase especially after the *First Indian War of Independence* in 1857 (*ibid.* xx-xxi), and having had independently developed in the 1850s, Bengali drama became a postcolonial movement from the very period of its inception.

In the second volume of The Encyclopaedia of Indian Literature, Amaresh Datta notes that Bengali theatre, which was soon to project overt or covert anti-imperialistic ideas, emanated out of English drama, and a number of Bengali aristocrats, who collaborated with the English imperialists socially, culturally, and economically, supervised the establishment of theatre-houses especially at their own palatial buildings or garden-houses in and around Kolkata, which was until 1911 the capital of India (1066). Among the theatre-houses founded in mid-19th century Kolkata were Prasannacoomar Tagore's *Hindu Theatre* (1831),

Nabin Chandra Basu's *Theatre* (1835), Kaliprashanna Singha's *Rangamancha* (1856), *Belgachhia Natyashala* (1858), *Pathuriaghata Banganatyalaya* (1865), *Shobha Bazar Private Theatrical Society* (1865), *Jorashanko Natyashala* (1865), and *Bagbazar Amateur Theatre* (1868). Datta dismissively notes that in these 19th-century Bengali theatre houses, "Shakespearean plays or English translations of Sanskrit plays were staged" (*ibid.* 1066). With the productions of Ramnarayan Tarkaratna (1822-86), Michael Madhusudan Dutt (1824-73), and Dinabandhu Mitra (1830-73), Bengali drama developed from being insipid copies of Eurocentric plays into independent critiques of 19th–century Bengali society.

As Michael Madhusudan Dutt gradually translated his own plays – most notably, *Ratnavali* (1858) and *Sermista* (1859) (and one by Mitra) – into English, Bengali theatre began to gain first national and thereafter international recognition and acceptance. Many plays of Rabindranath Tagore (1861-1941) were translated into English too, mostly by the litterateur himself. It was also in late-19th and early-20th century India that Indian English drama developed and matured. Early specimens included C.S.Nazir's *The First Parsi Baronet* (1866), D.M.Wadia's *The Indian Heroine* (1877) (based on the *First Indian War of Independence*), Ramkinoo Dutt's *Manipura Tragedy* (1893), and Krishna Iyer's *Lord Clive* (1913). T.M.J.Indramohan puts much more importance to the post-independence Indo-Anglian plays because they

> "have resuscitated […] [India's] socio-cultural and political dignity from the imperial compression. By and large the plays written after the end of colonialism are committed to champion the nationalist feeling and to inculcate a new vigour in the minds of the people with an awareness of their national pride and cultural values. They do not theorise any particular aspect but articulate the categories of social and psychic identity and their labile new deployments across the ideological spectrum and it is a discipline stands away from the superpower's hold and carve a niche of their own in the history of race, culture and politics"[1].

These, together with the translated versions of Bengali dramas, generated a considerable amount of anticolonial resentment among the the-then audience and readers. Indian Bengali drama – in original or translated versions – became postcolonial in periods of both inception and development. The present essay focuses on the issue of protestation in Indian Bengali plays written by arguably one of Bengal's greater postmodern playwrights, Badal Sircar (1925-2011), many of which have been translated into English by theatre-activists and academicians.

Composed in post-independence India, Sircar's plays are not only identifiably postcolonial in identity but also are discernible critiques of the debilitating divisions of society engineered by the English imperialists. In the 'introduction' to *Postcolonial Drama*, Gilbert and Tompkins trace the functioning of 'performances as anti-imperial tools' and write that postcolonial plays, just like the other antiimperial subgenres, seek to destabilise "the cultural and political authority of imperialism" (1, 3). The post-1947 Bengali plays – in original version and translation – perceptively cater to what Gilbert and Tompkins enlist as the features of typical postcolonial performances – responding to the experience of imperialism, acting performance for the continuation and regeneration of the colonised communities, and interrogation of the hegemony underlying imperial representation (11). Sircar's plays, in their exploration and criticism of Indian society partitioned on Marxist lines, question and demolish the essentialised concepts of the Indians, their customs, and their behavioural patterns in theatres produced by the White Western colonisers.

It might, however, be mentioned here that Dharwadker has interpreted postcolonial theatre studies as "[...] typical[ly] focuss[ing] on modes of textual and cultural resistance that appear after the formal end of colonialism rather than on the challenges to colonial authority during the period of foreign control. Given the theoretical preoccupation with the continuing effects of imperial processes, much of the criticism also concentrates on Europhone (primarily Anglophone) writing and performance rather than on productions in the indigenous language(s) of the former colonies" (*Acts of* 440). Truly, though the post-independence Indian English plays have been much more critically reassessed than the pre-independence dramas, the latter group is definitely more exhaustive and convincing in their portrayal of the decadence and miseries of pre-independence Indian societies than those written after 1947 because the former plays were written by litterateurs who had had lived through the debilitating colonial atmosphere. Sircar's oeuvre, presently widely rendered into English, gains importance because of the fact that the Bengali dramatist has had intently lived through the turbulence of both the pre-independence and post-1947 Indian societies, and his plays are truthful in their presentation of different problems of postcolonial India. They can be treated as sources of alternative power – the power of protestation against imperial dominance and the exploitation of the downtrodden. It may be mentioned that Deshpande has expressed doubt about the effectiveness of the postcoloniality of plays by such dramatists as Sircar, Mohan Rakesh (1925-72), Mahasweta Devi (b. 1926), Kavalam Narayan Panikkar (b. 1928), Vijay Tendulkar (1928-2008), Utpal Dutt (1929-93), Girish Karnad (b. 1938), Surendra Verma (b. 1941), Ranganathan Parthasarathy (b. 1930), and Arun Mukhopadhyay (b. 1937), which he considers are merely the usages "of the post-ideological world looking at the emergence of a political independence in the third world" (*Modern Indian* xiv). In contrast, Paul Poplawski lauds Sircar not only for his postcoloniality but also for ushering postmodernism in Indian drama (198).

Badal Sircar's plays perceptively bridge the points of Gilbert and Tompkin's observations and answer to Dharwadker's criticism. They are originally written in 'indigenous' Bengali and later translated, as mentioned earlier, into English – for example, by Girish Karnad in *Three Modern Indian Plays – Badal Sircar's 'Evam Indrajit'* (New Delhi: Oxford University Press, 1990), Suchandra Sarkar in *'Beyond the Land of Hattamala' and 'Scandal in Fairyland'* (Kolkata: Seagull, 2003), Soumitra Chakroborty in *Forum Three: Badal Sircar's 'The Other Side of History'* (2006), Samik Bandyopadhyay and Kalyani Ghose in *Three Plays: 'Procession', 'Bhoma', and 'Stale News'* (Kolkata: Seagull, 2009), and Subhendu Sarkar in *Two Plays: 'Indian History Made Easy' and 'Life of Bagala'* (New Delhi: Oxford University Press, 2010). N.S.Iyer includes him as one of the three great Indian writers (the others being Karnad and Tendulkar), who have had "contributed immensely to the development of Indian drama in [...] English" (138). In addition, Peter France writes how the New Delhi-based journal *Enact* has increased the readability of Sircar's plays (*The Oxford Guide* 464).

By relentlessly focussing on the commoners and downtrodden, Sircar's plays criticise a class and status-concerned India created by English colonisers, and lambaste the humiliation usually meted out to the financially-underprivileged Indians by the rich. Defining the basic tenets of Marxist criticism, Lois Tyson mentions the theory that all human activities can be explained "in terms of the distribution and dynamics of economic power" (54), and so can be the interaction between Sircar's different characters. If society witnesses a continuous struggle between the financially-privileged *bourgeoisie* and the economically-underdeveloped *proletariat* (*ibid.* 54), Sircar's plays are identifiably Marxist in their outlook because they try to exhibit how the poor and downtrodden are being constantly exploited by the rich and landed bourgeoisie. If Waugh describes the Marxist world as a world of 'class struggle' (*Literary Theory* 143), Sircar's is definitely a Marxist world where the financially-developed people constantly use their privileges to deny even the basic amenities to the impoverished mass. If the "capitalist world order [...] [is] [...] a discourse of lies" (*ibid.* 149), the struggle of Sircar's poor become multifarious – against the physical domination, cultural exploitation, and economic repressions promulgated by the bourgeoisie. Terry Eagleton notes that with the all-round developments in the Western World in the 1970s, Marxist criticism lost its popularity in Europe and North America (195). However, it continues to be relevant in the East – especially Asia and Africa – a region where Sircar's plays on class struggle are set.

For understanding the philosophy of Sircar, which is especially based on class struggle, readers need to refer to the concluding scene of his *Evam Indrajit* ('And Indrajit') (1962) – "a classic of contemporary Indian theatre" according to Deshpande (*ibid.*1). In the scene, the omnipresent 'Writer' urges a fatigued Indrajit to 'be on the road', fully aware that both of them are 'the cursed spirits of Sisyphus' who 'must go on with the pilgrimage' though there is 'no respite' (*ibid.* 249-50). This 'pilgrimage' includes the relentless class struggle for recognition and privileges. The fifty plays the leftist Sircar wrote, produced, or directed especially between the 1960s and 2003 – the year in which he was crippled by a road accident – did not attempt to revolutionise the society, but they revolutionised Indian drama by introducing the concept of the 'Third Theatre' that bridges the usual lacuna between performers and spectators.

Even when fully aware of his limitations in a hopelessly repetitive and conforming society, Sircar continued writing in order to make his audience and readers aware of the existential angst the common humanity is faced with on a daily basis. In fact, all his other critically acclaimed and widely translated plays, including *Sara Rattir* ('All Night', 1963), *Baaki Itihash* ('The Rest of History', 1965), *Paagla Ghoda* ('The Mad Horse', 1967), *Shesh Nei* ('There's No End', 1969), *Ballabhpurer Rupkatha* ('The Fairytale of Ballabhpur', 1972), *Spartacus* (1972), *Michhil* ('Procession', 1974), *Tringshya Shatabdi* ('Thirteenth Century', 1975), *Bhoma* (1976), *Hattamalar Oparey* ('Beyond the Land of Hattamala', 1977), and *Bashi Khabar* ('Stale News', 1979), undertake to question the integrity and aims of governance and exposes the hypocrisies of modern individuals without urging for any escapist or suicidal tendency. Linking the histories of oppressions and class struggles to the daily experiences of middleclass Indians, Sircar seeks to present a common panacea for the numerous maladies afflicting modern individuals. More often than not, he fails to locate the object of his quest – the definite procedure for ending the existential angst; but, similar to Sisyphus, he resumes his quest immediately. About *Evam Indrajit*, Amshan Kumar writes,

> "When Sircar all of a sudden turned away from mocking fun at the feudal ills to depiction of melancholic introspection in *Evam Indrajit*, he was feted by the class of audience owing allegiance to existentialism and philosophy of absurd. Leftist critics swiftly panned him for the projection of hopelessness in the play".[2]

In fact, Sircar first attracted attention as a light-veined playwright with a serious message with his *Evam Indrajit*, which was conceived in England, written in Nigeria, and published in 1965. The global responses to his most efficient existential theatre have had always been in superlatives. Cody and Sprinchorn write,

> "[...] [T]he play is about an ordinary man, Indrajit, who is about to become a commonplace man, a man with a name that rhymes with the Bengali equivalent of Tom, Dick, and Harry – Amal, Vimal, and Kamal. Indrajit can surrender to the routine of middle-class existence and become Nirmal. Instead, the Writer points Indrajit to the never-ending road that all human beings traverse, where the process of walking is the only product. [...] [*Evam Indrajit*] [...] shows the middleclass educated individual not as a vanguard of proletarian revolution but rather as a puerile entity trapped concentrically in its own spiralling drive for material gain and success. In doing this, Sircar found a way of dramatising the crisis of the middle-class Indian, as well as the crisis of humanity at large" (*The Columbia* 387).

Sitanshi Talati-Parikh applauds the way *Evam Indrajit* "moves back and forth in time, with a blending of stream of consciousness" and its exploration "of the concept of a play-within-a-play" (*Western Drama* 163).

Undergraduate Indian students majoring in English are almost always required to study *Evam Indrajit* as part of their curriculum. For them, the following observation by Natesan Sharda Iyer would almost certainly be helpful:

> "[*Evam Indrajit*] [...] is actually a theatrically effective and crystallised projection of all the prevalent attitudes, vogue and feelings and undefined frustrations gnawing at the heart of the educated urban middle class. In a way, *Evam Indrajit* is about the residue that consists of those 'who have failed to adjust and align and ceases to aspire and also those who are enmeshed in the day-to-day struggle for survival'. They revolt against the well-defined old religion and traditional values of life. They are doomed to live alone and suffer from existential loneliness. *Evam Indrajit* confronts the reader and its critics with a concrete pattern of poetic images that demonstrate literature about literature, play about the birth and development of a play, and thus demanding creative efforts of interpretation. The play compels the reader to interpret, analyse, and evaluate life for themselves" (142-3).

The play may also be reread as Sircar's crusade against the humdrumness of modern urban Indian existence and against the symbolic hegemony of commonality.

A considerable portion of the oeuvre of Sircar, whose formal first name was 'Sudhindranath', is occupied by the poignant anti-establishment plays he wrote during the 1970s' *Naxalite Revolution* in Bengal. They not only demonstrated his leftist credo, but also established him as a performative litterateur with an uncompromising attitude to every sort of domination and artificiality. E. Renuka and Sampa Bhattacharyya write that through such plays, Sircar especially "expose[d] some of the postcolonial problems that haunt the city [of Kolkata] – the unemployed, frustrated and angry youth, pestering beggars, black marketers, soaring prices, selfish political leaders, cutthroat religious fanatics, status-quoist administrators, and domineering magnates – all living in a marketplace-like society ridden with fake encounter deaths, human degradation, and so on" (*Postcolonial Theory* 151). These realistic and truthful representations endeared the playwright to numerous Western literary critics. Curiously, he had had remained relatively unknown to indigenous readers throughout his life.

Badal Sircar, later a non-practising Catholic Christian, was born on 15 July 1925 at Hatibagan of Bengal's Kolkata. According to his autobiography, *Purono Kasundi* ('The Old Mustard-sauce') (Kolkata: Lekhani Publishers, 2006), he was given the alternative name of 'Badal' or 'rain' by an uncle because he was born during the monsoon. His father Mahendralal Sircar was an associate professor of history at *Scottish Church College*, Kolkata, and his mother, Sarala Mona Sircar, was a scholarly lady who actively encouraged Badal Sircar to comprehend his own family's privileged condition and experience both affluence and intellectuality as he matured. Ironically, it was this very affluence that the dramatist would turn against in his later productions.

Sircar studied civil engineering at *Bengal Engineering College*, Shibpur, graduating in 1947, witnessing the 1943 *Bengal Famine* and the communal carnages of 1947. The dramatist was employed as a surveyor and planner until 1975, and as late as in 1992, he earned a postgraduate degree in comparative literature from *Jadavpur University*, Kolkata, and, later, the degree of *Doctor of Letters (honoris causa)*. Interestingly, in 2010, the leftist dramatist expressed his inability to accept the *Padma Bhushan* offered to him by the Indian government.

The developer of the so-called 'Third Theatre' was attracted to Bengali theatre in adolescence. According to Sircar, "Most

Bengalis do not read plays. I read them minutely. When I learned English, I began with the plays of George Bernard Shaw (1856-1950)" (Majumdar 98). His early plays were based on Shaw's satirical comedies. In 1941, he adapted and enacted a few scenes from Walford Graham Robertson's *The Slippers of Cinderella: An Impossibility in One Act* (1919). It was his "first entry into the dramatic arena" though moderately successful (*ibid.* 98).

The maturing dramatist, confessedly, was influenced by the respective humour and grimness of the plays by such European and American playwrights as Jean-Baptiste Poquelin (or 'Molière', 1622-73), Richard Brinsley Sheridan (1751-1816), Shaw, and Eugene O' Neill (1888-1953). The conventional Western dramas – the 'first theatre' according to Crow and Banfield, would later lead him into comparing and contrasting their aspects – especially their theatricality, suavity, and sophistication – with those of the Bengali folk-theatre forms – the *jatra*-s, and he found both the performative dimensions alienating and stiffening. About the form of European theatre popularised in Kolkata, Crow and Banfield write,

> "[...] [T]he colonialists brought with them their own cultural traditions and practices, at such time as relative peace, and unquestionable prosperity, allowed these luxuries. The first theatre, called simply the *Calcutta Theatre*, was built during the period of Warren Hastings's governor-generalship in 1779, and ran for more than three decades until an accumulation of debts forced its closure. In every way the numerous theatres that followed over the next 100 years were modelled on the then contemporary practices of English, specifically London, theatres. In spite, therefore, of the oppressive heat and humidity, audiences, conventionally attired, would gather in indoor venues, architecturally designed in congruence with the Drury Lane and Covent Garden theatres of the day, even if not quite as ambitiously scaled and ornamented" (112-13).

Though the 'Second Theatre' – the *jatra*-s, on the other hand, secularised over time, they employed prose dialogues that were both rude and over-dramatic. Moreover, as Crow and Banfield write, males played the female characters, and *jatra*-s were marked by 'over salaciousness' (*ibid.* 115).

Sircar abandoned both the forms for the 'Third Theatre', an innovation which brought performances away from the confines of the proscenium and placed them squarely among the squatting audience, where the props would be the interacting spectators, and the actors were expected to rely on their bodily movements than depending on make-up and gaudy dresses. Thus Sircar could easily break down the 'fourth wall' and introduce the concept of 'physical theatre' in Indian performative terminology. Deshpande writes,

> "Sircar could not simply have embraced the rural theatre. He was city-bred, and he did not want to be an impostor in the rural theatre. So he created what he called the *Third Theatre*. This was a theatre that lived and breathed among the common people, that spoke of their lives, that cried their tears and dreamed their dreams. This was theatre for social change. Later, he preferred the term *free theatre* to *Third Theatre*. Not only was this term less confrontationist, it was also more accurate"[3].

'Third Theatre', as a term, also symbolised Sircar's professed closeness to the members of the famous 'Third Estate', the commoners. The terms 'patha natika' (street performances) and 'aangan mancha' (space theatre) – the latter originally identified the "30 feet by 28 feet" room on the second floor of the *Academy of Fine Arts*, Rabindra Sadan, Kolkata, where Sircar's theatre group, *Shatabdi*, founded in 1976, began performing – also owed their popularity, if not their coinage, to the playwright. His group has been lauded for its advancement of experimental – rather *avant-garde* – theatre in Kolkata (Brandon 76). According to the dramatist himself,

> "In *Third Theatre*, you could not use furniture which would hide the performers. You do not use 'make-up', for your closeness to the audience would betray your preparations and your artificial dresses. No spotlight is required. *Third Theatre* is marked by three aspects: flexibility – it can be performed wherever you like; portability – you do not need to worry about electricity and the likes before performance; and cheapness – less props need less money" (Majumder 103-5).

Nivedita Tandon rereads street theatre and *Third Theatre* as postcolonial reactions against the "conservatism and elitism" of British conventional theatre (*Perspectives* 103).

Intent on becoming a theatre-writer of consequence, Badal Sircar left his employment in the 1950s, and after 1956, the year he produced *Solution X*, he briefly taught at Jadavpur. During this period, he became involved in leftwing activism, joining the undivided *Communist Part of India* (*C.P.I.*), but unlike the other noted Bengali thespians like Bijon Bhattacharyya (1917-78), Utpal Dutt, and Ajitesh Bandyopadhyay (1933-83), he was too soon disillusioned with politics, and though he preferred Marx all throughout his life, he was scarcely a radical. Rather, pragmatically trying to decide what was to be his most suitable vocation, he shifted to a small Entally flat in central Kolkata with his wife and two children. In 1957, he went to London for two years, ostensibly for furthering his engineering studies, but in reality, to be more acquainted with the different aspects of the English stage.

Sircar's visit to London helped him to witness several theatrical performances by professional English, Irish, and American actors. Superior performances by Charles Laughton (1899-1962), Michael Redgrave (1908-85), Margaret Rawlings (1906-96), and Vivien Leigh (1913-67) helped him to develop himself into an efficient dramatist (Majumder 100). Euro-American experimental drama had always influenced Sircar, and even at the height of his productivity, he continued to admit the influence of the British theatre director, Joan Littlewood (1914-2002), the American dramatist Richard Schechner (b. 1934) of the *Performance Group*, and the Polish experimental playwright Jerzy Grotowski (1933-99) in his transformation as a thespian. His attachment to Schechner, from whom he learnt the "intricacies and details of theatrical workshops", was particularly deep (Majumder 114). They corresponded frequently, and Sircar's 23 November 1981-letter to Schechner (printed in *The Drama Review* 26(2), Summer 1982-edition, and available on *http://humanitiesunderground.wordpress.com/2011/02/10/a-letter-from-badal-sircar/*) is frequently cited as one which summarises his theatrical history and reflects his credo.

Interestingly, though many of his play have been reviewed as Brechtian, and he himself adapted Bertolt Brecht's 1944 *Caucasian Chalk Circle* as *Gondi* ('The Circle') in 1978, he would not admit having to do anything with the German dramatist. His *Evam Indrajit* has often been reread in context of John Osborne's *Look Back in Anger* (1956). Importantly, though he uninhibitedly interacted with the Western thespians, he never wrote his plays in any language other than Bengali, from which they were later translated by various academicians. This insistence on following the indigenous language for literary composition also marks his conscious postcoloniality. To Schechner, he wrote:

> "What can I write? I am no writer of essays. I am a theatre man. I wrote some plays because I am a man of the theatre, not because I am a writer. I have to write in English, but English is not my language. My experiences with *Shatabdi*, in theatre, in the cultural jungle of Kolkata, my city; my experiences with other people, with society, with life itself in all its absurdity, sordidness and beauty-all these are no better than a chaotic mass of confusion, and a long history of trying to find a meaningful course, a rational path,

> through this chaotic agglomeration. I am looking back to locate and understand the path already traversed; I am looking ahead to project it to the future so that the next few steps can be taken".[4]

Before moving abroad, Sircar had founded an informal cultural club, *Chakra*, and occasionally organised the cultural festival of *Sammilani* (Majumder 100). In 1951, *Chakra* staged Sircar's play, *Bara Trishna* ('Great Thirst'), in which the dramatist himself performed. After returning from Britain, he was ready to produce *Boro Pishima* ('The Elder Aunt'), written in 1959. A year before, he had scribbled what later became the introductory section of *Evam Indrajit*, which he completed at the suggestion of his friend, Mukul Roy, while town-planning among the Igbos in the south-east Nigerian town of Enugu. He worked there for three years after experimenting in Paris for nine months on a French government's architectural scholarship, and temporarily settling down in Kolkata. In an exhaustive 2009 interview conducted by the dramatist Debashis Majumder and documenter Sudev Singha, Sircar pinpointed the five jobless months after his return from London as the precise period when the alternative 'Third Theatre' was conceived, with the dramatist becoming its 'first man'. It grew out of his prejudiced comparative study between the cinema and the theatre as mediums of entertainment (Majumder 101-02).

Having had nursed anti-naturalistic sentiments as a dramatist, Sircar identified the principal alienating factors between the spectators of proscenium theatres and its actors. The actors perform on a higher platform, whereas the audience sit on a lower level, with entrances different from the actors' provided to them. Actors remain at a considerable distance away from the last-row audience. Most importantly, as the audience are required to suppress their presences, the actors, performing under spotlights, are expected to be unmindful of the presence of spectators. This constitutes another kind of power-politics –

the power exercised by actors on their spectators. Always an anti-hegemonic crusader, Sircar, through his 'Third Theatre', proceeded to deconstruct the actors-audience divisiveness. There would be no spotlight and no cosmetic materials. The audience would encircle the performers, and even certain members from the spectators would go forward and perform in the area separated for actors. In 1970, when Kolkata was witnessing intermittent clashes between the Naxalites and state government law-enforcers, *Sagina Mahato*, originally written in 1969 by Gour Kishore Ghosh (1923-2000), was staged, to spontaneous applause. The Bengali spectators were introduced to Sircar's alternative theatre, which would quickly be popular all over India, especially in Manipur, Orissa and Kerala, and earn international recognition, beginning with Laos, Pakistan, and Bangladesh, and later spreading to the Soviet Union, Poland, Czechoslovakia, and the United Kingdom. It must, however, be mentioned that the Communist playwright, Safdar Hashmi (1954-89), did not like Sircar's plays which, according to him, were 'cynical' and 'tastelessly glorify his own sacrifices' (*Theatre of the Streets* 23-4).

It may be mentioned that Sircar, who began as a conventional dramatist attacking the exploitation of the common people, did not conceive his 'Third Theatre' as an alternative, proletarian-literary force until around 1972. His earlier plays like *Evam Indrajit*, *Sara Rattir*, *Baaki Itihash*, *Paagla Ghoda*, *Shesh Nei*, and *Ballabhpurer Rupkatha*, were written for and produced in the conventional proscenium theatre. Sudipto Chatterjee, in fact, identifies these conventional dramas as Sircar's "best" (*Not the Other* 215). Sambhu Mitra's theatre-group, *Bohurupee*, which first published his angst-ridden *Evam Indrajit* (later staged by *Saubhanik*), enacted two of his earlier plays – *Baaki Itihash* and *Pagla Ghoda*, the later easily belonging to the 'abstract-gothic' sub genre, with the woman on the funeral pyre professing her love for one of the three sorrowful men surrounding her. In the former, he questions the role of the middle class people in times of unrest and genocide throughout history and necessitates retribution as and when needed. As Dharwadker writes, "*Baaki Itihash* [...] use[s] figures from classical and medieval history to construct ironic counter histories for contemporary Indian audience or represent 'history' itself as an intolerable burden thrust on the late twentieth-century individual" (*Theatres of Independence* 15). In Sircar's plays, even after encountering numerous hardships, the protagonists do not commit suicide or abandon their class-struggle. That is the basic *Sircarian credo*: one needs to behave like Sisyphus in the existential crisis but cannot allow himself/herself to die and evade responsibility. Incidentally, Utpal Dutt's plays like *Louha Manab* ('The Iron Man', 1964), *Kallol* ('Sound of the Waves', 1965), and *Maha Bidroho* ('The Great Rebellion', 1989), are marked by their note of pessimism, as against Sircar's existential or 'straight' comedies.

Turning to Sircar's other proscenium theatres – in *Sara Rattir*, for example, a couple discover their mutual marital incompatibility after taking refuge in a mysterious house owned by an insomniac old man. G.J.V. Prasad writes, "[The play] [...] looks at the frustration and sense of longing in a woman, albeit in the framework of a man's world" (*Muffled Voices* 75). Sircar's productions were no different that this – to reiterate, they all deal with the problems, desperateness, and struggles of human existence. When he wrote *Spartacus*, based on Howard Fast's 1951 publication, it was a conscious movement away from the confines of proscenium. His first 'Third Theatre' was followed by *Michhil* – criticising the state's exercise of its administrative power to annihilate young Naxalites. In this play, the actors, moving in a circle towards the end of the play, began to directly seek audience participation. *Bhoma*, where the humdrum conversations of an apparently sophisticated society are interspersed with pathetic cries from the desperately-hungry Bhoma, until police arrive and silence the likes of him, followed *Michhil*.

In *Hattamalar Oparey*, the thieves Kena ('Purchase') and Becha ('Sell') find themselves transported to a utopia only to learn the value of requisition, and *Bashi Khabar* focuses on the tribal-struggle against the oppressive power of the state. While Eugene van Erven observes that *Bhoma* is a gripping "real-life story of a simple Bengali lumberjack named 'Bhoma'" (131), Amar Nath Prasad thus writes about *Michhil*, " [...] [It] deals with the theme of a real home or a real way of living in this world of various sorts of deviations and corruptions. The playwright imagines a new ideal world in which man does not live by exploiting others. There are two main characters in this play – the old man and *khoka* who represent the old and new generations respectively" (*Indian Writing in English* 253-4). It may be recalled that *Michhil* was enacted at *Curzon Park* by a group of infuriated theatre activists when one of their members, Probir Dutta, died of police firing on 20 July 1974, and, as always, Sircar himself was at the forefront of the theatrical procession. Later, in *Tringshya Shatabdi* and *Sukhpathya Bharoter Itihash* ('Immensely Readable Indian History', 1976), Sircar began to combine history and theatricality. He also experimented with Rabindranath Tagore's 1923 abstract play, *Rakto Karobi* ('Red Oleanders'), perceptively because "it was godless", and the left-aligned Sircar was vociferously an atheist (Majumder 113). It was staged by the *Pathasena* theatre group. Reviewing Sircar's mature plays – almost all of them literary crusades against every form of oppression – K. Nirupa Rani writes, "For Sircar theatre has become a real human event – 'a real meeting of human beings, not mask to mask, armour to armour, but man to man'" (*Aspects of* 286).

Badal Sircar, who remained an uncompromising and non-elitist crusader against every sort of hegemony – be it societal, literary, economic, or political – all throughout his literary career, died of cardiac arrest at his Maniktala, Kolkata-residence on 13 May 2011: the very day West Bengal witnessed the end of the thirty-four-year-old rule by the leftists and the establishment of the rightist *Trinamool Congress*-led government. He was diagnosed with colon cancer in 2010. The leftist, who had earned the sobriquet of an 'ultra-revolutionary-Marxist-playwright' in the 1970s for staging his anti-government plays like *Rupkathar Kelenkari* ('Scandal in Fairyland', 1974) and *Gondi* in *Curzon Park* every Saturday, began his serious societal crusade by protesting against commonality in *Evam Indrajit*, and throughout his career, he tried to bring to the forefront though his theatre the plight of the poor and downtrodden. If the posterity is to remember the name of any Indian dramatist who most successfully countered and thwarted the capitalist-funded literary ventures to anoint Indians with Western philosophy, the name of Sircar will always be mentioned among the foremost of the reactionaries.

References:

1. Indramohan, T.M.J. "Postcolonial Writing: Trends in English Drama". *The Indian Review of World Literature in English* 2(2), July 2006 – *World Literature Online*. Accessed on 27 May 2011 *<http://www.worldlitonline.com/july-06/article2.pdf>*
2. Kumar, Amshan. "His Austere Brand of Theatre". *The Hindu* (*Arts – Theatre*) 26 May 2011. Accessed on 28 May 2011. *<http://www.thehindu.com/arts/theatre/article2050740.ece>*
3. Deshpande, Sudhanva. "The Outsider: Badal Sircar (1925-2011)" *Pragati* 16 May 2011. Accessed on 31 May 2011. *<http://www.pragoti.org/bn/node/4397>*
4. "A Letter from Badal Sircar". *Humanities Underground*, 10 February 2011. Accessed on 31 May 2011. *<http://manitiesunderground.wordpress.com/2011/02/10/a-letter-from-badal-sircar/>*

Bibliography

Aspects of Contemporary World Literature. Ed. Reddy, P. Bayapa. New Delhi: Atlantic Publishers and Distributors Pvt. Ltd., 2008.

Brandon, James R. *The Cambridge Guide to Asian Theatre*. Cambridge: Cambridge University Press, 1993.

Crow, Brian, and Chris Banfield. *An Introduction to Postcolonial Theatre*. Cambridge: Cambridge University Press, 1996.

Dharwadker, Aparna Bhargava. "Acts of Authority/Acts of Resistance: Theatre and Politics in Colonial and Postcolonial India (Review)". *Modern Drama: World Drama from 1850 to the Present* 48 (2), Summer 2005: 440-44.

Theatres of Independence: Drama, Theory, and Urban Performance in India since 1947. Iowa City: University of Iowa Press, 2005.

Eagleton, Terry. *Literary Theory: An Introduction.* 2nd edn. New Delhi: Maya Blackwell, 2000.

Erven, Eugene Van. *The Playful Revolution: Theatre and Liberalisation in Asia.* Bloomington: Indiana University Press, 1992.

Gilbert, Helen, and Joanne Tompkins. *Postcolonial Drama: Theory, Practice, Politics.* London and New York: Routledge, 1996.

Indian Literature: An Introduction. Eds. Dev, Anjana N., Bajrang B. Tiwari and Sanam Khanna. New Delhi: Pearson Longman, 2006.

Indian Writing in English: Tradition and Modernity. Eds. Prasad, Amar Nath and Kanupriya. New Delhi: Sarup and Sons, 2006.

Iyer, Natesan Sharda. *Musings on Indian Writing in English – Drama. Vol. III.* New Delhi: Sarup and Sons, 2007.

Literary Theory and Criticism: An Oxford Guide. Ed. Waugh, Patricia. New Delhi: Oxford University Press, 2006.

Majumder, Debashish. *The Most Important Aspect is the Connexion between Audience and the Performer:* An Interview with Badal Sircar. Boyer Desh 6(2), April-June 2010: 96-122.

Modern Indian Drama: An Anthology. Ed. G.P. Deshpande. New Delhi: Sahitya Akademi, 2000. Reprint 2004.

Muffled Voices: Women in Modern Indian Theatre. Ed. Subramanyam, Lakshmi. New Delhi: Har-Anand Publications Pvt. Ltd., 2002.

Not the Other Avant-garde: The Transnational Foundations of Avant-garde Performance. Eds. Harding, James Martin, and John Rouse. Ann Arbour: University of Michigan Press, 2006.

Perspectives and Challenges in Indian English Drama. Ed. Tandon, Neeru. New Delhi: Atlantic Publishers and Distributors, 2006.

Poplawski, Paul. *Encyclopaedia of Literary Modernism.* Westport-Connecticut: Greenwood Publishing Group, 2003.

Postcolonial Theory and Literature. Eds. Rao, P. Mallikarjuna, Rajeshwar Mittapalli, and K. Damodar Rao. New Delhi: Atlantic Publishers and Distributors, 2003.

Theatre of the Streets: The Jana Natya Manch Experience. Ed. Deshpande, Sudhanva. New Delhi: Jana Natya Manch, 2007. Rpt. 2008.

The Columbia Encyclopaedia of Modern Drama – I. Eds. Cody, Gabrielle H., and Evert Sprinchorn. New York: Columbia University Press, 2007.

The Encyclopaedia of Indian Literature (Devraj to Jyoti). Vol. II. Ed. Datta, Amaresh. New Delhi: Sahitya Akademi, 1988. Rpt. 2005.

The Oxford Guide to Literature in English Translation. Ed. France, Peter. Oxford: Oxford University Press, 2001.

Tyson, Lois. *Critical Theory Today: A User-friendly Guide*. 2nd edn. New York and London: Routledge, 2006. Rpt. 2008.

Western Drama through the Ages: A Student Reference Guide, Vol. I. Ed. King, Kimball. Westport-Connecticut: Greenwood Publishing Group, 2007.

3

Badal Sircar's Evam Indrajit:
Issues of Writing, Reading and Narrativity in the Context of Existential Politics

Anjan Dasgupta

Badal Sircar's *Evam Indrajit* is a remarkable play which can be read from so many perspectives. There are multi-layered meanings that emerge from the text which provide lot of food for thought. The interesting issues include narrative design, the plot or the plotlessness, the absurdist strain, social location, the unmistakable postmodernistperspectiv, alienation and the political aspects that are insuperably grafted in the text.

In this paper I will try to look into the narrative design imbedded in mythical pattern which consciously raises issues of writing and reading and also intentionally subverting issues like a linear narrative and the inevitable question "What happens next?" The traditional structure is not encouraged, the problem of reading and responding also take us the theoretical premise of reader response. Kermode's debate on the sense of an ending is also relevant. First; we need to see what actually happens in the play.

The play with the writer who tries to look for a subject to write on. He rues over the fact that "I have nothing to write about". The word 'nothing' in fact recurs almost in a Godot like pattern and disturbs us raising typical existential question. And central to the Genre of the Theatre of the Absurd. Ionesco suggests:

> Absurd is that which is devoid of purpose...Cut off from his religious,metaphysical, and transcendental roota,man is lost; all his actions become senseless, absurd, useless. (Ionesco 20)

There is an expectation of something different on Indrajit among the common branch of Amal, Vimal, Kamal and Nirmal. So when the fourth one says his name is Nirmal,the author is not prepared to accept. He mentions this on correction that his name is Indrajit. The name Indrajit has obvious connotations of rebellion. Indrajit has an archetypal image of a rebel and one who is honest and can afford to take up the charge against a host of uncertainties. There is a typical existentialist dialogue when the author asks in a repartee like session of questions about the death of Indrajit. Indrajit chips in 'Not dead yet' (p.199). The writer wants to ascertain, 'Are you sure'. This Godot like uncertainty pervades the entire play and this happens in the purview of an absurdist play.It is not the absurdist writer's concern to find out a meaning. It is interesting when Alan Schneider, who waws to direct the first American production of Waiting for asked Beckett what he understood by Godot; he answered, "If I knew, I would have said so in the play" (Schneider, 24). So the search for the writer rests on an Indrajit who can lie different from Amal,Vimal,Kamal and Indrajit. But the attempt seems quite futile as revealed through among other things a puppet show. There is a very interesting scène in the play which involves Amal,Vimal,Kamal and Indrajit trying to take up propositions of serious academic pursuits, physics, poetry, the essay, cricket, football, cinema and other 'interesting propositions.' The topics vary from the film hero Yul Brynner and Marlon Brando to Einstein, George Bernard Shaw, Pramathanath Bishi and their academic and intellectual pursuits. There is an intellectual exchange of ideas, but nothing concrete turns out or neither is extended fully towards completion. The author's intention itself is to convey a sense of incompleteness and chaos. This dialogue is accompanied with a slow repetitive pattern on the tabla, showing the boredom and continuity which does not promise any change. This phatic communion is not intended to reach anywhere but it is aimless and very much rooted in the absurdist tradition. Indrajit wants to go to some place, a place where he wants to run away:

> "Don't know, some place, you know, somewhere far away. I do not know what will be there-jungle probably, or desert, or iceberg. Birds, penguins, ostriches, wild animals, kangaroo, jaguar. Strange people - Eskimo, Maori........". (204)

There cannot perhaps be a better absurdist dialogue as it were. The narrative goes forward but it does not follow the traditional questions of narrativity or linear progression in the strictest sense. The inevitable question 'what happens next?' is subverted time and again intentionally in a typical post structuralist pattern. The character, Manasi, for example, is multidimensional in ways more than one. She comes on stage playing different roles; different dimensions, sometimes as the friend and mentor of Indrajit, sometimes as his wife; every time Indrajit acting as the anima of the author or the protagonist Indrajit. She is the 'every woman of sorts'; she is at the centre of interest. She is also at the centre of uncertainty as the writer quizzes Indrajit about Manasi:

> About Yourself and Manasi : What is she to you?
>
> Indrajit: Sister?
>
> Writer (pause) Sister?
>
> Indrajit: Well, cousin then. (210)

The entire discourse is full of incertainty. Indrajit finds everything 'meaningless' sharing the existential uncertainty which pervades all the play. Indrajit suggests, "That all these minutia-they are all meaningless" (p. 211). Sircar is bothered aboutr aboput the issues of, 'Who am I?' and as Eslin asks, 'What does it mean when I say-I?'(Eslin-43). Badal Sircar's *Evam Indrajit*, we must add is a wonderful reworking of the Indrajit myth in the absurdist tradition. Sircar, who composed the play sitting in France itself where Absurd Drama was first enacted, finds in Indrajit, the mythological hero of Ramayana who fought but lost, a symbol of alienation and lot other things which shall be taken up late in this article.

If we look at the myth of Indrajit we shall remember that he used to find from behind the clouds so the enemies have a tough task to get the better of him. Similarly Nirmal Kumar Roy refused to be the part of the common flow of humans around him. He takes the guise of a name in his search of someone different. It is significant that Indrajit is an extremely pious individual an upright individual who fights against the Rama and his battalion with a unique gusto and austerity. He stands tall against his peers and is respected deeply by friend and foes alike. Michael Madhusudan Dutta finds a lot of reasons to sympathise with Indrajit identifies him as a wronged rebel like a King Lear 'more sinned against than sinning'type of a hero in his epic, "Meghnad Badh Kavya". How Sircar places this myth into the context of a postmodern absurd drama is something very interesting. The myth making capacity of the modern and post modern artists of course contribute in a major way but there are other issues also which need to be explored in some detail. In his introduction to the monumental work on absurd literature, Martin Esslin points out:

> 'If the critical touchstone of traditional drama not apply to these plays, this must surely have been due to difference in objective, the use of different artistic means to the fact, in short, that these plasys were both creating and applying a different convention of drama.'(Eslin; ed. 4)

He further adds:

> 'The Theatre of the Absurd is involved in the relatively few problems that remain: life deal isolation and communication and it can by its nature only communicate one poet's most intimate and personal intuition of the human situation his sense of being,his individual vision of the world'. (Eslin, ed.4)

Sircar catches this intense disillusionment and aimlessness which Albert Camus noticed long before in 1945 in his *The Myth of Sisyphus:*

> A world that can be explained reasoning, however is a familiar world. But in a universe that is suddenly deprived of illusions and of light, man feels a stranger. This is an irremediable exile, because he is deprived of memories of a lost homeland as much as he lacks the hope of a promised land to come. The divorce between man and his life, the actor and his setting truly constitutes the feeling of Absurdity. (Camus, 18)

In this absurd play we find a detailed analysis of a prolonged aimlessness; the 'exile', which Camus has talked about. If we consider the definition of Absurd Theatre find in the Penguin Dictionary we can attribute the feature mentioned there easily to the play:

> Term applied to a group of dramatists in the 1950s who did not regard themselves as a school but who all seemed to share certain attitudes towards predicament of man in the universe:essentiallysummarised by Albert Camus in his essay 'The Myth of Sisyphus' (1942). This diagnoses humanitty's plight as purposelessness in an existence out of harmony with its surrounding (absurd literally means out of harmony. (Law, 16)

Sircar in his play tries to show the pathos of a young man, his purposelessness, and an existence of harmony. Ionesco, who inspired Sircar intensely calls his own plays as 'antiplay'; in which the topic adopted in traditional plays are intentionally subverted. This is exactly what Sircar does. We need to consider once more the analysis of Esslin:

> If a good play must have a clearly constructed story these (the absurd dramas have no story or plot to speak of, if a good play is judged by subtlety of characterisation and motivation these are often without recognisable characters and present the audience with almost mechanical puppets; if a good play has to have a fully explained theme which is neatly exposed and finally solved, these often have neither a beginning nor an end, if a good play is to hold the mirror up to nature and pot ray the manners and mannerisms of the age in finely observed sketches, these seem often to be reflections of dreams and nightmares; if a good play relies on witty repartee and pointed dialogue, these often consist of incoherent babblings. (Eslin, 22)

Sircar's play fit the bill in so many ways. Sircar when asked in an interview whether *Evam Indrajit* is a political play or not he said he never considered, it so and did not know of existentialism. In fact the absurdistsa were very keen upon distinguishing themselves from the existentialists as Eslin explains:

> It is this striving for an interrogation between the subject matter and the form which it is expressed that separates the Theatre of the Absurd from the Existentialist Theatre. (Eslin, 25)

He was trying to recreate traditional myth in the modern context. There is however the undeniable Sartrean angst as the play points out repeatedly, "Our existence is a pointless particle of dust". The pay is replete with prolonged despair, disillusionment and hopes of the protagonist Indrajit who like his mythological namesake seeks to keep an alienated existence. Indrajit does not want to conform or follow the beaten track.

Like Berenger, the protagonist of Ionesco's play, Rhinocerous, who is the only human amongst others who have become rhinos. There is that adamant refusal to conform. Like Pirandello, Sircar also adopts the play within a play in an entirely different realm. Just as Camus adopts the Sissyphus myth to portray a psychological realism where external conflict reveals internal chaos without any concrete characterisation and a realisation that there is "no exit" and no escape from the humdrum affairs of life which Indrajit seeked to avoid by rejecting his biological functions in his pewrvasive search to write a play. He wants to do something meaningful in life like his namesake Indrajit. It is a typical absurd play such as "Ionesco's" Amedee"or Beckett's "Wating for Godot" in that it exemplifies the hollowness and futility of a pseudo-modern existence. The play keeps on echoing that "our existence is a pointless particle of dust" (p. 233). Therefore the play is unconsciously coloured with Satrean Existentialism. The theme is evolved through the dreams, despair and disillusionment of the protagonist Indrajit.The theme of identity crisis is echoed by the very title "and Indrajit". He is .... "and Indrajit", a part of the whole. He is described in terms of society and not in terms of his own existence. He prefers to be called Amal, Kamal or Vimal and conform to the dictates of society or the doctrines of tradition. His identity is yet again questioned by his teachers by a mere roll number. He can therefore easily pose as Amal and answer his roll-call.

The monotony and mechanical nature of the contemporary times is stressed by the repetition of "one-two-three", words like "From home to school. From school to college. From college to the world" and "after files tea-Then files-then snacks- then files-then tea." and phrases like "going round". (p. 213/225). The language of *Evam Indrajit* transports us to the world of Absurd Drama with its cyclical and repetitive pattern. The stichomythic design adds to the phenomenon where single lines or parts of lines are spoken by alternate speakers. The utterance of comments of desperation with lack of emotion add to the Absurd. Amal, Kamal and Vimal become cogs in the wheel of society. He attempts to impart meaning to the daily activities of life, love marriage, profession and prevents himself from submission to a humdrum existence.

Therefore, the play is in the absurdist tradition in that we do not comprehend anything significant, meaningful and traditional in it. Neither does it possess a logical or coherent plot. Amal asks, "What is the plot?" writer answers, There isn't one (p. 207). Sircar talks of the 'happily lived ever after endings' as the Writer conjectures, "They lived so happily that there was no more story to tell" (p. 228). Indrajit rues at the end of the play, "what's the point of finishing it? It won't ever get complted. Its end is its beginning" (p. 249). The celebration plotlessness is a calculated strategy which works in tandem with the absurdist's thought that language often fails as a medium of communication. The inadequacy of language echoes the lack of meaningful human associations. The language verges on word-play and is playful at times. The dialogue becomes purposefully elliptical. There is no realism, and the play portrays a psychological realism, where external conflict reveals internal chaos. There is no concrete characterization. The various characters around appear to be the projection of the protagonist himself. It is in such an age that *Evam Indrajit* holds relevance.

The very title "Evam Indrajit" or "And Indrajit" exemplifies modern man's state of identity crisis. He prefers to be addressed as Nirmal, like Amal, Kamal or Vimal and conform to the dictates of society. The stichomythic dialogue and repetitive phrases add to the idea of a humdrum existence. The structure of the drama reminds one of the same. People are caught in a cycle of time in which the events change, but people are the same. The aunt finds it strange that the writer needs to write relegating basic biological functions. Amal, Kamal and Vimal in short and broken sentences give us a picture of disillusioned picture of post-independent India. Their broken words reflect the 'broken images" of India. Vimal suggests that in such a state of affairs, they must adopt the others' stand:" If I am alive, all is well.' Camus surmises, 'One asks, oneself, why is bhe alive?' (Camus, 29). In *Evam Indrajit*, the structure of the play is cyclical, echoing the main idea of the play: the monotony of a mechanical existence. The plays often deal with the middle-class and their problems, frustrations and conflicts. when he finds inspiration in the form of a woman named Manasi. Manasi is the Indian counterpart of Jung's Anima, an entity serving as a pointer to the collective consciousness. The very title Evam Indrajit or 'And Indrajit' exemplifies that Indrajit's identity is not 'just Indrajit' but 'and Indrajit and is described in terms of society and not in terms of his own existence. Sircar; perhaps unconsciously enters the terrains of Sartrean existentialism as he must make his oprotagonist realise that such attempts are actually quite futile and meaningless. Asha Kashekar in her analysis points out that in the post independence Indian playwrights one finds a steady disintegration of aspiration and optimism. (Kashekar, 14).

Badal Sircar makes his opinions very clear into what terrains he is trying to enter into:

> Indrajit: The influence of the of the Indian sprit on ancient Indian literature can be seen in the profusion of interpolation and the way description theoretical analysis and unrelated details continually hamper the flow of the main story. (212).

The concept, entirely Indian certainly has a clear ring of post modernity, the entire method of how to deal with the concept of plot, structure and wholeness. Going back to the story we find the frustration of the educated unemployed and a nagging sense of insecurity and uncertainty whether it comes to choosing a job or an interview for a prospective job. The writer conjectures on the choice of a particular interview; "Yes, but do you know I'm sure that is a wrong policy. When you badly need a job you must go to the interview for the worse job first. The chances are better there." (p. 221).

The complex issues of language are also taken up. The writer says, "I have to put into language the drama of these atoms going round and round. The language is senile and words are battered and maimed." (p. 221). The very issue of language and the efficacy of language as a medium of communication gets central importance. There are occasions in which language fails as a viable mode of communication. For example in Waiting for Godot, we find the huge load of communication on Vladimir and Estragon, the waifs. To a rather inocuous question seeking help for some people who have fallen down, "What are we waiting for? the bland non contextual answer, "We are waiting for Godot," comes as a surprise. Sentences and scenes may be short, broken and at times, totally meaningless reminiscent of the Theatre of the Absurd. Language here leads to fragmentation and a fractured identity, just as is the echo with which Act 1 ends. Amal, Vimal and Kamal are on the stage, but the light is focused only on the writer, who, in an almost omnipotent prophetic tone, declares,

> We are here,still here,here on earth. Amal, Vimal, Kamal stand up. Ring the bell frantically. But the dark deepens, leaving only the Writer in light..
>
> I am divided. I am broken into pieces, into atoms.I'm a symphony composed of atoms....
>
> The earth is crushed but it's still alive
>
> The century's old but it listens still. (221).

Act II finds the protagonists all working in some capacity or the other. The scene in which the writer, now a peon in the office in which these people work passes a file between these people. They hurl it between tables, 'thrice' and 'faster each time.' The continuous and recurrent activity has polyvalent meaning. It is a pointer to the post modern existence, which leads to nothingness, as it were. We are reminded of that famous comment on Waiting for Godot which says, "In Godot nothing happens twice", so is a typical existentialist pattern the nothingness is celebrated as a way of life. Indrajit pines:

> "To seek a break in this unchanging rhythm of death is perhaps the most foolish and futile attempt of Man in this world"....... (p. 233).

Act II ends with more absurdist discourse talk where we find Indrajit unable to find an answer "I don't know anything ... but I can't find an answer. I am tired now..... Nor can I do anything". (237).

The writer shares the tireness. ".../What's the use of all these words?.../ My quests are tired.../My efforts limp.../I am very tired...... (238).

Act III finds another repartee accompanied by a game of cards on the process of democracy and other political issues, family issues, domestic problems, Peculiar unrelated questions are juxtaposed almost to the effect of antithesis and oxymoron. When the 'writer' mentions 'Calcutta, London, everything goes round and round like a wheel'. Still it is not a proper wheel', we are reminded of T.S. Eliot's parade of city names in the Waste Land (1922). Indrajit rues that there is no sense of achievement. This is the case of wishfulfilment that never happens or materialises. There is almost a Camus like nihilism, Indrajit is unable to have faith in life and concludes that such life is meaningless and equivalent to death. There is an essential irony about the whole thing which occurs on different planes. The typicality of existence and occurrence is asserted when Indrajit ensures he has married someone else; albeit with the same name Manasi much to the surprise of the writer. Indrajit expresses the typicality of existence and individuals when he surmises, 'Manasis come and go'. There is a brilliant conglomeration of words, sense of an attempt to equate everything. In a mindboggling exchange of terms, isms, film heroes, relations the list is endlessness; the circularity and the nonchangeability of things is highlighted. The existence itself is in jeopardy; all concepts get mixed up, confusion reigns. Here is a sense of separation; as Adamov writes, "I am separated. What am I seperatyed from- I cannot name it. But I am separated" in a footnote he adds, "Formerly it was called God. Today it has no name." (Adamov, 19). Much later Kundera would write his 'The Unbearable Lightness of Being (1983)'. He deconstructs the famous assertion of Nietzche which rues life as being too heavy to be beared. He feared that if our lives recurred and history repeated itself, then the burden of existence would have been to unbearable for us. Kundera searches for this apparently light life which becomes unbearable and which he terms, 'symbol of burden'. Far from the magic realist tag thrust upon him, this is a very realistic observation with which Badal Sircar also is agreed. There is an optimistic cum pessimistic end. There is uncertainty but the basic faith in the uncertainty is there. Two or three points need to be made with reference to the text before we pass on to a more generalised discussion. First we need to take up the statement made by the Writer on the plot of the play, "Well, you see there is not much difference between the beginning and the end. Its a circular play" (248). It makes a lot of comment on the absurdist radiation, that he takes up. The Indrajit myth is perhaps most powerful here. The desperate attempt of an individual seeking to be different; seeking to be an Indrajit does not quite shape up here. It is sad that way.Indrajit realises he too would follow the beaten track sooner or later. The repetitiveness of Indrajit's daily routine is no different from that of Amal, Kamal, Vimal. There is no escape, the writer rues very pathetically. There is every possibility of threads dissipating. But then 'one has to carry on' (247). Here we find Amal as aspiring to take an exam which will get him the membership to the Institute of Bettermanship which should give him a promotion.

There is a basic irony about the whole thing. Vimal is looking for a cement permit for his house, Kamal has hit upon an 'excellent business' idea 'absolutely full proof'. Indrajit is frustrated; 'Everyone! This is everyone! Amal, Vimal and Kamal' and then there is the final acceptance of the protagonist; his final admission, 'No, Manasi, don't call me Indrajit, please don't. I am Irmal. Amal, Vimal, Kamal and Nirmal'. The acceptance is the anticlimax of the play. It sort of settles down the indomitable spirit of a rebel. Even the Writer cannot accept; "You and I can't be Nirmals"(p. 249). He adds, "We are the cursed spirits of Sisssyphus". We have to push the rock to the top-even if it rolls down." (p. 250). Indrajit is now shattered. The endless road is in front of them but there really sems to be no respite from asny of these humdrum affairs.

The protagonist eventually realizes as in Sartre's "No Exit" that there is no escape. The fulfillment of his love too does not provide him with a refuge for escapism. His visit to London further frustrates him and he verges on suicide; he fails in this regard too. He concludes: "The past and present are two ends of a single rope."

The play ends on a note of discord. There are bundles of frustrations. There seems to be no end to this cycle of insufficiency and uncertainty. The very desire to be Indrajit is in itself very confusing. Why Indrajit? Why not someone else? Indrajit was a loser at the end of everything. He was a person who sought identity by hiding himself. The post-modern man perhaps does just that. There is no redeeming hope or no optimism. Nirmal wants to be Indrajit and in that attempt also he is a failure.He does not want to follow the beaten track and so he wants to be like the mythical Indrajit; a non-conformist; a fighter, a loner, a tragic hero type but in his notattempt he loses, by giving a fight as his mythological counterpart but by surrendering to some complex social paradigms, far beyond the hero's control. Nirmal's attempt to be different is suppressed in this postmodernist Absurdist tradition which Sircar manages quite successfully. Camus handling of the Sissyphus myth is a very close inspiration as mentioned earlier. Myths get represented, presented and turned and tossed in this complex post-modernist narrative and absurdist worldview. There is an incantation at the end, like a prayer:

And hence

There's no end

There's no hope,

Of fulfilment

By the holy shrine

At journey's end,

And have faith

In the road,

The endless road,

No shrine for us

No god for us

But the road,

The endless road.

This is an open ending if there was any. The road motif recurs in the play as it portrays the absurd situation most potently. No plot is developed or fulfilled; there is some optimism at the end underlying a deep pessimism but Sircar does not lose the basic faith amidst all the chaos. Sircar remakes the Indrajit myth,explores issues of writing and reading; subverts traditional narrative designs and creates a play well within the absurdist tradition.

Bibliography

Primary Source :

Badal Sircar, *Evam Indrajit, in Modern Indian Drama, An Anthology*, New Delhi, Sahitya Akademi, 2000.

Secondary Source :

Alan Schneider, *Waiting for Beckett*,,Chelsea Review, New York, 1958.

Albert Camus, *Le Mythe De Sisssyphe*, Paris, Gallimard, 1942.

Arthur Adamov, *L'Aveu*, Paris, Edition du Sagittaire, 1946.

Aparna Bhargava Dharwadker, *Theatres of independence: drama, theory, and urban performance in India since 1947.* University of Iowa Press, 2005.

Asha Kasbekar, "*Badal Sircar and the Poor Theatre*". *Pop culture India!: media, arts and lifestyle*, ABC-CLIO, 2006.

Eugene Ionesco, *Dans les armes de la ville*, Louis Barrault, Paris, 1957.

Eugene Ionesco (translated into English by Derek Prouse), *Rhinoceros and Other Plays*, New York : Grove Press, 1960.

Jagannath Ghosh, *Badal Sircar Natya Chinta*, Bama Pustakalya, Kolkata, 2002.

Jean Paul Sartre, trans.Wade Baskin, Citadel Press, new York1967.

Jonathon Law, *Penguin Dictionary of Theatre*, Penguin, 2001.

Martin, Esslin. *The Theatre of the Absurd.* London: Pelican, 1968.

Martin, Esslin. ed. *Absurd Drama*, London, Penguin, 1965.

Oscar Brockett, & J. Franklin Hildy. *French History and Drama, 1940-1968. History of the Theatre*, 9th ed. Ed. Boston: Allyn and Bacon, 1968.

Samuel Beckett, *Waiting for Godot: A Tragi, comedy in Two Acts*, New York: Grove Press, 1954.

Milan Kundera, *The Unbearable Lightness of Being*, Faber & Faber, London, 1984.

4

Myth, Gender and Sexuality: A Reading of Karnad's *Naga Mandala*

Sutapa Saha

Karnad's plays usually adopt mythical fabrics which he always deconstructs by questioning the politics of power. Like the Classical dramatists, he also does not invent plots, but weaves complex dimensions into pre-existing narratives. In *Yayati* he re-tells the age old story of the king who in his blind yearning for eternal youth does not dither to seize the youth and vitality of his son. *Hayavadhana* is an elaboration of a tale found in *Kathasaritasagara* that deals with the crisis of incongruous disagreement between the opposites in human life. *Naga Mandala* is dramatization of two folk tales of Kannada. At the heart of the play is the gender discrimination and the marginal position to which the Indian women are pushed that forms the elementary component of the socio-cultural identity of the country. Women and men are defined and constrained by the roles they are assigned. The set of conventions and regulations that an individual has to confirm to is principled here mainly by bigotry and hypocrisy. The play questions the double standard of the Indian society, the liberal standpoint that it takes in case of a man contravening the social norms, while implementing the same mercilessly in case of a woman.

The zeitgeist of *Naga Mandala* is 'Mandala' which consists of a triangle and a square, rather a triangle within a square. The three points of the triangle are the three characters of the drama

Rani, Appannna and Naga, the eternal triangle of an adulterous situation presenting the wife, the husband and the lover. The lover is a Cobra, the Naga endowed with the feelings of genuine love for Rani, the wife of the husband Appanna. The process of the transformation of Naga into a human being may remind the readers of the age-old Snake-Myths and the Kerala Naga-Cult. The meaning of the play is deeply rooted in the reader-spectator's cult(ural) consciousness which is the storehouse of rich symbolical narratives. They point towards the realms of nature , the cultural history and the mental patterns, they work beneath the surface of the rational and civilized mind. Karnad was probably the first to feel the necessity of visualising theatre on the basis of indigenous Indian traditions. The reconstruction of the myth actually poses a few questions to the advanced, civilized and rational mind, and Karnad locates the existential dilemma in the protagonist's self-knowledge.

When Sleep (Nidra), Food (Ahara), and Copulation (Maithuna) are the three basic needs of life, the question is raised of the legitimacy of pleasures when it comes to women. Rani's marriage remains unconsummated because her husband is enamoured of another woman and so reluctant to spend time with his wife. While Appannna's relation with the concubine remains unquestioned, Rani has to go through the Snake-ordeal to prove that she has not indulged in adultery. After the ordeal she is attributed with Divinity. But woman's desire must be understood separately from reproduction, motherhood or divinity. Over the ages History has witnessed patriarchal control over female sexuality. The admirable sexuality is ascribed to respectable women, whose ideal destiny is reproduction and motherhood and the degrading sexuality manifest in the prostitute. Caught between the whore and the naïve girl-woman i.e., Rani, there seems to be a very little space in order to manoeuvre the sexualized female body. Women are physically 'induced into femininity by a patriarchal culture and then are accused of perpetuating that process i. e, what women should do or what is demanded of women or what they are expected to do. Rani is expected to remain imprisoned in her husband's house without any love relationship, under the vigil of a dog and a mongoose, only cooking her husband's lunch, and remain lonely and yet at the same time expected to be unadulterous. Women's desire, sexuality and pleasure are viewed as fallen values.

To comprehend the cultural representation of womanhood and women's self-images, one has to explore the realm of ideology and consciousness while keeping in view the constraints of politics and economy and the processes which make for the social and political construction of gender. Construction of 'sex' and 'gender' supports the various regimes of power. Ideologies of womanhood are created as much by the realm of sexuality as by the realms of race (in the orthodox social hierarchy of the Hindus, the women and the Sudras are the two lowest categories).

During the 19th century, European and American culture also insisted on dividing femininity into angelic and demonic, virtuous and vicious types, implying the difference between good and bad woman. But the fact is that not even respectable females can suppress their inexhaustible eroticism or desire. If reproduction and motherhood are natural and acknowledgable, then it also has to be acknowledged that sexuality also articulates a fundamental human need and natural urge irrespective of men or women.

Women are expected only to obey their husbands, follow her husband like his shadow. The 'Dharma' or the duties of an ideal wife virtually meant a woman's surrender to the dictates of her husband, and subjection would continue even beyond the death of the husband, as marriage is conceived to be a relationship of eternal bondage. It was this eternal concept of marriage which once had rationalized prohibition on widow marriage. This prohibition implied a total control over the mind and body of the woman. Even for Vidyasagar, the falling standards of public morality and the increasing tendency towards adultery and foeticide-were two most important reasons for removing the prohibition of widow marriage. Unable to lead a life of self-denial, widows indulged in 'illicit' sex and thus put to shame all the three lineages of their husband, father and mother. The growing sexual anarchy in society was attributed only to the inability of the widows to restrain their libido. So it was necessary to regulate female sexuality into a socially legitimate channel, i.e, marriage. And for this it was essential to remove the prohibition. With all respect due for Vidyasar, the reform still sounded like ensuring social discipline and patriarchic control over women's bodies and desires. Even the Prudish Victorian culture did everything it could to silence sexuality – from divising technique to prohibit masturbation in women and children to putting draperies to hide the sexual suggestiveness of piano legs.

Out of Oedipus and castration complex a woman gives up her wish for a penis and puts in place of it a wish for a child, disillusioned with her clitoris, she focuses instead upon her vagina and thus fulfils what is culturally expected of femininity. Effect of institutions, practices of power operate in the binary frame of masculine 'subject' on the female 'other' and thus keeps undercover the inner truth of female desire. But Karnad's play suddenly exposes this autonomy as illusory. There are indications in the play which uncovers the fact that Rani makes love with the Naga deliberately which subverts the tradition of preserving the chastity of a woman. Rani has good many reasons to doubt that the Naga (transformed into her husband's body) is actually not her husband Appannna, but she hesitates and never questions this fact, because she does not want to be deprived of the heavenly bliss that she has been enjoying every night with the Naga – "No I won't, the pig, the whale, the eagle– none of them asks why. So I won't either. But they ask for it again. So I can too, can't I?" Naga is the symbol of supernatural power who fulfils the desires of the devotees. Naga is also the phallic symbol who employs the myth of life to educate Rani and initiate her into the pleasure of sex.

In Indian myth, the Sanskrit word 'Naga' is associated with element of water symbolising emotion, love, motion and life. Naga has its feminine attribution when paired with mothering i.e, creation. Shedding of skin symbolises casting off of the old self which is a powerful symbol of rebirth and renewal. Naga is a masculine symbol associated with the phallus of lightning with a tremendous assertive power. Dual snake imagery can be looked upon as the language of science. Observe the formation of DNA and how it forms a perfect serpentine double hellix–the transmitter of genetic information within the nucleus of the living cell– the image of orgasm that has been so devoutly worshipped since ages. Naga, the Cobra is symbol of 'Kundalini' power, a cosmic energy coiled and slumbering within men. In Hinduism Kundalini is a coiled serpent i.e, the residual power of pure desire. Naga also represents 'freedom' in Hindu mythology as because they can never be tamed. Naga represents fertility and creative life force, sexual desire and passion.

Karnad opts for the symbolic representation of Naga that not only educates Rani about sex, but liberates her from the shackles of suppression and repression to a great extent. Sex seems to be the road to salvation in Karnad, which is an important 'Purusartha' that paves the obvious path of liberation and freedom for Rani. Rani performs as per her human nature or 'Swadharma' by yeilding to the Cobra. "The Cobra simply looks at the bird's eyes with its own sight. The bird stares and stares ... unable to move its eyes ... it stands fascinated, watching the changing colours in the eyes of the Cobra." "Frogs croaking in pelting rain, tortoises singing soundlessly in the dark, foxes, crabs, ants, rattlers, sharks, swallows even the geese! The female begins to smell like wet earth. And stung by her smell, the King Cobra starts searching for her queen... It is there and there and there, everywhere".

A woman's self is defined in terms of her body and further reduced to her sexualised body that sees her body as her self. Rani's preoccupation with her mirror at first hardly allows to see her self. The gestalt that appears on the silvered surface is what grants her 'I' its identity. But in the beginning the 'I' is nothing more than a projection, and the reflection is far from real 'more constituent than constituted'. Then the image becomes the 'alienating destination' of the 'I' and places the 'I' in a 'fictional direction'. Given the *stade du miroir*, the 'I' adopts 'the armour of an alienating identity' and 'I' only becomes into being in the field of the other. Women's subjectiveness is regulated since they are constantly required to define themselves only through the 'male other'. Even Michael Madhusudan Dutta's 'Veerangana Kabya' draws the mirror-stage of Kaikeyi, the bad queen who accuses King Dasarath of not keeping his promises made to her, because she thinks that old age has robbed her of her youth and physical beauty and she has lost any kind of attraction for the king. And she feels unworthy of herself. Even 'Surpanakha', the subaltern demonic female reminds the readers of her love for the Highborn Ramanuj even after the humiliating castration of her nose by him who thinks her unworthy of Royal love. Women are only the vehicle of urges and cannot wish to be anything else than what men expect them to be. Men must resist any kind of enslavement by women, even the 'Elite Nazi soldiers also feared being engulfed by destructive female desires'. Men take the offensive before these women can put their horrible plans into practice. All her life a woman must drag her desire and her body like a monstrous fetter imposed on her spirit. Appanna's frowning indifference and rejection of any sexual relationship with Rani and his control over the body of the concubine show the diametrically opposite ways in which the female body is used–Rani as the new bride tries to draw Appanna's attention to her bedrecked reflection in the mirror, and when Appanna slams the door on her, the same mirror throws to her signals of her body's unattractiveness. Rani feels unworthy because of her unconsummated body and the concubine also feels unworthy because her only use is her body. It is only after her relationship with Naga, Rani picks up her mirror again and her 'I' enters history. The fragmented body image now forms its totality. Motherhood now becomes the truest sign of her cultural authority. The meaning of motherhood within the terms of a masculine culture and sense of motherhood out of natural human instinct and desire make her realise the grave injustice of the entire situation- "I was a stupid ignorant girl when you brought me here and now I am going to become a mother, I am not a parrot, not a cat or a sparrow. Why don't you take it on trust that I have a mind and can explain this charade to me?" The ordinary woman with normal desires even makes her son perform the dutiful ceremonial rites for his father after the Cobra (Naga) is dead.

The modern return to myth by Karnad de-mythcizes the husband-wife marital condition in Indian cultural context. Rani sheds her skin like the Naga to cast off her old self behind and is transformed and reborn with a cosmic energy. The element of water associated with the Naga now finds its alchemical and magical counterpart in the image of the inverted triangle which is an ancient symbol of femininity, a representation of female genitalia. Gender, creativity, Lunar, Yoni, Shakti, subjectivity, culmination–all are associated with this image. The eternal triangle denoting adulterous situation is juxtaposed with the inverted triangle of female desire. It is also the juxtaposition of two opposing dimensions – suppression of femininity by power and liberation of femininity by sensuousness. Rani's body that has been the site of confinement, violence, regulation and communication of the victimized gender-self, that same body is used by Rani to rebel, to subvert and to negotiate her space.

Bibliography

Bristow, Joseph, *Sexuality*, Routledge, New York, 1997.

Butler, Judith, *Gender Trouble*, Routledge, New York, 1990.

Dodiya, Jaydipsinh K. and K. V. Surendran, *Indian English Drama – Critical Perspectives*, Sarup & Sons, New Delhi, 2000.

Elam, Keir, *The Semiotics of Theatre and Drama* (1980), Taylor and Francis e-Library, 2005.

Foucault, Michel, Hurley, Robert, Trans. *History of Sexuality: The Use of Pleasure* (vol 2).

Hall, Gray and Clare Birchall, *New Cultural Studies: Adventures in Theory*, Edinburgh Univ. Press, Edinburgh, 2006.

Karnad, Girish. *Three Plays*. New Delhi: Oxford University Press, 1994.

Mukherjee, Tutun, ed. *Girish Karnad's Plays: Performance and Critical Perspective*, Pencraft International, New Delhi, 2006.

Ray, Bharati, *From the Seams of History: Essays on Indian Women*, OUP, London, 1995.

Tandon, Neeru, Ed. *Perspectives and Challenges in Indian English Drama* Atlantic Pub & Dist., New Delhi, 2006.

5

"(Political) Methods in Madness": A Study of Power Politics in Girish Karnad's *Tughlaq*

Joy Mukherjee

> "The power which establishes a state is violence; the power which maintains it is violence; the power which eventually overthrows it is violence."
>
> – Kenneth Kaunda, First President of Zambia.

In a country named after a political ruler (King Bharata), nothing can be more dear to the heart of the people of India (or Bharatbarsha) than politics. The country has ever been tossed by various political conflicts since times immemorial. The great epic *Mahabharata* projects the intrigues and counter intrigues of two aspirant groups–the Kauravas and the Pandavas–in order to usurp political power. The *Ramayana* also has the theme of conflict for political power. So we can say that political writings are as old as the history of Indian writing itself. In Indian drama also political themes have found great importance. The eminent drama personality Girish Karnad is famous for using indigenous material for his writings. In his second play *Tughlaq*, first produced in Kannada in 1964 and later translated into English, he delves deep into the history of medieval India to fetch up a controversial personality before his spectators' eyes. The very time the play deals with is replete with political scuffles and the basic conflict of the play, in one sense, is the fight over the possession of the throne.

The history of medieval India is stained with gore. After the Turk and the Afgan invasion during the eleventh and twelfth centuries, the Delhi Sultanate was established. During the next few centuries up to the arrival of the British, Delhi witnessed many murders, secret killings and other acts of violence under the temptation of gaining power. The Tughlaq dynasty (1320-1414) was not free from such acts of violence. To remain in power was a matter of maneuvering the arms and muscle strength as well as one of shrewd jugglery of brain power. By choosing a slice of Indian medieval history as his theme, Karnad naturally invites the theme of power-politics in his *Tughlaq*.

Tughlaq centres round the tussle for power between the king and the various power groups. Muhammad Bin Tughlaq was one of the most meritorious kings ever to ascend the throne of Delhi. He had deep knowledge in philosophy, logic, mathematics, medicine and even calligraphy. He was well versed with several languages like Persian, Arabic, Turkish and even Sanskrit. But even such a genius had to come down to the condition of a base intriguer to remain in power. On the other hand, the king had many enemies–the unhappy feudal lords–who had their own strategies for dethroning him. This conflict forms an interesting episode in Indian history and Karnad's play dramatizes this very power game.

The play opens to show King Tughlaq as an idealist. He is running after a vision of a unified India without the division of caste and religion. He has waived the jiziya tax to bring equality between the two principal communities of India, and he desires to establish the rule of justice in his kingdom without any consideration of might or weakness, religion or creed. Guided by his lofty idealism, he has taken the decision of shifting his capital from Delhi to Daulatabad and warns his subjects against taking it as a "mad whim of a tyrant" (Scene I, p. 149) as he has solid reasons to back up this decision. He wants to "build an empire which will be the envy of the world." (Ibid) But behind this idealist there is a dark history. Tughlaq is said to have taken the path of heinous conspiracy in order to come to power. He is said to be guilty of the crimes of patricide and fratricide. Exactly at the prayer time when Tughlaq's father, brother and other devotees were completely unarmed, an elephant went mad and the melee took the lives of the father and the brother. This cleared Tughlaq's way to kingship. The event is just hinted at in Karnad's play in the very first scene where a young man wants to prove the event to be an accident. "I tell you it was an accident", he says–but others object to his view and take it as an act of absolute deliberation. Power politics is such a game that pays no heed to even personal relationship.

Exactly like the path shown in Machiavelli's *Prince*, Tughlaq clears all the thorns that grows in his path and would lead to his future bleeding. Sheikh Imam-ud-din is a staunch critic of Tughlaq's rule and is engaged in uniting the masses against the king by publicly accusing him of the crimes of patricide and fratricide. As Zia-ud-din Barani reports to the Sultan, "He says the Sultan is a disgrace to Islam." (Scene II, p. 157) Under Imam-ud-din's instigation, there are widespread riots in Kanpur and half of the city is said to be on fire. Tughlaq has to use his shrewd brain to meet up the challenge. There is more news of trouble in the state as Ain-ul-Mulk has risen in revolt after the king has withdrawn him from the Governorship of Avadh and made him the Governor of Deccan. Now, Tughlaq decides to pluck one thorn with another.

Power politics is more a game of brain than one of physical strength. Everyone is using his cunning and shrewdness to overpower the opponent and only the fittest survives. In this game, courage, honesty and justice play no role as in *Tughlaq* Najib says, "Courage, honesty and justice! My dear Barani, we are dealing with a political problem!" (Scene II, p.158). Najib informs the Sultan that Sheikh Imam-ud-din "has a striking resemblance to you" (Scene II, p. 160). Tughlaq utilizes this valuable piece of information with his own wicked planning. He first destroys the credibility of the Sheikh by arranging for him a public meeting in Delhi when he comes here and forcing the public to stay indoors. When nobody is seen responding to the Imam's call, the Sultan makes him accept his offer of becoming his envoy to Ain-ul-Mulk. In the royal robe, royal turban, royal slippers, and sitting on the royal elephant, the Sheikh looks exactly like Tughlaq. When he approaches the enemy party along with some soldiers, Ain-ul-Mulk attacks and kills him, mistaking him to be the Sultan. His murder is graphically reported by Ratansingh:

> Ratan Singh: I couldn't understand what was happening. Neither did the Sheikh, obviously. His face was twisted with fear but he was shouting at the top of his voice asking us to stop. He didn't stand a chance. Arrows poured into him and within minutes he looked a gory human porcupine. (Scene IV, p. 173)

Ratansingh considers the death as a murder: "Sheikh Imam-ud-din was murdered, you know. In cold blood." (Scene IV, p. 173). The king was hiding behind some hills and attacked the party of Ain-ul-Mulk all of a sudden. This strategy of the king completely overwhelmed his enemies and the rebellion was quelled with the arrest of the Ain-ul-Mulk.

Machiavelli spoke of the lion-fox theory while writing on the essential qualities of a successful ruler. Tughlaq seems to be a combination of lion-like strength and fox-like cunningness. His way of dealing with Ain-ul-Mulk may bear witness to this fact. Even after catching him in his snares, he lets him go back to Avadh as the governor. As he says to his Step-mother and Najib, he pardons Ain-ul-Mulk merely for his ability to detect a flaw within minutes in his solution of a famous chess problem over which he spent days. Muhammad says, "I have just solved the most famous problem in chess. Even al-Adli and as-Sarakhi said it was insoluble. And it's so simple–" (Scene II, p. 154). This shows the artistic aspect in the great intriguer's character. The chess is also a symbol of the political game of power in which Tughlaq has just defeated Ain-ul-Mulk. He is, therefore, able to kill two birds with one stone and emerges as more powerful a ruler.

Power is a fruit over which there is always a tug-of-war. One who is on the throne has to face oppositions from the aspirant power-groups. The nobles are quite dissatisfied with various decisions taken by Tughlaq. They cannot digest the fact that the Hindus are exempted from paying jiziya tax. They are highly displeased at the unholy murder of Sheikh Imam-ud-din and are sacred at the Sultan's decision of transferring the capital from Delhi to Daulatabad. In Scene V, one Amir says, "But Daulatabad is a Hindu city and we'll be helpless there. We'll have to lick his feet" (p. 174). They are, therefore, eager to usurp the power themselves. This leads to the conspiracy of the nobles and the lords of the court. The Amirs, Sheikhs and Sayyids who are working against the dictatorship of the Sultan, are so powerful and influential that even the trusted courtier Shihab-ud-din comes to join their party. "You have persuaded me to do what I had never sworn to do", he says. (Scene V, p. 179) As Ratansingh proposes, they plan to kill Tughlaq at prayer time when the entire palace is unarmed. But the Sultan has the information of the whole plan and is able to take necessary measures to frustrate it. During the prayer Shihab-ud-din and the Amirs get up and take out their daggers to kill the Sultan. But Hindu soldiers rush into the room, surround the Amirs and arrest them. Tughlaq, however, remains engaged in his prayer, as if he is unaware of everything that happens around him. After completion of the prayer he talks with Shihab-ud-din and stabs him with his own hands in ferocious anger. He then says to Barani: "Are all those I trust condemned to go down in history as traitors?" (Scene VI, p. 185). He also sends orders of execution for all the escaped Amirs and Sheikhs. But the real trick is played when Tughlaq issues orders to make public announcement that there was rebellion in the palace and the nobles of the court tried to kill the Sultan and in his effort to save him, Shihab-ud-din died a martyr's death. This makes Barani comment: "Oh God! Aren't even the dead free from your politics?" (Scene VI, p. 185).

In this game of politics, the ultimate winner is Sultan Tughlaq. In *Macbeth*, Malcolm describes the state of Macbeth's country in the following words:

> Malcolm : I think our country sinks beneath the yoke;
>
> It weeps, it bleeds; and each new day a gash
>
> Is added to her wound... (Act IV, Scene iii)

Just like Macbeth's realm, Tughlaq's country is seen to be lying in a pool of blood. The reason of such bloodshed, of course, is very different in the two cases. When Tughlaq's step-mother accuses him responsible for futile deaths, he confesses that behind everything there is his desire for power:

> Tughlaq: (*shouting.*) No, they were not futile. They gave me what I wanted–power, strength to shape my thoughts, strength to act, strength to recognize myself.
>
> (Scene X, p. 204)

How power-politics brings about split within the group of nobles, has been traced by Karnad in *Tughlaq.* To win the favour of the king or to acquire influential position in the court, they engage in conspiracy against each other. In this matter, they heed no personal relationship, nor are they guided by any sort of morality. This is proved when Ratansingh betrays the group of nobles who conspired to kill the king. In this, he forgets all bonds of love and affection with Shihab-ud-din who adopted him as a brother, and sends him in the mouth of death by giving Tughlaq the information about Shihab's involvement in the plot. Behind this treachery also there is the story of power-politics.

Shihab-ud-din's father killed Ratansingh's father and usurped his Jagir. Ratansingh avenges by plotting thus the death of Shihab.

Apart from the centre of power, there grow up some epicentres of power too. These are the minor power groups which try to dominate the ruler. When more than one group start working in the same interest, there comes conflict and violence. This is seen in the case of Tughlaq's step-mother and Najib. She makes a frank confession before the Sultan that she has Najib poisoned. Tughlaq realises that this is because of her desire to have control over the king that made her kill him: "Get rid of Najib, so you could control me?" (Scene X, p. 204). Najib was slowly having influence over Tughlaq and she could not accept it. So, Najib becomes another victim in the game of power. But even the step-mother cannot have her mission fulfilled as Tughlaq sentences her to death: "Tell the Nayab Vizier I want her stoned to death publicly tomorrow morning" (Scene X, p. 205). No body is safe in this dangerous game of power.

Between the minor characters also there works the power-game. The two common men Aziz and Aazam are shown to be friends. They resort to conspiracy for their personal profits. They are able to cheat even the Sultan and frustrate his aspirant plans with their shrewd maneuvering of the affairs. Aziz disguising as Vishnu Prasad, a Brahmin of Shiknar, brings charges before the Kazi-i-Mumalik against the Sultan of illegally confiscating his land, and is able to get some land along with a handsome compensation. He also joins the Civil Service under the Sultan and takes Aazam as his associate. They are able to amass a huge amount of money when the citizens of Delhi are being taken to Daulatabad. Finally, Aziz kills Ghiyas-ud-din Abbasid, the descendent of Khalif Abbasid when he comes from far Arabia as the Guest of Honour of the Sultan, and poses to be Ghiyas-ud-din himself to avail all the facilities and comforts of the court. Thus a puny dhobi is able to cheat the shrewd king with his own sharp presence of mind.

But when Aazam decides to desert Aziz and escape through a tunnel in the fort, he is killed by the confidants of Aziz. When the shrewd Sultan recognises the imposter and charges him with the murder of the holy saint, he claims that he is 'Your Majesty's true disciple' as "he has spent five years of his life fitting every act, deed and thought to Your Majesty's words." (Scene XIII, p. 217) Aziz's arguments are successful in winning Tughlaq and he is sent to Deccan as an officer in the Sultan's army. The powerful man should be well aware how and when to use his power and when not. Thus Tughlaq can be ruthless with the rebel nobles, especially with Shihab-ud-din, but is kind in his treatment of the dhobi (washerman).

It has been argued that no Indian playwright can do what Shakespeare has done with British history or Brecht with European history. Karnad's present play is a successful adaptation of Indian history into drama. As Holinshed provided Shakespeare with the materials he needed to compose his historical plays, Ishwari Prasad supplied the basic framework for *Tughlaq*. Bedre R. T. and Meera M. Giram record the story behind the composition of *Tughlaq*:

> "It was during a conversation with Kirthinath Kurtkoti, the writer of the *History of Kannada Literature*, where Karnad made up his mind to write a history play. Kurtkoti complained that no Indian playwright could do with our history what Shakespeare did with the British history and Brecht did with the history of the West." (*yabaluri.org/Triveni/CDWEB/girishkarnadstughlaqjul2007.htm*)

But what has made the play famous is its contemporaneity in the Indian political scenario. K.R. Srinavasa Iyengar rightly detects a 'modern' approach in Karnad (Iyengar *735*). Bedre R.T. and Meera M. Giram hold the play to be a commentary on the deterioration of the Indian political situation after the time of Jawaharlal Nehru. Girish Karnad in "Introduction" to *Three plays* remarks:

> In a sense, the play reflected the slow disillusionment my generation felt with the new politics of independent India, the gradual erosion of the ethical norms that had guided the movement for independence, and the coming to terms with cynicism and real politik. (p. 7)

But even if the play is shorn of all the allegorical meanings inherent in it, the play remains a fine presentation of power politics. U.R. Anantha Murthy writes on *Tughlaq*, "Both Tughlaq and his enemies initially appear to be idealists; yet, in the pursuit of the ideal, they perpetrate its opposite. The whole play is structured on these opposites: the ideal and the real; the divine aspiration and the deft intrigue" (Murthy, U.R. Anantha, "Introduction to *Tughlaq*", *Three Plays*, OUP, New Delhi, p. 144).

References:

1. All the textual references are from Girish Karnad's *Three Plays,* Oxford University Press, New Delhi, 1996.
2. Iyengar, K.R. Srinivasa, *Indian Writing in English*, Sterling Publishers Private Limited, New Delhi, 2001, p.735.

Internet links

1. "Girish Karnad's *Tughlaq*: A Study in Existentialism and the Absurd", Bedre R. T. and Meera M. Giram, in http://*yabaluri.org/Triveni/CDWEB/girishkarnadstughlaqjul2007.htm, accessed on 14.5.12.*
2. "Girish Karnad's *Tughlaq* : A Nietzschean Enigma, *Rajesh Kumar Sharma*, in http://litarkay.tripod.com/tughlaq.htm, accessed on 14.5.12.
3. "Girish Karnad explores Tughlaq's character", S Manikutty and Sampat Singh, in http://articles.economictimes.indiatimes.com/2004-11-05/news/27379866_1_girish-karnad-tughlaq-hindus
4. "A Perspective on Symbols in Girish Karnad's *Tughlaq*", M. Jagadeswari in http://www.languageinindia.com/april2012/jagadeeswaritughlaq.pdf, accessed on 30.4.12.

6 Girish Karnad's Flowers: Contesting the 'Code of Piety'

Joydeep Bhattacharya

Religious austerity on the basis of the purity of body and mind is one of the suppressive narratives that curtail individuality within the monolith of religion. Religions tend to become most intolerant whenever they face any aberration from their self-formulated code of piety. The Brahmin discourse of piety is one such example that was configured in the Vedic era, consolidated largely during the post-Mughal and British periods (Bayly 370) and has been historically operational for centuries. This 'purity-conscious-culture', which is exclusive and elitist, is simply another mode of asserting the Brahminic supremacy in the caste hierarchy and, therefore, maintained both with consent and coercion. The subjective desire of an individual is ruthlessly curtailed here for the sake of an objective system, and man and woman alike are subjected to this normative model of purity. Under this rigid law of existence, the human subjectivity becomes circumscribed and helplessly conformist. Girish Karnad's monologue *Flowers* (2004) provides an excellent critique of this age-old normative excess with a view to exposing the unnecessary preoccupation with an impersonal world of rigid rules and a notion of inviolable piety. Although the 21st century urbane India might find the issue of Brahminic purity/impurity irrelevant, caste or casteism is still an unavoidable reality for the larger section of the society and so is purity-impurity dichotomy, drawing lines between higher and lower castes. Karnad's exploration of a Brahmin subjectivity looking for its identity inside a highly ossified system of rules therefore holds importance, as it tries to begin a dialogue with the formation of an individual self in a highly religious/casteist location.

In Karnad's dramatic canon, *Flowers* is a novel experiment in form for being a monologue. It has uniqueness also in its subject because it shows the difficulties of a circumscribed life of religious austerity that constrains the natural desires of, even, male sexuality. The Brahminic ideals, which come to rely on the piety of a coherent mind-body, is confronted with a Brahmin-cum-human subject split between the callings of tradition on the one hand and his life-long repressed desires on the other. The confrontation is immensely productive as it unveils the un-accommodative nature of religious configurations based on a superficial manifestation of purity and their suppressive understanding of human mind. Karnad makes use of the folktale of Veeranna, popularised by the Kannada writer T.R. Subbanna in his novel *Hamsageethe* (1952). Veeranna was a married priest, who lied about his mistress's hair in the 'prasada', called it God's hair and discovered, to the surprise of all, that God (the 'Shivalinga') indeed sprouted long silken hair. When a tuft of hair was pulled out to verify its originality, blood began to trickle from the wound of the 'lingam'. Submerged into a sense of sin, Veeranna committed suicide. In his typical style of appropriating the resources of folklore to understand modern experiences, private and public alike, Karnad recasts the legend of Veeranna. The purpose is to critically read a male subjectivity which is highly regulated by an ascetic regime of Brahminic discipline. The irony, which lies in the fact that a male/Brahmin-made system has become oppressive to one of its members who never consciously contemplates dissention, undermines the very qualitative nature of the system itself. Its mode of operation becomes debatable for its misplaced emphases that disregard the human subject for the sake of impersonal rules and misconceive a notion of piety and pollution.

The monologue of the unnamed priest presents a ritualised life dedicated exclusively to the service of the 'Shivalinga' in the village temple. It is his private domain secured by the indissoluble vigil of age-old customs and traditions. "I have lived here all my life and discouraged all friendly attentions from the world outside" (243), states the priest. He knows the 'linga' since his childhood and can brag about making the shrine the favourite place to the ruler of the land by virtue of his exquisite skill of floral decoration of the divine incarnation. The daily ritual of flower art over the 'linga' which is a "plain phallic stump with a smooth crown and a rough-hewn vulva for the base" (244) is his sort of worship of and assimilation into the divine. When the rite begins, there remains he and his God, nothing else of the universe; so much so that "the linga is my step-wife" (244), as complaints his wife. He decorates the 'Shivalinga' everyday and performs all the rites with such mechanical perfection that all the world outside becomes lost into insignificance. But this adulation of the divine symbol betrays the circumscribed existence where life has become mechanically ritualised and monotonous within the ossified wall of norms. Behind the praise and admiration of the devotees as well as of the ruler, inevitably lies his suppressed desperation gasping for a free space.

The culture of purity and pollution of the Brahminic ideals is pervasive. It does not only limit itself within the temple precinct but also proliferate in other domains to determine subjectivity. The domestic world of the priest is an extension of his temple. His home, which comprises his parents, wife and two children, exhibits the powerful presence of 'dharmic' refinement, restraint and the internalisation of the code by all the members, including his wife. It is a Brahmin's domain which must be made different from a lower caste house, say a Dalit one as we find in Vijay Tendulkar's *Kanyadaan*, where drunken fathers beat mothers and make love with them before their children, all in their muddy gutters (44). In such a context of religious/caste regulation, woman's role seems to bear upon a dual oppression; one springs from the immediate situation of religious/caste supervision, and the other comes from the traditional obedience to patriarchy which chiefly formulates these disciplinary systems. Wifehood, in the priest's home, is quite normally subjected to such dual regulation that produces a dutiful, pious wife who even shivers at the thought of a full-fledged sex with her husband lest it should awake the entire household and, even, she might see herself naked beside her husband. When the tired body of the priest comes back home after the end of the strenuous ritual in the temple, it meets a woman's body equally (or even more) circumscribed by the binary of piety and pollution. The suppression of subjective desire multiplies resulting in a loss of free space for all.

The only "breach in the invisible defences" (245) occurs when Ranganayaki, the affluent prostitute with bright teeth, dusky skin and a mole on her left breast, visits the temple and catches the eyes, which are hitherto unfamiliar with what it means to be the lust for a woman. The corollary emasculation fast creeps in, but the "fire raging in my loins" (Ibid) is hard to control. Then starts a passionate affair uncapped after years' repression. Suddenly, the mind begins to un-coat customs and runs to the prostitute's house after the evening 'puja' to re-utilise the flowers on her bronzed nudity. Tradition appears to be weak and cannot hold against this outburst of passion inasmuch as Ranga's body and her house provide a better alternative to both, the 'linga' and the Brahminic home. The magical curves, indents and shapes of her body, which inflame the imagination of a floral artist, are missing in the smooth, bland and stony phallus. He wonders, "Why didn't the Lord offer a form which inflamed invention like Ranga did?" (250). The living quality of the object of worship weighs more than the visibly lifeless stony stump that cannot even give a slightest note of appreciation to his brilliance. His heart still beats for the 'linga' since he grows with it, but Ranga's body kindles the hidden fire within and therefore proves irresistible. The prosititute's house, on the other hand, totally undermines the customary validity of the Brahminic home. The rigidly formulated domesticity on the line of piety-pollution dichotomy seems to be a circumscribed state of existence where the idea of sex-for-pleasure is summarily rejected as incompatible with Brahminic purity. It is a home where human instincts are to be conditioned according to the given standard. The priest laments,

> At home, we all bathed in the open, in the corner formed by the neem and the banyan trees in our backyard, so my wife covered herself with a sari even when she bathed. On the days I wanted her, I would give her a look she had come to recognize and late at night when everyone was fast asleep, she would crawl up to my room for a *furtive scuffle* in bed which demanded the minimum of uncovering. There were our two children and my old parents in the house and you never know who might call out for help. (my emphasis) (248-49).

The basic problem, however, lies somewhere else. The discursive home administers the construction of a particular wife who, the priest continues, "would have died of shame than be seen naked, even by herself." (249). Such codified categories fall in sharp contrast to the prostitute whose socio-cultural position makes her immune to similar regulations, she being conditioned by her category of 'impurity'. Her status of an outsider to this regime of purity renders her alluring to the repressed priest, who now finds the 'linga' as simplified dullness and his dharmic and chaste wife as a "wet rag" (253) with "all excitement for life drained out of her" (Ibid).

If the priest's unbridled involvement with Ranganayaki devalues the rigidity of religious imposition on human subjectivity, his miraculous acquittal from the alleged blasphemy is another way of undermining the oppressive system. As the news of his nocturnal adventure spreads all across, the ruler plans for a sudden visit to the temple at the late hour of night to confirm his alleged absence. He has to free all the flowers from Ranga's naked body and run back frantically to the temple in order to reuse them on the holy 'linga' before the ruler comes in – an act of unpardonable desecration of the divine. But God seems to be upset over the Brahmin's disobedience as the ruler discovers a long strand of hair tangled in the flower given to him for his 'prasada'. It is a blatant evidence of his heinous sin of redecorating God with the "polluted discards" (256) of a prostitute's body and subverting the norms of purity and impurity. In a moment of tumultuous consciousness, he replies, "If we believe that God has long hair…He will have long hair" (257). It is the only reply that he could give under such circumstance. But the system demands, "Prove it" (Ibid). After twelve days when the door of the inner sanctum opens, all awe-struck eyes witness "waves of jet black hair" (258) billowing out from the 'Shivalinga'. When a courtier pulls out a tuft of hair from it, the inanimate stone-stump bleeds. General scepticism suddenly gives way to mass hysteria over and veneration of the priest and lifts him to the status of a saint.

Paranormal miracle adds to the ironical power of folk tales, which are known for their plurality of meaning and contestation from within. The use of such miracle is in plenty in Karnad's many other plays. *Naga-Mandala*, for example, shows the subversion of social norms through Rani's magical acquittal in the snake-ordeal. The mysterious hair of God has a similar purpose that seeks to question the basic mode of configuration behind the deification of the 'distracted' priest. First, it seems to draw a 'divine validation' of the Brahmin's alleged immorality. Although he is blasphemous to the society and fallen even to his own eyes so long conditioned by irrevocable customs, God, most surprisingly, perhaps thinks otherwise. To Him, the priest's piety remains intact even after his sexual laxity, which is the most dreaded sin from any religious standard. God's different judgement seems to undermine this social system of validation that misplaces its emphases. Piety of the soul is overlooked for a recognisable piety of the body with an aim to creating a normative category. God's judgement can be taken for the authorial intervention in the irrational. Under the paranormal garb, Karnad hits at the religious absurdities and busts religion's 'logic' of piety and pollution. Again, the mysterious hair exposes the cognitive deficiency of the institutionalised religion. The easy transition from scepticism to veneration suggests its fallacy about the purity and contamination of human soul. The punitive crowd promptly becomes apologetic about their misreading of the priest and ready to believe in his asceticism. Their switch-over, which apparently glorifies Brahminic austerity, originally exposes the unnecessary preoccupation with unalterable rules and serves to de-legitimise their understanding of religion.

The final blow to orthodoxy is provided by the self-immolation of the priest – an act that seems to derive the most important significance of the miracle. The divine intervention can be interpreted as God's recognition of the priest's self-purity and also the fallacy of religious faith. But it seems also to present a case where an individual is shelled back into the square one – the circumscribed condition which he tried to transcend and where subjective liberation is a foreign idea. His deification owing to the miracle brings more restriction than before. He is "the state saint now, to be prized, protected and shown off to visiting envoys" (259). He loved God and still loves him. All he wanted was the courage to live like a normal human being, even "to live in disgrace" (Ibid). But there lies the limitation of the institutionalised religion. It remains suppressive and contractile even in its glorification. It makes him saint but unmakes his normal life. In this perspective, God's recognition of his innocence seems to be problematic. To God Himself, the priest might seem innocent and therefore He rescues him from punishment. But God's magical act ultimately proves suppressive because it causes more restraint on the priest's life. To the common people, the divine hair proves that the priest is still 'pure'. Thus, it glorifies the prevailing narrative of purity and pollution. Ideally, God's act might justify the priest, but in reality it re-asserts the norm of purity, which the priest opposes. The self-immolation at the end is therefore the priest's disavowal of this rigid orthodoxy. He dies not because of any fear for social castigation or sense of sin. He dies to protest. "God must understand I simply cannot live on His terms" (260).

Flowers can be viewed as a study of how religious orthodoxy can heavily restrict subjectivity. The Brahmin priest's psychological conflict between erotic love and religious responsibility, which is presented in the dramatic of the "triangulated desire" (Dharwadker xxxii) between a man and two women, ends in his self-immolation. His repressed life looks for a break from rigidity and exposes an equally repressed domesticity where his wife betrays the burden of double conformity, one to the traditional patriarchy, other to the Brahminic/religious obsession with piety. For the priest it becomes ironical because he has to suffer at the hand of a system which has been historically formulated by the male prerogatives. Aparna Dharwadker rightly comments that *Flowers* is the first work in the genre of folk-based plays and a small but important shift in Karnad's dramaturgy for its focus on male rather than female sexuality (xxxi). But, its significance multiplies when it is read as a text on Brahminic/religious excesses over male desire/ subjectivity. It then begins to exhibit the process of contesting the 'incontestable', relying chiefly on folklore's strength of irony. The style of monologue seems to befit the situation because it beautifully captures the sense of a lone act of confessional self-defence in the court of socio-religious persecution. As the priest goes near the temple tank to "seek in the narrow confines of that hollow the answers that God has denied" (260) him, he rewinds his past experience in a long utterance that leaves multiple questions before the authority, bestowed with the sole power of questioning. He is alone in his 'impure' act, and his loneliness is created by his lone figure on the stage. The monologue has all the potentials to be successful on the stage, but lot will depend on the individual execution of the actor in the priest's role.

Bibliography

Bayly, Susan. *Caste, Society and Politics in India/From the Eighteenth Century to the Modern Age,* Cambridge & India: Cambridge University Press, 2005.

Dharwadker, Aparna Bhargava. Introduction. *Collected Plays.* Vol. 2 by Girish Karnad, New Delhi: OUP, 2005. vii-xxxix.

Karnad, Girish. *Collected Plays,* Vol. 2, New Delhi: OUP, 2005.

-- *Three Plays: Naga-Mandala, Hayavadana and Tughlaq.* Trans. Karnad. New Delhi: Oxford University Press, 1994.

Tendulkar, Vijay. *Kanyadaan,* Trans. Gowri Ramnarayan. New Delhi: OUP, 1996.

7

Did You Feel Such Contemporary for me, Such Abhorrence?: The Dalit Situation in Karnad's Hayavadana

Kaustav Chakraborty

> Noble is your aim and sublime and glorious is your mission. Blest are those who are awakened to their duty to those amongst whom they are born. Glory to those who devote their time, talent and their all to the amelioration of slavery; glory to those who will reap their struggle for the liberation of the enslaved in spite of heavy odds, carping humiliation, storms and dangers till the downtrodden secure their human rights.
>
> – Dr. B. R. Ambedkar

Division of labour is found in all the societies of the world, its basis being inequality of men in intelligence, talent and culture, difference in needs of the people living in a civilized society and in their physical circumstances. It was present in ancient Egypt, Mesopotamia and Greece and even in the Indus Valley civilization because a complex city-based society cannot exist or be formed without some sort of division of labour. Manu who is ordinarily but erroneously considered to be the founder of Caste System in India (if there was such a historical person) lived no more than two thousand years back. And *Manusmriti* was written much after the castes (Not caste system) had evolved as a historical process and when the society, under the influence of Buddha's teachings, was rather developing 'anti–caste' tendency, threatening the privileges of dominant communities. The priestly class, the ruling class, the professional or agriculture based communities, the menial class and the outcastes had already emerged with their characteristic style of life, with their 66 privileges or deprivations from region to region with different nomenclatures. Originally castes could represent tribes belonging to different races/groups as they entered India from outside, separated mainly by different spoken languages, traditions, customs and professions etc. and later because of geographical and situational factors as they settled down in different parts of the country. Functional/occupational groups also consolidated themselves into castes with passage of time. It only required brilliant mind from amongst the educated community to analyze the situation and give it a systematic form in writing which in due course came to have an all-India format and Manu appeared on the scene. (No body could divide men by force overnight and set up a system of the type of caste formations of Manu's description, which were unequal in status and income etc.) He gave it a formal religious shape by grouping various interest groups into four main castes, viz. *Brahmins, Kshtriyas, Vaishyas and Shudras*, leaving vast majority outside the caste system, who were called *Anaryas /Avarnas / Dasyus / Das / Chandalas/Antajyas/ Panchamas*. While the first three castes were *Aryans*, the *Shudras* and the outcastes were the aborigines whom the *Aryans* subjugated, the *Shudras* being 'broken' people and the outcastes being Buddhist rebels as proved by Dr. Ambedkar in his writings. The outcastes have also been called *Ati-shudras* (utmost shudras), U*ntouchables, Depressed classes, Harijans* and *Scheduled Castes* from time to time. Nowadays these people call themselves *Dalits* which means 'Crushed People'. It is about these people that Dr. Ambedkar speaks in his book 'Annihilation of Caste', and these are the people who raised their voice at the 'World Conference Against Raceism in 2001'. The position of the *Shudras* in the Hindu scheme of things is deplorable but worse is the position of the outcastes.

However, Manu converted the natural system of division of labour into an unnatural one by imposing arbitrary rules against social mobility, especially the rule of caste being fixed permanently by birth, by sharp stratification based on too many privileges and rights for the higher castes and too many 67 handicaps for lower castes and by banning upward social mobility altogether. Because the whole scheme was so unnatural, they sold this morbid philosophy in the name of God. The *pursha Sukta* of the Rig Veda and other similar entries in the other three *Vedas* are later interpolations, when the caste system had been more or less established. That was just to convert the unholy polity into a holy one in the name of God. The theories of transmigration of soul and of *Karma* were invented to justify the graded inequality of castes, to justify the privileges of *Brahmins/ Kshtriyas* and to pacify the *Shudras* into acceptance of their deprivations as their destiny.

It does not help very much either to argue that caste is a colonial creation, and hence all that we see around us is really a motley crowd of hastily cobbled identities of very recent vintage. While it is true that identities, including caste identities, change over time, it would be incorrect to go to the extreme of asserting that caste itself is a colonial creation. Such a point of view not only makes the Hindus appear bigoted, which they are, but also stupid, which may not always be the case. It is as if the inhabitants of India had no identity worth the name prior to colonialism, and were one large, undifferentiated mass. The British changed all this, or so the story goes, and Hindus were calmly driven into all kinds of caste, religious and sectarian corals at the behest of colonial prodding. Yet, in a significant way, colonialism did make a difference. The way British officials understood caste obviously also affected the way caste was practised, and this led to some quite innovative relations between different jatis all over India. From the earliest moves of the Asiatic Society to the legal codification achieved by Henry Maine, the Brahmanical view was privileged as the correct interpretation of Hindu culture and custom. This is what gave Brahmans a larger than legitimate role in the conception of Indian society. a feature that is only recently being challenged from a variety of quarters. In *Hayavadana*, Devadatta, the only son of the revered brahmin, Vidyasagara, is "comely in appearance, fair in colour" whereas the son of the low-born ironsmith, is "dark and plain to look at". The lower caste people are the upper caste Hindus' 'Other'. But the 'Other' is not only separate and different like the member of another ethno-cultural, religious or linguistic group. This 'other' is a part of Hindu society, and yet apart from it. These caste identities are in fact the indications of absence. Each of these high and low castes represent what the other lack. Devadatta, on account of his brahminical lineage, has been portrayed as 'unrivalled in intelligence':

> Having felled the mightiest pundits of the kingdom in debates on logic and love, having blinded the greatest poets of the world with his poetry and wit, Devadatta is as it were the apples of every eye in Dharmapura (106).

Kapila, being a base born, marvels only at bodily items in order to suit as a perfect 'other' of the cerebral brahmin "...in deeds which require drive and daring, in dancing, in strength and in physical skills, he has no equal" (106). The notion that members of a certain caste share certain characteristics by the very fact of their birth seems to be just as important an ideological device as the notions of ritual purity or 'karma', and seems to operate at all levels of the caste hierarchy. Berreman has noted that:

> low castes hold particular stereotypes about each other which are shared to varying degrees by high castes. Blacksmith are considered physically powerful, Bajgis are considered hard working and clever.... Shoemakers are considered degraded in every respect. (*Hindus of the Himalayas*, 220)

Dr. Ambedkar as well has precisely stated:

> Caste system is not merely a division of labourers–which is quite different from division of labour–it is an hierarchy in which the divisions of labourers are graded one above the other. (*Writings and Speeches*, 67)

Moreover, the brahmins tactfully conceal their lack by colonizing the consciousness of those from the inferior castes. The brahmins have succeeded in convincing the low-castes to see the situations in the way they want them to see. Accordingly, Devadatta hardly appreciates the expertise of Kapila. With no sense of remorse, Devadatta can state that he has simply forgotten to come to the gymnasium though Kapila had asked him to witness how, in a wrestling, he "caught Nanda in a crocodile-hold". Kapila, on the contrary, not only praises Devadatta eloquently but even repeats the very language of the high-caste to project himself insignificant and greatly indebted:

> And I'll say it again. If it wasn't for you I would have been no better than the ox in our yard. You showed me that there were such things as poetry and literature. You taught me... (118).

The stereotypical assignment of intellectual/refined qualities to Devadatta, a high caste Brahmin, and that of the coarser/physical skills to Kapila, only because he is the son of Lohita, is essentially caste oriented. According to Berreman the ideological effect of this stereotyping is generally conservative and further damaging for the lower castes:

> The members of various castes are often said to be suited to that caste and no other by their very nature. To give advantages to low caste would be useless, as they would not be able to make use of them. (*Hindus of the Himalayas*, 220).

Kapila's evaluation that without Devadatta's guidance he "would have been no better than the ox in our yard", his acute interest in 'poetry and literature' and his declaration: "Even my parents aren't as close to me as you [Devadatta] are. I would leave them this minute if you asked me to" (118) point out another aspect of caste psychology. Apart from the emotional attachment, the unconscious motive that pulls Kapila incessantly towards Devadatta, despite the latter's maltreatment, is that of getting hold of the upper-caste norms. K. Kapadia has commented that,

> this adoption of upper-caste norms is, instead, an attempt to appropriate a prestigious cultural style that, they feel, enhances a change in their low-caste status. (*Siva and her Sisters*, 11)

It seems that Kapila, in his endeavour to adopt the upper-caste norms, has overlooked the fact that in the entire history of caste ridden India, the lower castes have never been allowed to specialize in the knowledge and the skills of the higher caste. Kapila's catastrophe can be equated with that of Ekalavya in *Mahabharata*, which reveals the fact that the educational competence of the talented individual among the lower castes has only brought victimization and penalty.

Louis Althusser in the article entitled *Ideology and Ideological State Apparatuses* has talked about the materiality of ideology i.e., how ideology determines not only what we think but also what we do. The extent of Kapila's inferiority complex which is the consequence of the age old misinformation can be understood if we carefully speculate his actions in the beginning of Act One:

> Devadatta: Sit down.
>
> (This is of course exactly what Kapila wants. He sits down on the floor).
>
> And don't speak...
>
> (Devadatta gets down on the floor to sit beside Kapila. Kapila at once leaps up and gestures to Devadatta to sit on

> the chair. Devadatta shakes his head but Kapila insists pulls him up by his arm. Devadatta gets up).
>
> You are a pest.
>
> (Sits on the chair. *Kapila sits down on the ground (happily…)* (119).

The uneasiness from which Kapila suffers when Devadatta comes down to his level to sit on the same floor and the way he feels relieved and 'sits down on the ground happily' near Devadatta's feet, who is now sitting on the chair, clearly disclose how, through constant casteist proliferation and torture, the lower caste people have been convinced with the caste-ideology that they can not and should never be at par with the superior castes. One such document of dissemination, *Manusmriti*, the foundational text that laid down the code of conduct for Hindus, states that the lower caste is born from the feet of the Lord while "from His mouth He created the priests, from His arms the ruler, from His thighs the commoner" (Verse 31). *Manusmriti* further affirms that when a brahmin is born, "he is at the top of the earth, as the lord of all living beings, to guard the treasure of religion" (Verse 99); whatever there is in the universe, the brahmin "deserves all of this because of his excellence and his high birth" (Verse 100). There verses show how literature and myth, created and perpetuated by brahmins, seek to justify the social hierarchy and sanction their superiority. Stanley Rice accurately observes:

> If then, it be admitted that brahmans, at least in the earlier stages, became the superior caste by reason of their priestly office and all that is thereby implied, it is not unnatural that they should have made use of their position to glorify themselves, as the priesthood has shown itself apt to do in other countries. That they did this in extravagant fashion, claiming privileges unheard elsewhere and even arrogating to themselves the position divinities may be admitted (122).

Kapila and Devadatta have been described as two friends with 'one mind one heart':

> The world wonders at their friendship. The world sees these two young men wandering down the streets of Dharmapura, hand in hand, and remembers Lava and Kusha, Rama and Lakshmana, Krishna and Balarama.
>
> (*Sings.*) Two friends there were – one mind, one heart (106).

However, there are shadow lines of demarcation and inequality that forbids them from becoming complete friend. Even, the Bhagavata's repeated stressing of the obvious "Two friends there were one mind, one heart" ironically hints at this reality. This can be further explained if we notice the difference of attitude and expression between Kapila and Devadatta, during their interaction. Like a typical classist, Devadatta asks:

> What do you know of poetry and literature? Go back to your smithy–that's where you belong (119).

He explicitly delivers his irritations and annoyance without thinking how it would hurt Kapila:

> Dava Datta: You call yourself my friend. But you haven't understood me at all...(*irritated*) Don't start on that now. You said it fifty times already...Why don't you go home? All I wanted was to be by myself for a day. Alone. And you had to come and start your chatter (118-19).

Kapila, on the other hand, naively conveys his emotional attachment in unequivocal terms:

> Don't you know I would do anything for you? Jump into a well–or walk into fire? Even my parents aren't as close to me as you are. I would leave them this minute if you asked me to (118).

Kapila's sincerity is again revealed in his earnest attempt in tracing out Padmini's house. Even regarding this Devadatta has been skeptical:

> But should I have trusted this to him? He means well–and he is a wizard in his smithy, in his farm, in his fields. But here? No. He is too rough, too indelicate. He was the wrong man to send. He's bound to ruin the whole thing (Anguished) (122).

Kapila proves how mistaken Devadatta has been in his estimation of his companion. Kapila's self supposition has been relatively accurate:

> My dear Devadatta, your cloud-messenger, your bee, your pigeon is sitting right in front of you and you don't even know it? You wait here. I'll go, find out her house, her name... (122).

Kapila further exhibits his genuine fondness for his pal by easily slaying himself, after discovering that Devadatta has already slaughtered himself before the goddess Kali:

> Kapila: You've cut off your head! You've cut off your head! Oh my dear friend, my brother, what have you done? Were you so angry with me? Did you feel such contempt for me, such abhorrence? And in your anger you forgot that I was ready to die for you? If you had asked me to jump into fire, I would have done it. Pf you had asked me to leave the country, I would have done it. If you had asked me to go and drown in a river, I would have accepted. Did you despise me so much that you couldn't ask me that? I did wrong. But you know I don't have the intelligence to know what else I should have done. I couldn't think–and so you've pushed me away? No, Devadatta, I can't live without you. I can't breathe without you. Devadatta, my brother, my guru, my friend...(*Picks up the sword*).

You spurned me in this world. Accept me as your brother at least in the next. Here, friend, here I come. As always, I follow in your footsteps.(*Cuts off his head. It's an easier death this time*) (138-39).

Padmini, who goes in search of the friends, is approved by the goddess who favours her with the blessing of life of the two friends; but she commits an error. Padmini happens to transpose the heads with the result that there are two men now–one with Devadatta's head and Kapila's body and the other with Kapila's head and Devadatta's body. Since head is superior according to *shastras*, Devadatta scores a point over Kapila. Kapila is the ultimate loser in this ludicrous bargain of mixing up of heads. He has lost not only his body to Devadatta but also his peace on account of the *vasavas* lodged in Devadatta's body. His mundane logic that body being the real person Padmini should belong to him is spurned by both Devadatta and Padmini. Finally Devadatta and Padmini go back to the city where Devadatta enjoys the benefits of Kapila's well-trained body. Kapila, who feels hurt and cheated remains in the forest to train the brahmin's body dancing by his head like a corpse and shape it into form.

Padmini, the wife of a brahmin, stumbles on the opportunity of relishing Kapila's 'ethereal shape', even maintaining her caste-superiority. She in fact seizes the scope of having the best of the two men–Devadatta's head and Kapila's body. In her endeavour she deprives Kapila of his skills and enables Devadatta to exploit Kapila's physique, till it once again grows delicate with time. In this connection we must also not forget that every visible error or apparently unmotivated act, according to Freud, is the outcome of the unconscious/repressed desires. The notion that human beings are motivated, even driven by desires, fears, needs, and conflicts of which they are unaware that is, unconscious was one of Sigmund Freud's most radical insights, and it still governs classical psychoanalysis today. The unconscious is the storehouse of those emotions, desires and unresolved conflicts we do not want to know about because we feel we will be overwhelmed by them and thereby try to repress them. This repression, however, does not eliminate our suppressed emotions. Rather, it gives them force by making them the organizers of our current experience: we unconsciously behave in ways that will allow us to "play out", without admitting it to ourselves, our conflicted feelings about the emotions we repress. Thus, for psychoanalysis, the unconscious isn't a passive reservoir of neutral data, rather it is a dynamic entity that engages us at the deepest level of our being:

> Our unconscious desires not to recognize or change our destructive behaviours–because we have formed our identities around them and because we are afraid of what we will find if we examine them too closely–are served by our defenses. Defenses are the processes by which the contents of our unconscious are kept in the unconscious. In other words, they are the processes by which we keep the repressed, repressed in order to avoid knowing what we feel we can't handle knowing (Lois Tyson, 15).

Hence, Padmini's 'mistake' is in fact the outward manifestation of the well-defensed desire of experiencing the thrill of both the men that she had been repressing in her unconscious.

Towards the end of the play, Padmini walks with her child into the embrace of Kapila and claims the child to be the child of both Devadatta and Kapila. Before performing sati, Padmini once again displays her caste-consciousness. She entreats the Bhagavata to give her child to the hunters residing in the forest, by telling them it's Kapila's son so that they will bring him up; when the hazardous task of bringing up a child till he is five years old is complete, then he should be taken to the Revered Brahmin Vidyasagara of Dharmapura. Although Padmini had once regarded the child to be the son of both the men, she clearly utilizes Kapila's identity only to hand over the well-nourished child to Vidyasagara as Devadatta's son so that the child might he considered as the progeny of the upper caste brahminical ancestry. In this connection the observations made by A. Jagamohana Chari is noteworthy:

> In Karnad's Hayavadana, the metaphysical dialectic or discourse we come across consists in its essence in the statement made by Devadatta: "According to the *Shastras*, the head is the sign of a man" and also later in Padmini's utterance: "Must the head always win". If we examine the logic which is pre-given, Devadatta's head should succeed in explicating Kapila's body to his and Padmini's satisfaction, after it is hooked on to Devadatta's head. But after about a year his head fails to enjoy the liveliness of the body. Its litheness begins to wear off owing to the lack of the physical labour. Consequently Devadatta loses Padmini to Kapila once again. And Kapila who finds the brahmin's body a drag and a torture trains it by hard physical labour in the forest. And he "lives" unlike his friend. The subversionist folk element in the play also plays on this text "live" into a disruptionist comment on the quality of life of the city, the knowledge of *Shastras* and *Varnashrama dharma* as dead and oppressive...a brahmin head is the repository of abstract ideas divested of all sensuousness. Abstract ideas of ritualistic nature which tradition has sanctified are useful for a brahmin like Devadatta in exercising authority or dominance over a non-brahmin like Kapila. But he finds in reality or in his experience sensuous pleasures of the body inescapable. So he discovers the lie inherent in his own being. He refuses to come out of it because it represents the mystique on which the class/caste thrives. Kapila too, who has bowed to the hegemonistic mystique yields to the lie and sacrifices his own passion for Padmini, when he cuts off his head in Kali temple (Dodiya, 234).

Both Devadatta and Kapila are victims of the metaphysical mystique which is at the base of *Varnashrama dharma*. Even the name Kapila, that means 'the dark one', is the signifier of the caste hierarchy, for the name itself gives the impression as if he is the inferior/impure/other of the brahmin Devadatta, whose name itself makes him appear superior and blessed for Devadatta means, the offering that befits God. In this relation we can recall Verse 98 from *Manusmriti* which confirms that the very birth of a brahmin(born to be a priest) is the eternal physical form of religion; for he is born for the sake of religion and is fit to become one with ultimate reality.

Girish Karnad is deeply concerned with the social deformity of the caste Hindu society. Questions have often been raised whether at all a non-Dalit writer like Karnad can give an authentic documentation of the subaltern reality. As the Dalit writer Sivakami states:

> Most nondalit writers feel and contend that they are better storytellers on dalits than dalits themselves...In other words, they still view the work of art as a safe play of skill coupled with the aesthetics that they are accustomed to. (*Touchable Tales*, 24)

Despite these criticisms we must not forget that apart from Karnad we have a host of writers like Mulk Raj Anand and Arundhati Roy who do not belong to the deprived caste/class yet have effectively depicted the realities of these downtrodden through works like *Untouchable* and *The God of Small Things*. The essential humanism in Karnad has stimulated him to expose the evils of caste system not only in this drama but also in other plays like *Tale-Danda*. *Tale-Danda* tells the story of a community settled in a small kingdom within the present day boundaries of Karnataka, in 1168 A.D. The year marks the ascendance of Basavanna, a saintly person and a major proponent of the Bhakti movement, who draws thousands of 'sharanas' or the devotees from mainly the economically oppressed lower caste, by his secular and egalitarian preaching. The members of the upper caste, however, become alarmed and the growing resentment surfaces when Kalavati, a brahmin's daughter is given in marriage to Shalivanta, a cobbler's son. The enraged Brahmins are held in check by King Bijjala. The king's ambitious son, Soyideva, takes the advantage of the explosive situation. He incarcerated the King and usurps the throne. Basavanna realizes that the movement that he has nurtured has gone berserk. He dies, a broken-hearted man. The sharanas are ruthlessly crushed and Soyideva rules in a land where the caste system regains its sway.

In *Hayavadana*, Karnad illustrates how the consciousness of and the participation into the caste politics of power has rendered the friendship of Kapila and Devadatta, incomplete. Swami Dayananda has aptly described caste as "an anachronism that had long outlived its usefulness, a force that is working for the disruption of Hindu society and a cancer that is slowly poisoning the very life blood of the nation" (Pandey, 74). The deep rooted feelings of caste that are imbedded in the psyche of the people induce the playwright to admit:

> In Karnataka as elsewhere in India, a man has only to open his mouth and his speech will give away his caste, his geographical origins, even his economic status. (Introduction, *Three Plays*)

The only relationship that finds completeness is that of Padmini's son and Hayavadana. The Kapila-Devadatta liaison has been partially poisoned by the malignant *Varnashrama dharma*, whereas the unawareness of it enables the child to associate himself unreservedly even with a horse an attachment that brings fulfillment to both of them. The child, who is found not to be able to laugh like a human child, laughs only when the horse, born of a princess and a 'gandharva' cursed to live like a horse until he loved a human, laughs a real laughter to make the child laugh and in the process it gains its completeness by getting rid of the human voice. This mutual affection further exposes how inhuman the caste system is the social distortion that alienates friends and leaves human-relationships incomplete.

As Homi K. Bhabha says, nations are themselves narrations in which specific identifiers are employed to create an exclusive and homogeneous conception of the national tradition. Such signifiers of homogeneity always fail to represent the diversity of the actual national community for which they purport to speak and, in practice, usually represent and consolidate the interests of the dominant power groups within any national formation. The myth of a national tradition is employed not only to legitimize a general idea of a social group (a people), but also to construct a modern idea of a nation state in which all the instruments of state power (e.g. military and police agencies, judiciaries, religious hierarchies, educational systems and political assemblies or organizations) are subsumed and legitimized as natural expressions of a unified national history and culture. Texts like *Hayavadana* show how, the dalits have miles to go for seeking acceptance from the wider society by creating and legitimizing a space for themselves within the nationalist narratives and the desolation gets accurately echoed in the following lines:

> Who am I
>
> Don't scratch old wounds
>
> Who am I
>
> Not what you think I am
>
> I have grown up playing in the dust of my alleyways
>
> I have learnt to fight for myself at an age when others dream dreams
>
> I am that winsome bud which blooms on my forefathers' graves

And must smilingly endure every punishment merely because it exists. (Ishrat Aafreen)

Bibliography

Ambedkar, Babasaheb. *Dr. Babasaheb Ambedkar: Writings and Speeches,* Bombay: Government of Maharashtra, 1987.

Anand, S. ed. *Touchable Tales: Publishing and Reading Dalit Literature,* Pondicherry: Navayana, 2003.

Berreman, G. *Hindus of the Himalayas,* University of California Press, 1963.

Bhabha, Homi K. 1990. Nation and Narration, London: Routledge.

Bouglé, C. *Essays on the Caste System,* trans. D. Pocock, Cambridge University Press, 1971.

Dodiya, Jaydipsinh, *The Plays of Girish Karnad: Critical Perspectives.* Prestige, 1999.

Kapadia, K. *Siva and her Sisters: Gender, Caste and class in Rural South India',* Boulder, CO: Westview Press, 1995.

Karnad, Girish. *Collected Plays (Volume 1).* Delhi: Oxford University Press, 2005

— *Three Plays.* Delhi: OUP, 1994

Mukherjee, Tutun. *Girish Karnad's Plays: Performance and Critical Perspectives,* Pencraft International, 2006.

Pandey, D. *The Arya Samaj and Indian Nationalism,* New Delhi: S. Chand, 1972.

Rice, Stanley. *Hindu Customs and their Origins.* Delhi: Low Price Publications, 1993.

Smith, K. Brian and Dongier, Wendy ed. *The Laws of Manu (Manusmriti),* Penguin Books: India, 2000.

Tyson, Lois. *Critical Theory Today,* Routledge: India, 2008.

8 Interrogating Gender Stereotypes in the Plays of Vijay Tendulkar

Arpita Dasgupta

"Why can't men limp behind? Why aren't women ever the masters? Why can't a woman at least ask to live her life the same way as man?" cries out Sarita in Vijay Tendulkar's *Kamla.* At the same time, while voicing protest against the oppression of women, her utterances seem to uphold paradoxically, the male bias in the 'gendered' distribution of power as she says: "Why must only a man have the right to be a man?" "Those who do manly things should be equal to men. Those who don't, are women. And there will be some among them who have beards and moustaches too. Isn't being Prime Minister of India a manly thing? And isn't it an effeminate thing to grovel at that Prime Minister's feet?" Such age-old gender stereotypes have been explored in the plays of the journalist turned playwright Vijay Tendulkar "with an honesty and depth that often scared the audiences away", to quote his eminent contemporary Girish Karnard. However, it rarely gets more complex and intriguing than Silence! The Court is in Session, Sakharam Binder, and A Friend's Story where "the ideological construction of gender" which "keeps the male dominant" to quote Gayatri Chakravorty Spivak is alternately challenged and vindicated, and in the process essentially problematized.

In *Shantata! Court Chalu Aahe,* translated by Priya Adarkar as *Silence! The Court is in Session*, an apparently independent, nonconformist woman Leela Benare, is pitted against an orthodox, patriarchal society. With the professed aimof 'spreading enlightenment', apart from having 'some fun to do with a court' the members of The Sonar Moti Tenement (Bombay) Progressive Association arrive at a nearby village to theatrically depict the trial of American President Lyndon B Johnson for producing atomic weapons. To pass the time before their 'proper show' on stage, they decide to enact a mock-trial against one of the members of their troupe. The accused chosen when she herself is backstage, in preference to other willing candidates, is Leela Benare, regarding whom, as Ponkshe and Karnik, two of the actors whisper, there is some secret to be divulged. A lawyer by profession, Sukhatme declares: "There's not much difference between one trial and another. But when there's a woman in the dock, the case does have a different complexion". Sharing this general excitement "to see what the trial of a woman is like" is ironically, the other female member of the troupe, Mrs. Kashikar, whose abject subordination to her husband only emphasises male domination in society.

Accordingly it is the 'gendered' social status of Miss Benare, as per conventional middle-class values, that serves as a yardstick for judging her conduct as an individual. Investigating the charge of infanticide, the mock-trial finds her guilty of a much more serious crime, 'unmarried motherhood', and imposes on her the punishment of abortion! In so doing, her personal life is intruded upon in the most indecent manner and very soon the 'mock-trial' assumes much serious proportions, bringing malicious fun to all participants, except the woman concerned.

Meant to expose and discipline the libertine Miss Benare, the mock-trial reveals in turn the hypocrisy and moral depravity of the orthodox middle class society. Accusing Benare of infanticide, Sukhatme as the prosecution lawyer grapples for choicest expressions to glorify "woman as the mother of mankind. Our culture enjoins us to perpetual worship of her" he says. The trial then veers towards a ruthless dissection of Benare's character with reference to her illicit relationship with a married Professor Damle, which has achieved fruition in her womb. This in turn digs up her adolescent affair with her maternal uncle and establishes her in the court as an immoral, promiscuous woman. Denouncing grown-up, unmarried, girls as a "sinful canker on the body of society", Mr. Kashikar, the judge and also a witness in the mock-trial prescribes child marriage as a corrective measure and toying his line, as always, his spouse further opines "It's the sly new fashion of women earning that makes everything go wrong." In the course of the trial Miss Benare learns that she is on the verge of losing her job and the child in her womb, as ordained by the court, shall be destroyed. Thus the patriarchal court endeavours to discipline the errant, self-assertive woman, abiding by the 'rule laid down for us by tradition': 'Na stri swatantryamarhati' i.e. 'Woman is not fit for independence.'

The muffled voice of woman, in this case Leela Benare, is allowed ten seconds for self-defence just before the verdict. What follows is a monologue in which Miss Benare pours her heart out. In an unabashed manner she talks about her longings, betrayals she suffered, scoffs at the 'ferocious look', 'worn-out phrases', 'unsatisfied desires' of the so-called 'cultured men of the twentieth century' and strongly declares : "My private life is my own business. I'll decide what to do with myself; everyone should be able to!" Not yet aware of the oncoming verdict, she now wants to give birth to her 'son' who apart from his mother, must have "a father to call his own- a house- to be looked after- he must have a good name!"

It is here that the non-conformist, iconoclastic and hence punishable stand of Miss Benare becomes ambivalent, problematic. Wary of being an unwed mother, she attempts, though in vain, to enter into a matrimonial alliance with useless, undeserving men like Ponkshe and Rokde; thereby succumbing to the male-centred norms of social recognition. Her desperation is also glimpsed in her playful advances to the innocent villager Samant. It is interesting to note, that she refers to her unborn child as her 'son'. Does this imply she has gone through a gender detection test of her foetus, a medical test not without legal complications and completely banned in certain parts of India with high rate of female infanticide?! Why did she with her progressive views feel the need for this test? And if there is no specific medical knowledge behind this utterance, then its male bias is all the more surprising and paradoxically significant in the given context.

In the first Act, she is presented as an essentially lively, spirited woman, whose strong personality is yet to be ravished by the mock-trial. Even then, as she sings or recites a portion of a poem with full vigour and zest for life, is audible an underlying cry for a secure, settled life. While alone with Samant, before the arrival of her co-actors, she sings: " Oh, I've got a sweetheart/ Who carries all my books/He plays in my doll house,/And says he likes my looks/ I'll tell you a secret-/ He wants to marry me/ But Mummy says, I'm too little/ To have such thoughts as these." In view of the later revelations, this seems to hark back to her adolescent experience with her maternal uncle. Assuming her co-actors as the 'children' in her class, the teacher Benare states "There is a battle sometimes, where/ Defeat is destined as the end,/ Some experiences are meant/ To taste, then just to waste and spend..." through a poem which, significantly helped Tendulkar to conceive her character. She is caught unawares by her co-actors in a mock-trial at a point when she is singing about the stolen nest of a 'poor little sparrow', albeit in a cheerful tone, that will recur as a poignant background score at the end of the drama!

Thus from the very beginning, as has been noted, Tendulkar provides subtle hints of the vulnerability of this otherwise strong woman. Her modern, progressive, emancipated outlook to life is offset by the vestiges of patriarchal ideology she has subconsciously retained. Miss Benare is caught at the crossroads of upcoming women emancipation and reigning patriarchal orthodoxy. Unwittingly she partakes of both the worlds which contributes to her angst-ridden state and accounts for her apparently ambiguous remarks: "I thought I should just laugh and laugh till I burst... And I used to cry my guts out." "Life is a something that's nothing- or a nothing that's something." "There's great joy in a suicide that's failed. It's greater even than the pain of living." She hates, despises her body which overshadows her mental refinement, even her sentiments, emotions in the eyes of man. At the same time she also loves and is grateful for the passionate moment "so beautiful, so blissful, so near to heaven!" as a 'witness' of which, 'a tender little bud' is flowering in her body. Torn between conflicting urges, Miss Benare displays a wide range of attitudes that culminate in her agonizing refusal to accept the shocking verdict: "No! No! No!- I won't let you do it- I won't let it happen- I won't let it happen!" While the other characters move backstage to prepare for their 'actual' show, reeling under the effect of her mock-trial, "Benare feebly stirs a little. Then gives up all effort."

Bearing striking similarities to Benare and embodying a greater anomaly in the conservative society is the masculine female Sumitra in *Mitrachi Goshta*, translated by Gowri Ramnarayan as *A Friend's Story* . Her entire personality has "a natural, aggressive masculinity, but with a figure irresistibly attractive to men." Having grown up with boy playmates this intelligent as well as attractive girl is good at sports, smokes and cycles her way through the college campus, heedless of the interest she generates among the students- nerds and scamps alike. In an attempt to feminize her as per conventional norms, her family members arrange a match for her. On meeting him she feels "no physical thrill" though "the decent boy" feels "it all". A "girl is a girl after all" to quote Sumitra; nurtured by a male-dominated society with its fixed set of rules, she retains a basic need to conform to the accepted norms. Sumitra therefore tries to rectify her supposed 'deficiency' in her own preposterous way, the failure of which even leads to her suicide attempt. On returning from hospital, she cross-dresses for a male role in a drama that further complicates the situation. Her naturally different instincts reigning supreme, she falls in love with Nama who playes her love interest and has a steady boyfriend in Manya Dalvi, while her domineering presence on stage deeply arouses Pande, the roommate of Bapu, the narrator and Mitra's only friend!

No longer wary of her 'difference', Sumitra rebelliously determines to consummate her lesbian urges. Fiercely possessive of her 'lady love' she will not brook any impediment to their relationship: be it her rival Dalvi, the friendly counsel of Bapu, or for that matter Nama herself, if she dares to move apart and get married. "Nama can't get away. I hold her in the palm of my hand" says Sumitra actualizing as if the theatrical command of her 'male role' over her 'delicate and doll-like' heroine. The imbalance of power between them is apparent in Nama's anguish: "She doesn't allow me to edge in a word, as if she's always right, what she likes is the best... Everything has to be decided by her. And I must agree without any reservations". However, based on the false premise of gender crossing, this pseudo-male-female power equation is doomed from the very beginning. Thus while ditching girls like Nama happens to be the 'man' Dalvi's 'business' much like Benare's Damle, the 'lesbian bitch' Mitra has to leave college for her genuine passion and Nama's honour is salvaged through matrimony in Calcutta.

Then comes the final and most disturbing twist in the drama. Wrecked at the loss of Nama, Mitra takes a destructive plunge to assert her femininity that though not unnoticed , had paled before her 'not normal' proclivities. Through the eyes of Bapu, we find her frequenting a club in 'outrageous costume' and make-up. Scoffing at the status of 'a good little girl', she prostitutes herself to the officers in a drunken state, crying out in desperation : "I'm a human being, I have my will...I'll do what I like". The final words on her lips show her as a lonely individual pining for her estranged friend even more than her lost love. The wheel comes full circle as she again attempts suicide, this time with success. Thus she renounces the callous world that understands nothing but strict conformation to its 'man-made' rules.

While in *Silence! The Court is in Session* and *A Friend's Story*, Tendulkar presents two 'different' women's difficulties in the male-centric society; in *Sakharam Binder* he looks beyond the boundaries of social sanction with astounding, almost obscene frankness, raising disturbing questions about social institutions, gender politics.

A book binder by profession, Sakharam is a man who is proud of his supposedly radical, unorthodox views. Compelled by the abuses of his Brahmin father to run away from home at the age of eleven, he introduces himself as "a Mahar, a dirty scavenger" as a defiant rejection of the casteist hegemony. Scoffing at the married men in the village who don't "have the guts to do a thing openly!", the unmarried Sakharam lives in, by turn, with those homeless women who have fallen apart from their husbands. He offers each of them shelter with the additional promise of 'a sari, a choli and fifty rupees. Plus a ticket to where she wants to go' on leaving him and his house. "Everything good and proper, where Sakharam Binder is concerned", he asserts. Yet, while in his house, the woman must not forget that he is the 'master' there. "The others must obey, that's all. No questions to be asked." The play begins with the arrival of Laxmi, the seventh woman he brings home, whom he tells categorically: "You'll have to be a wife to me, and anyone with a little sense will know what to make of that." A rebel and orthodox at the same time, Sakharam believes not in marriage but in the imbalance of power/ lopsided distribution of power in orthodox marital relationship which he intends to continue in his house without the bonds of wedlock! Bereft of any other option, the 'abandoned', helpless woman, in most cases, cannot but accept this ignominy in order to survive in this patriarchal society.

Such is the case with Laxmi who has been discarded by her husband for her inability to conceive by him. A docile, submissive woman, accustomed to the rigours of male domination, she puts up with the excessive demands and accompanying assaults of Sakharam to the best of her ability. In so doing, she brings about interesting changes in Sakharam. The apparently atheist Sakharam who "is not scared of God or of God's father!", starts worshipping the deities, takes regular bath, wears clean clothes and seldom indulges in drinking bouts. He even brings home an image of Lord Ganesha, he had earlier made fun of, on the occasion of Chaturthi. Tired of her after a year he parcels her off, but has to acknowledge this traditional, religious woman "left a mark before she went away."

A complete contrast to Laxmi, the next woman to enter Sakharam's house is Champa, an outright rebel against the male-dominated society. Refusing to bear her husband Fouzdar Shinde's tortures, she for a change has walked out on him and even beats him up when he endeavours repeatedly to bring her back from Sakharam's place! Accordingly, she strongly challenges the authority of Sakharam in his own house; refuses to perform domestic chores, drinks, curses and orders him around. Smitten by her fiery, sensuous charms, he accepts her dominance in lieu of physical pleasure she provides in an inebriated state. He stops worshipping deity, going to work as the gross sensual elements are rejuvenated in him under her influence. Cast off, this time by her nephew, when Laxmi returns to Sakharam he shouts "I don't want you or your God in my way.... Pick up that picture or I'll kick it".

Sakharam thus to a considerable extent is influenced and shaped by the woman he lives with. At the behest of Champa when he agrees to keep Lakshmi in his house, the three characters become enmeshed in a vicious triangle that leads to disastrous consequences. The strain of cohabiting two opposing forces embodied by the two women has a telling impact on Sakharam; he becomes 'an impotent ninny' as figured out by Champa. This is indicative of his waning dictatorship, certain fall from his earlier position of eminence. He now has no control over the proceedings as Champa becomes sexually involved with his friend Dawood Miyan, and Laxmi too, finds a 'friend' in Fouzdar Shinde. With the once menacing 'man' out of the fray, the locus of power now oscillates between the two women that builds up the tension of the drama and takes it to its most disturbing climax. As the outspoken woman with an enviable influence on Sakharam, Champa's precedence over Laxmi is obvious but not necessarily ultimate in this temporal world of fleeting changes. Thus the 'cornered' Laxmi finds a way to regain her control on Sakharam's household. She poisons Sakharam's mind with her malicious inputs about Champa's sexual revelry with Dawood. Unable to digest this insult to his already injured manhood, Sakharam in a fit of anger strangles Champa. The murder leaves him completely bewildered and dependent on Laxmi who now comes forward to cover up the act. The curtain falls on the action with the docile woman exhibiting 'masculine' traits as she starts digging a grave with a shovel to bury Champa's body in the kitchen, when Sakharam proves unequal to the task! Reflecting on this unexpected ascendancy of Laxmi, Vasant Palshikar opines "Actually the play Sakharam Binder is not about Sakharam. Initially, the playwright may have intended to make Sakharam the protagonist. But the play slips from his hand; it becomes the play that focuses on the character of Laxmi, and at this point, she becomes the protagonist of the play."

Sakharam Binder finally essays out an ambivalent relation to the stereotyped notions of gender and its corresponding associations of power. Each of the three central characters : Sakharam, Laxmi, Champa, has his/her own period of domination and subjugation. In the process the traditional notions of male-female attributes are donned in, exchanged by them with different effects. The womaniser Sakharam is rendered impotent; Champa is initially empowered then choked by her feminine sensuality; and Laxmi, most interestingly, appears androgynous as she works her way to the pinnacle of power. From the oppressed surrogate wife of Sakharam, the jealous weakling in the triangle, to the dominant accomplice in Champa's murder- she displays it all. The play ends with Laxmi, the new centre of power, trying to enthuse a distraught, shaken Sakharam she takes as her husband, by saying: "I've been a virtuous woman. My virtuous deeds will see both of us through." We are left wondering whether the gender stereotypes are overhauled, modified or reasserted.

Capturing "human behaviour, elusive and ever changing", the plays of Tendulkar thus explore the issue of gender with all its complexities, ambiguities and uncertainties. Be it the unwed mother Benare, lesbian-turned-whore Sumitra or the live-in partners, Sakharam, Champa, Laxmi, Tendulkar's characters come in headlong clash with the strictures of the conservative society that reveal their strength as well as weakness. In the process the staple male-female relation with their binary opposite attributes appear reversible; not necessarily mutually exclusive. Coming back to the question from Tendulkar's *Kamla* with which this article began, it may be answered that within the broad framework of the lopsided distribution of power between the sexes, too deep rooted to be overhauled in a trice; men too limp, at times even behind the most docile, conservative women; as the characters cross gender redressing to some extent, the fundamental inequality in the human world.

Bibliography

Ramnarayan, Gowri, "An Interview with Vijay Tendulkar" *Frontline*, March 27, 1992.

Spivak, Gayatri Chakravorty, "Can the Subaltern Speak?" in *Marxism and the Interpretation of Culture*, ed. Cary Nelson and Lawrence Grossberg, London, Macmillan, 1988.

Tendulkar, Vijay, *Collected Plays in Translation* New Delhi, Oxford University Press, 8th. impression, 2011.

Web-Links

http://www.outlookindia.com/article.aspx? 237547

http://www.the-criterion.com/v2/n1/Shailaja.pdf

http://www.tjells.com/article/84_ThePlaywrightAsASocialCritic.pdf

9 Vijay Tendulkar's Silence! The Court is in Session: A Study of Power Relations

SK Lutfar Rahaman

Vijay Tendulkar, who deserves to be called a multi-faceted creative genius because of his attempt at writing various genres such as short story, article, one-act play, drama, screen-play, literary criticism and translation, has now earned recognition not only as a prolific Marathi playwright but also as a leading Indian dramatist. Tendulkar was born into a lower middle-class Brahmin family in Bombay in 1928 when, as M .K. Naik observes (1984:114), the Gandhian whirlwind began to sweep over the length and breadth of the land, upsetting all established political strategies and ushering in refreshingly new ideas and methods that shook Indian life in several spheres to the core and when Marxism, soon after Russian Revolution, caused flutter in some regions of India. He first emerged as a journalist in the capacity of a sub-editor of a Marathi weekly, *Navbharat*, published from Pune. His emergence as a dramatist began with *Grihasth in* 1955, though his second play *Shrimanth* brought him recognition as a dramatist. Thereafter he never stopped writing plays because, as he has confessed, everything came to him in the shape of a play. He has to his credit thirty-two full-length plays, twenty-four one-act plays in addition to his plays for the children. Before his death on 18 May, 2008, awards and honours like Sangeet Natak Akademi Award, Padma Bhusan and Katha Chudamani were bestowed upon him for his immense contribution to the literary field. A man of rare calmness and quietude, hiding his sensitiveness and critical acumen behind his beard and spectacle he never forgot to keep harmony between form and content in his dramatic works by making his characters speak in natural language so that they never sound artificial. With his anti-essentialist mindset and new-found social consciousness he has focused on themes ranging from the alienation of modern individuals to contemporary political complexities, from social-individual tensions to complexities of human characters, from man-woman relationships to interpretation of historical episodes. He has made himself different from the previous generation of Marathi dramatists by writing such notable plays as *Manas Navache Bet (An Island Called Man), Shantata! Court Chalu Aahe (Silence! The Court is in Session), Ghashiram Kotwal, Gidhade (Vultures) Shakaram Binder, Kamala,* and *Safar*. As a dramatist, Tendulkar deserves to be bracketed with other Indian dramatists writing in Indian languages such as Mohan Rakesh in Hindi, Badal Sircar in Bengali and Girish Karnad in Kannada. All of them have earned reputation as dramatist of high calibre by any standard, but in respect of variation in dramatic creations Tendulkar has slight edge over them. Varieties in his creations are noticeable because of the fact that without sticking to any ideological solution of the problems of life, Tendulkar has depicted the problems of life which he has observed minutely from close or distance. In his works there are more problems of life than their solutions. In most of his works he has tried to show how all past references have lost validities in the fast-changing world scenarios. *Shantata! Court Chalu Aahe*, the English version of which is *Silence! The Court is in Session* is no exception to this case. This three-act play which may be called Tendulkar's magnum opus is undertaken to explore power relations between men and women, between the dominant and the marginal.

Shantata! Court Chalu Aahe was written in 1967 when in America radical feminism came to the fore with a vociferous slogan-'personal is political' and when in the post-Independence

India nationalist ideology which was built around false essentialisms of home/world, spiritual/material, East/West, masculine/feminine, refused to make the woman question an issue of political negotiation with the West (Partha Chaterjee, 1995). In the colonial period Indian women spontaneously participated in the Gandhian Movement with the hope of getting emancipation from patriarchal domination and gender discrimination. A worthy representative of the Gandhian age Kamaladevi Chattopadhyaya herself puts it:

> Women with pale eyes and blushing cheeks, who had been gently nurtured behind silken curtains, women who had never looked upon a crowded street, never beheld a strange face...flung themselves into the blinding glare of day, unshaded and unprotected.... They faced perils and privations with a happy light in their eyes and a spring in their limbs. Almost overnight their narrow domestic walls had given away to open a new wide world in which they had a high place (cited in M.K. Naik, 1989:116).

But in the post-Independence period the women's aspirations remain partially fulfilled. Women are granted the right to franchise and given access to education and individual profession, but still they are equated with private sphere and required to maintain the inner sanctum of home. According to R Radhakrishnan, our mode of understanding is implicated in our mode of partisanship, and our mode of partisanship is an expression or function of our location-what that location includes and excludes (R Radhakrishnan, 2007:192). In consequence of this, in Indian nationalism, he observes, inside/outside perceptions are indeed very much alive. There is no trans-ideological free-space of arbitration to adjudicate among multiple non-synchronous boundaries. In making use of the inner/outer distinctions as a way of selectively coping with the West, nationalist rhetoric makes 'women' the pure and ahistorical signifier of 'interiority'. 'In the fight against the enemy from outside, something within gets even more repressed, women becomes the mute but necessary allegorical ground for the transaction of national history.' They are persuaded to 'take on the name of a vast inner silence not to be broken by the rough and external clomour of material history' (Ibid). All these have bearing upon the text of Tendulkar's play, *Silence! The Court is in Session.*

In the post-colonial period with his knowledge of Patriarchy, which, according to Jana Sawicki, (1991) is 'the name of global effect of domination made possible by a myriad of power relations in the micro-level of society', Tendulkar, in this play, has explored the man-woman power relationship and how torture on woman has been rationalized though cross-examinations in a judicial court. While exploring these he critiques the Hindu patriarchal meta-discourse-*na stri swatantriya marhati*(woman not fit for independence). He also constructs an oppositional feminist discourse in order to resist patriarchal power that underpins nationalist ideology towards its refusal to give an unmarried woman the status of motherhood. The resistance is constituted in four different terms: in terms of strong refusal of patriarchal verdict, in terms of sobbing, in terms of silence and in terms of song.

Though the play is gyno-centric because of its main focus on an unmarried expectant woman, it embodies more stories than one. The stories are woven in a crisscross way by the threads of the lives of a cross-section of urban middle-class people. In weaving their stories Tendulkar explores the power-relations- which, according to Foucault (Foucault in ed james d.faubion, 1994:17), are 'the most deeply invested experience in the history of human culture'- from which no culture has yet been emancipated. Perhaps Tendulkar knows that all ideologies are more or less inadequate for social criticism in the fast changing world scenarios. Maybe because of this fact he, like a genealogist, has resurrected the low ranking knowledges of a cross-section of men and women. Particularly through the retrieval of the subjugated knowledge of an unmarried expectant woman and her refusal to be governed by the patriarchal court of law Tendulkar has made an attempt at exposing the exploitation of Mother India by the Indian intellectuals who were believed to protect its purity in the post-Independence period.

Silence! The Court is in Session, a play of three-act, has a double structure which symbolically resembles the two spheres of life: public and private. In introducing such a form Tendulkar serves his two purposes. In the public sphere he asserts his anti-imperialist mindset by constructing a mock-trial of American President Johnson who is projected as a threat to humanity because of his policy of proliferation of nuclear arms. In the private sphere he exposes the double standard of patriarchal Indian judiciary.

As the play opens, we find Benare equipped with anti-imperialistic consciousness, committed to spread the enlightenment ideas through theatre against American imperialism that has manifested itself through proliferation of nuclear arms. In this project she dominates her male and female associates belonging to Sonar Moti Tenement Progressive Association, an amateur theatre group in Bombay. Intelligent and witty Benare exposes their weaknesses and relegates them to an inferior position in their absence before Samant, a local man. In caustic terms she exposes Mr and Mrs Kashikar to Samant by saying that Mr Kashikar is the Prime-objective and Mrs Kashikar is actually Mrs-Hand-that rocks-the-cradle. She ridicules Mrs Kashikar in her absence because the latter is childless. In order to fulfill her desire of being mother she has adopted Balu Rokde who, in Benare's view, though educated by them, is treated like a slave. Sukhatme, as a lawyer, 'keeps swatting flies with legal precedents'. Mr Ponkshe, as she tells Samant, is 'the great scientist! Inter- failed!' Even she does expose the hypocrisy of Prof Damle with whom she has an affair. In her view, he may be an intellectual, taking pride in displaying his bookish knowledge, but he is scared to face the problem of real life. Besides these, she reveals to Samant her attitude to life without mincing the matter. As she tells Samant: 'Forget about the sage Tukaram. I say it – I, Leela Benare, a living woman, I say it from my own experience. Life is not meant for anyone else. It's your own life. It must be. It's very, very important thing. Every moment, every bit of it is precious-'(8). Benare here valorizes her personal life and freedom over all other things. She does not like anybody to poke nose into her personal affairs: "Who are these people to say what I can and can't do? My life is my own – I haven't sold it to anyone for a job! My will is my own. My wishes are my own. No one can kill those- no one! I'll do what I like with myself and my life! I'll decide… (5)." Her utterances make it clear that she is not an ordinary traditional woman; rather she is an anomalous character, very assertive in respect of leading her life on her own terms.

'However, because of the absence of the two regular actors, the group of the players belonging to Sonar Moti Theatre Association, Bombay, decides to induct Samant, a local hand in the regular performance as the fourth witness. Since there is enough time to pass before the enactment of the regular play on the mock-trail of President Johnson, they intend to play a game of words by staging a rehearsal of a trial on some other issue of which everything will be imaginary except the accused. In the course of the rehearsal all the amateur players who are failures in real life enjoy a sort of their second life by overthrowing the boundaries between the official and the private through the disruption of the etiquette of the court of law. The frequent call for order by the judge makes no effect on the participants in the court-proceedings. Lack of seriousness from each player including the judge creates peals of laughter in the courtroom, which appears to be converted into a domain for spitting pan. The judge gets engaged in picking either his ear or tooth with his tooth-pick during the proceedings. He is found busy chewing *masala pan* letting others also do it in the court without the sense that he is violating the propriety of the court. The adjournment of the court for spitting *pan* for a quarter of a minute and Ponkshe's use of smoking-pipe and letting out the curls of smoke in the witness box are found to be grotesque parody of the discourse of the court of law. The other grotesque elements are the judge's frequent tiffs with his wife in the open court and his conversion into a witness for informing the court about Benare's dismissal from teaching job by her school authorities. This sort of joyful affirmation of the collectivity gets jolted because of their tendency to suspect each other. The body of the text of the rehearsal is found to develop and move in an irrational way with the dialogues and gestures of the characters. The mock-trial on infanticide has two sides: positive and negative. On the positive side, it allows the amateur players to enjoy a joyful affirmation of change, an ecstasy of collectivity. On the negative side, the joyful game turns into a hunt for woman for torture. In the name of fun, jester and humour they accuse one of their colleagues of infanticide under section 302 of Indian Penal Code and thrust her in an absurd situation. In this connection it is pertinent to note Mary Louise Pratt's observation of the construction of traveling colonial discourse. For being colonial subjects, the Western travelers, as Louise Pratt observes (cited in Sara Mills, 1997:115), were privileged to enjoy the status of 'knowing subjects'. In that capacity they described the inhabitants of a colonized country not in terms of presence but in terms of absence in the colonial traveling discourse. In a similar fashion, Benare's colleagues, for being the subjects of the patriarchal ideology that considers woman not fit for freedom, construct Benare with the accusation of infanticide against her in her absence.

The rehearsal gradually takes the form of a play-within-a regular play which reminds us of Shakespeare's *Hamlet.* In *Hamlet*, Hamlet scripted the play and had it enacted by some hired professional actors in order to be ensured as to whether King Claudius was the real murderer of his reverend father. His mission was to liberate Denmark from its corrupted ruler and to set everything in right order. It is true that in *Silence* Tendulkar, unlike Hamlet, does not present the play in ready form. But, as Arundhuti Banerjee argues, he very adroitly allows the actors and actresses to improvise 'the courtroom drama to build a serious theatre as Ibsen had adopted romantic drama as a receptacle for indictment of society' (Arundhuti Banerjee in *V. Tendulkar: Five Plays*, OUP, 2003). In spite of the difference between Hamlet's play-within-play and that of Tendulkar which has emerged out of the rehearsal, we find a resemblance between Hamlet's objective and that of Tendulkar. As in Elizabethan heroic culture Hamlet was against sexual corruption, so in post-colonial condition Tendulkar seems to have undertaken a task of exposing the hypocrisy and sexual corruption of the so-called progressive intellectuals who were expected to protect Mother India from contamination of all sorts.

However, as Foucault argues, we constitute ourselves as subjects acting on others. On this account we may say that in play-within-a play Benare's colleagues make an attempt to constitute themselves as subjects by acting on Benare. They try to use Benare as a site on which they want to inscribe masculine meanings and enact their masculine desires. As Foucault observes (Foucault in ed. James d.faubian, 1994:48), in Western culture torture on body has always been rationalized through judicial system. What Faucault says of Western culture is also applicable to all cultures. In post-Independence period Indian court of law which is shown to be in complicit with the Hindu patriarchal ideology tortures a young unmarried woman for her demand for personal freedom and the status of motherhood. Benare's co-actors try to constitute Benare though their gazes. First, they try to gain pleasures looking at her bodily gestures and movements. Secondly, they represent Benare as an erotic content without performing themselves any erotic action apart from looking at her. Thirdly, they treat the body of Benare as an object by denigrating her into a position of an accused of infanticide under Section 302 of Indian Penal Court.

The sadists always derive pleasure from seeing someone else's pain. For being sadists, Benare's co-actors and co-actress increase torture on her through their acts of interrogations and witnesses. Rokde testifies that he found Benare in Prof Damle's house as the night was falling. Rokde's testimony arouses curiosity in the minds of the on-lookers. Perturbed by Balu's evidence Samant wonders if the scandal is scripted as part of the text of the play or it is something that has to do with the real life of Benare. Kashikar and Sukhatme enjoy Benare's perturbation. For some more pleasure they demand from Rokde, Ponkshe, Karnik and Samant more information about Benare. None in the courtroom protests against the insult flung on an unmarried woman in the public. All of them derive pleasure from seeing Benare in pain and ignominy, although the possible exception is Samant, who undergoes a transformation from a spectator to an actor, from a witness to a sympathizer of Benare. Mrs Kashikar tortures her by opposing her acts of singing, dancing, laughing and running after men. With the mention of Damle's name, Benare's attacking gesture turns defensive. In spite of her protest that her personal life is being dragged into the game, they continue the trial with a suspicion that she has a liaison with Damle. Balu retaliates by exposing her affair with Prof Damle. Karnik humiliates Benare by digging out her past affair with her maternal uncle and the suicidal attempt she made while the love failed to consummate in marriage. Ponkshe oppresses Benare by divulging her pregnancy by Prof Damle and by disclosing the secret marriage proposal she made to him inside a family room of a restaurant. All her hopes that her urban friends would not jettison her into deep troubles are dashed to the ground. She finds her co-actors and co-actress throw all urban decency and decorum to the wind and they are in conspiracy to soil and vilify her character. Samant unwittingly tortures Benare by giving witness against her. In the witness-box he manufactures his evidence just by reading out a passage from a novel which happens to be akin to Benare's personal life. With this witness of Samant, the entire situation of the courtroom turns grave. Benare is booked to bay. In a frantic reaction to Samant's testimony, Benare lets the cat out of the bag. Her protest voices recede into silence with the banging of the judge's gavel. Instead of countering their accusations against her, she becomes edgy and wants to escape the awkward situation by leaving the hall. As a corollary of this, she unwittingly falls into the trap of her predators, who now think Benare has committed an infraction for being pregnant out of wedlock. "An infraction', according to Foucault, 'is not a wrong committed by one individual against another, but an offence or injury done by an individual to order, to the State, to the law, to society, to sovereignty, to the sovereign" (Foucault in ed. D. faubian, 1994: 43). Benare is thought to have done an infraction because in Hindu patriarchy unmarried motherhood is considered illegal and it is this sort of patriarchy that enjoins the nationalist ideology to consider "Mother and Motherland / Both are even Higher than Heaven" (30).

Sexuality, as Foucault argues in *History of Sexuality, vol.1*, 'is disobedient to power and a dense transfer point of power relations' (Foucault, 1990:103). Adapting Foucault's view on sexuality, it may be said that having enjoyed pre-marital sexuality with a married man like Prof Damle, Benare has disobeyed patriarchal power. Not only that, after pregnancy, she wants to enter into the institution of marriage in order to make illicit licit, the forbidden permitted. Here it is pertinent to note Sudhir Karkar's observation on motherhood. As he argues, a young Indian wife's situation in terms of family acceptance and emotional well-being changes dramatically once she becomes pregnant. The prospect of motherhood holds out a composite solution for many of her difficulties. Her low social status as a bride and a new comer, the humiliating relationship with other in her husband's family, her homesickness and sense of isolation and the unfulfilled yearnings of her sexual self, which are tangled up in a knot begin to be solved with the prospect of motherhood (S.Karkar in Ghadially Rahana, 1988:65). For being pregnant, Benare has the prospect of becoming mother. But her social status is denigrated because of her gestation out of wedlock. For elevation of her status she tries utmost to marry any other man, even though impregnated by Prof Damle Already the latter has denied having any responsibility for that pregnancy. Even neither Ponkshe, nor Balu, whom she proposed to marry her for becoming the father of the child in her womb comes forward to bear the onus of the unborn child because of their complicity with Hindu patriarchy. Rather they betray her by revealing the marriage proposals she secretly offered to them. The judge in an absurd way enters into the witness-box and tortures her psyche by furnishing information of her dismissal from the teaching job by the school authorities. The judge derives pleasure seeing her attempt at committing suicide out of excruciating pain for the loss of her financial freedom and security. The prosecutor, the defense council and the judge roll into one to rob her off the status of motherhood.

So the court argues that Benare should not be allowed to demolish the solid foundation of social body. If she is permitted to retain the illegitimate baby growing in her womb out of wedlock, the purity of motherhood and motherland shall be profaned. The court therefore allows her a time of ten seconds to defend her case before passing its final verdict. It is nothing but the rationalization of torture on woman through judiciary system.

However, Benare is not cowed down by the judicial torture. She is highly enlightened and knowledgeable about the victimization of women in Patriarchy. Mrs Shiris Pai's poem has consolidated her consciousness about women's precarious life in andro-centric world. In this world woman is plunged on an unknown dangerous path where she comes across a life of turbulence mixed with hope and despair. Her hopes and despairs are burnt out with a deep wound in her heart to bleed. Fed up with repetitive life she sometimes tries to veer it of her own accord. Because of this, she has to face obstacles of different sorts in society, yet she continues her struggle for having a free life. In all cases she incurs defeat. In spite of her full knowledge about woman's precariousness and defeat, Benare wants to lead her life on her terms. So once she is given the chance of defending her case, she does not let the opportunity slip out of her hand. She exploits the allotted time to inscribe her oppositional consciousness against patriarchal judicial power. She emerges as a new woman breaking her horrid silence created by the banging of the judge's gavel. She narrates her whole life in different trajectory and recreates her own self. The critic like Arundhuti Banerjee argues, her last speech is a sort of self-justification rather than a creation of her self (A. Banerjee in *V.Tendulkar: Five Plays*, OUP, 2003). But Ms Banerjee has missed the point that even though it is a self justification, in it she dares to apply reason to justify her position in society. 'Power' according to Foucault, 'is not repressive but productive'. 'Where there is power there is resistance and yet, or rather consequently, this resistance is never in position of exteriority in relation to power' (Foucault in Jana Sawacki, 1991:20, 56). On this view, it may be said that in allowing Benare to recount her life, Tendulkar resurrects the 'subjugated knowledge' of an unmarried expectant woman and thereby creates a resistance to patriarchal judicial power. Emanuel Kant defined 'enlightenment' as the courage to use one's reason (James Schmidt and Thomas E. Wartenberg in *Critique and Power* by Michael Kelly, 1994: 290). With the logic of enlightenment, Benare in the witness-box re-inscribes the history of her life. Her courage to apply her reason in favour of the deed she has done is highly praiseworthy. Marginalized, excoriated, yet she is not afraid to interrogate the oppressive hierarchies of power. She describes the so-called cultured persons in disapproving terms: "They are the mortal remains of some cultured men of the twentieth century. See their faces- how ferocious they look! Their lips are full of lovely worn-out phrases! And their bellies are full of unsatisfied desires" (74). The very fact of a woman speaking out before all the cruel persons in the court is highly subversive of patriarchal hegemony: It accrues power to her self. Measuring her life on her own scale, Benare confesses in the court that though life appeared a burden to her, she tried to make it joyful by landing herself in the job of teaching, which was never allowed to be interrupted by her pent-up sorrows and despairs. As a teacher, she discharged her duties faithfully and sincerely. She always tried to instill sense of beauty and purity in the minds of her students. She wonders to know why then the school authorities are going to sack her from teaching job. Then asserting her autonomy, she challenges the court not to interfere into her personal life, which she thinks is her own business. Then unhesitatingly she admits of her love with her maternal uncle. Love was blind then. So for falling in love with him she is not to blame. As she interprets, in their orthodox house in the prime of her youthful life she came in contact with her uncle, the only young male person in that house. They reciprocated love with each other. Through that exchange of love she got the recognition of her youth and beauty. She then was mere fifteen; it was not within her knowledge that marriage with maternal uncle would not be permissible in Hindu patriarchy. The marriage with him was thwarted by her mother and other members of the family. Out of despair, she wanted to commit suicide. From feminist point of view, suicide allows a woman to exercise her right over her life. Suicide, according to Showalter, is a grotesque fantasized female weapon, a way of cheating men out of dominance (Showalter, 1977:250). Through her attempt to commit suicide Benare wanted to escape patriarchal dominance. But she could not because she was saved from that dangerous attempt.

Thereafter Benare thought her love with Prof Damle would be different. She worshipped him as a god, but the latter, instead of receiving her worship, enjoyed her body that played an ambiguous role. It at once pitted Benare into a danger of pregnancy and enabled her to enjoy a moment so beautiful, so blissful, so near to Heaven. It is that body which is now bearing the fruit of love. Not only that, it is for the body that she would have reproductive power as well as the status of motherhood. Here it pertinent to note Julia Kristiva's comment on pregnancy. As Kristiva says, in pregnancy woman can recover a repressed relation to semiotic maternal through the profound psychic experience of giving birth to a new born child. In her view, pregnancy involves a kind of pleasurable, creative linking with other. This mode of relating, Kristiva says, involves a potential reconstruction of human social relationships, one in which a new relation to the semiotic body, its pleasures, and its dismantling of fixed oppositions (self/other, man/woman) can overturn existing masculine culture. Kristiva contrasts the Lacanian symbolic, the social and sexual system of the Law of Father, with semiotic which, in her view, is a realm of pre-linguistic experience-including bodily drives, feelings and rhythms experienced by the child in its pre-Oedipal relationship to the mother (Kristiva in Anthony Elliott, 1994:136-138). Adapting Kristiva's view on gestation, we may say that pregnancy has provided Benare with a sense of wholeness, a redoubling of her body, a separation and co-existence of self and other. This is the rationale for which she valorizes her pregnant body over all other things. In addition, she perhaps believes that the son she would give birth to would protect her from the oppression in male-dominated society. In making an unmarried expectant woman construct this sort of confessional discourse Tendulkar grants her the right to narrate a marginalized life in patriarchal society. The self-justification of this sort is no doubt a challenge to the patriarchal ideology that considers woman not fit for independence and refuses to grant an unmarried expectant woman the status of motherhood.

But the patriarchal court of law brushes aside all her arguments. It tries to prove her as a promiscuous woman on the ground that she has become pregnant out of wedlock and thereafter made attempt at getting married to another man for the protection of an illegal baby. The court also argues that unmarried motherhood has always been considered illicit and illegal by Hindu religion and traditions. Even though we find that in *The Mahabharat* Kunti was unmarried when she gave birth to Karna and in *The Bible* Mother Mary was a was virgin Mother. Both of them have been granted the status of motherhood by two different religions. Here lies the discrepancy between myth and reality. Since the inner sanctum of Indian polity has been defected from Western culture, and since the woman is equated with the private sphere, woman is expected to bear the responsibility for building up high moral values in society. On this ground, the court adjudges her guilty of having attempted to dynamite the sacred institutions of marriage and motherhood. The court therefore passes a severe verdict that the child growing in Benare's womb out of wedlock shall be destroyed, even though she shall retain her body. In opposition to this male-defined verdict she articulates her feminist rage exploiting available patriarchal terms: "No! No! No! - I won't let you do it- I won't let it happen" (76). Here it is relevant to note Camus's definition of a rebel. According to him, a rebel is one who says 'no'; but whose refusal does not imply a renunciation (The Rebel, 1951, Rep 2000). By saying 'no' to myopic patriarchal verdict Benare makes herself a rebel. Ethically Benare considers her rebellion a virtuous act because she cannot let a baby be destroyed by any one by any means when she knows the baby in her womb is innocent and the fruit of love.

After Benare's refusal to be governed by the patriarchal verdict, all her colleagues try to change the seriousness of the matter uttering palliative words. But it is beyond their understanding that the wound on woman's chastity can never be healed with palliative words. As the door of community hall opens, they come in contact with the public world and begin to behave like the progressive people. They try to dismiss the entire episode of the trial as game. But Benare remains unresponsive to their appeal. So they fail to veer the course of the play in other direction.

However, after her saying 'no' to the patriarchal verdict, Benare adopts another tactical position. She begins to sob. Sobbing may be considered to be a sign of anguish for her uncertain future. It may also be construed as one of the subcultures of the women to raise protest against patriarchal oppression. After her sobbing, Benare also sinks into silence. Her silence does in no way mean that she has admitted defeat in her fight against patriarchal oppression. Protest may have many forms. Silence is a sort of non-violent protest against the victimization of woman by man. Silence may be treated as her muted discourse. Here it would not be an exaggeration to note Elaine Showalter's observation on the muted discourse of women. In a classic article, Feminist Criticism in the Wilderness, (1998:259-262), borrowing from feminist historian Gerda Lerner and anthropologists Shirley and Edwin Ardener, Showalter points out that woman's culture is not so much a subculture as a dual perspective of living and participating in a dominant male culture with boundaries that overlap, but do not entirely contain the non-dominant muted culture of women. She thus views male and female experience as two overlapping circles with much of the women's muted circle falling within the boundaries of the dominant circle but with a small crescent of experience that she dubs, following Edwin Arderner, a wild zone, or no man's land of women's culture. It is entirely off-limits to man, where women know the male crescent, if not through personal experience, at least through myth and legend. Men have no experience or knowledge of the female crescent precisely because there is so little women's art known to men. Adapting Showalter's view on muted discourse, we may treat Banere's discourse of silence as no-man's land to which no man has any access. Spatially, here Tendulkar has granted her full autonomy. Metaphysically, he has empowered her to lodge a non-violent protest in the form of silence against oppressive patriarchal judicial system that maintains myopia towards male infraction.

A dramatist of progressive mindset, Tendulkar perhaps knows that restructuring of power relations between men and women in heterosexual society can never be made possible by snatching power from male by female. It is possible through negotiation for which an understanding between pro-woman and pro-man people should be encouraged. Women are different not only from men; they are also different from one another by class, race, caste, religion, sexual practice and so forth. Again there are many factors, which divide women and also unite some women with some men and vice versa. This is what we find in this play. Though oppressed by her husband, Mrs Kashikar unites with her husband and the tormentors of another woman, who is none other than her female colleague Benare. On the contrary, being disillusioned with the tormentors of Benare, Samant displays a good gesture of co-operation with Benare. His act of putting the green cloth parrot in front of Benare seems to indicate that he has no hesitation in respect of taking charge of an unborn child while its father's name has already come to the fore in the court. The parrot which Samant was bearing for his own nephew is now placed for an unborn baby whom he seems to be going to treat as his another nephew In Samant's act which seems to symbolize a brother's sympathy for his distressed sister, Tendulkar seems to drop a hint that the society with a heavy patriarchal bias where proper justice can not be expected is going to be defected by a society of fellow-feeling. Besides this, as Raymond Williams observes, in any cultural moment there can co-exist residual, emergent and dominant elements (Raymond Williams, 1977:121-127). By this Raymond Williams means culture is neither unitary phenomenon nor homogeneous unit that can be located in a single category. At any given moment dominant culture may be the most powerful one, herein can be traced some less powerful elements that either resist the dominant culture or run counter to it. Tendulkar, through Samant who contrasts the sadistic urban middle-class people by showing gesture of co-operation with Benare, explores an emergent culture of fellow-feeling in opposition to the patriarchal oppressive middle-class urban culture. Samant's gesture of co-operation with a female victim invokes a unity of the marginalized and victimized people in post-Independence India. A post-colonial dramatist, Tendulkar gives this sort of hint in the last lullaby which we are made to hear in Benare's voice wafting from some unseen place. Here Tendulkar envisions an inextricable bond between mother and son by making the mother tell her son of her oppressor. Apart from this, in this song Tendulkar's post-colonial oppositional voice seems to merge with the marginalized feminist voice in order to dub the greedy exploiter of innocuous love of unmarried women like Benare as 'crow', which pretends to be innocent, even though it has surreptitiously destroyed the nest of sparrow, symbolizing the chastity of woman. According to Foucault, ' in disciplinary techniques ways of knowing are equated with the ways of exercising power over individuals' (cited in Jana Sawacki,1991:22). In labeling the so-called progressive Indian intellectuals like Prof Damle as crow, which in Indian mythology came to be associated with demonic spirit, Tendulkar tries to raise consciousness of the marginalized and victimized people, irrespective of class and gender, against the intellectuals who want to catch fish but dislike to touch water. After Independence Indian politicians and intellectuals were expected to protect the sanctity and purity of Mother India. Instead of doing that, infected by the Western codes and conducts of life they are coming to pollute its pure body and ignore its precarious condition. Like Hobbes's *Leviathan* in which Hobbes has kept the ruler outside the purview of rule of law, Indian court of law maintains stony silence about the corrupt sexual practices of Indian intellectuals like Prof Damle and lets them move freely in the society. But Tendulkar explores their corruption in manifest form, showing how their furtive extended erotic act beyond married life has come to pollute the inner sanctum of Indian polity in the post-colonial condition. The title of the play has two parts: one is *Silence* which is punctuated with exclamation mark and the other being, *The court is in Session.* In the first part there is an ironical twist which implies that the court may remain silent about male sexual corruption and that it may silence the woman's marginal voice against it, but the dramatist is not silent; he is very agile and vocal against it. He therefore wonders to know in exclamation why the Indian women whose forbears participated in the freedom struggles against colonial power for autonomy and freedom are maintaining stony silence while they see one of them has been more sinned than sinning by the heavily biased Indian judiciary system. Through the song that encodes the victimization of woman by man, Tendulkar seems to send a covert message to all Indian woman to break their silence against patriarchal oppression while he finds in America the white women raise stout protest against patriarchal sexual politics with a vociferous slogan-'personal is political'. He seems to be asking in exclamation why are the Indian women not coming forward to oppose the victimization of woman by man, if they do not differ with Virginia Woolf's view in *Three Guineas* that a woman has no country, no nation, and no culture except one that gives a call for a fight against patriarchal domination of all sorts? Apart from this question, the text of the play also raises an implicit question: if the crow is not ousted from the inner sanctum of the society, how can the patriarchal authority preserve the purity in it?

Bibliography

Banerjee, Arundhiti (ed). Vijay Tendulkar's Collected Plays in Trans, New Delhi: Oxford University Press, 2003.

Chatterjee, Partha. *The Nation and its Fragments*, New Delhi: Oxford University Press, 1993.

Camus, Albert. *The Rebel* trans Anthony Bower, London: Penguin Books, 1953, Rep., 2000.

Elliott, Anthony. *Psychoanalytic Theory: An Introduction.* Oxford, UK & Cambridge, USA: Blackwell, 1994.

Foucault, Michel. *Power/Knowledge: Selected Interviews* (ed) Colin Gordon, Herfordshire: Hervert Press, 1980.

Foucault, Michel. *Power* ed, James D. Faubion, Vol-3, Allan Lane: The Penguin Press, 1994.

Foucault, Michel. *The History of Sexuality: An Introduction, Vol.1* trans. by Robert Hurley: New York: Vintage Books, 1978(1990).

Ghadially, Rehana. *Women in Indian Society A Reader*, New Delhi: Sage Publications, 1988.

Kelly, Michael: *Critique and Power*, Cambridge: The MIT Press, 1994.

Mills, Sara. *Discourse*, London: Routledge, 1997.

Naik, M.K. *A History of Indian English Literature*, New Delhi: Sahitya Akademi, 1985.

Radhakrishnan, R. *Between Identity and Location : The Cultural Politics of Theory*, New Delhi, Orient Blackswan, 2007.

Sawicki, Jana. *Disciplining Foucault*, London and New York: Routledge, 1991.

Showalter, Elaine. *A Literature of Their Own: British Women Novelists from Bronte to Lessings*, New Jersy: Princeton University Press, 1977.

Showalter, Elaine. 'Feminist Criticism in Wilderness' in (ed) *The New Feminist Criticism*, New York: Pantheon Books, 1985.

Tendulkar, Vijay. *Silence! The Court is in Session*, New Delhi: Oxford, 1978.

Williams, Raymond. *Marxism and Literature*, Oxford: Oxford University Press, 1977.

10 Corruption and Tragedy of Power in Vijay Tendulkar's Ghashiram Kotwal

Grishma Manikrao Khobragade

Tendulkar's original writings in Marathi deal with the issues related to contemporary social, political, cultural and economic life in Maharashtra. His play *Ghashiram Kotwal* is a story of the conflict between Ghashiram Savaldas, a North-Indian Brahman from Kanauj and Nana Phadnavis, the Chief Minister of the Peshwas, and the play may be considered as a tragedy of power. Tendulkar himself thus points out about the historical perspective of the play and his own point of views:

> This is not a historical play. It is a story, in prose, verse, music, and dance set in a historical era. Ghashirams are creations of socio-political forces which know no barriers of time and place. Although based on a historical legend, I have no intention of commenting on the morals or lack of them, of the Peshwa, Nana Phadnavis or Ghashiram. The moral of this story, if there is any, may be looked for elsewhere. (Tendulkar, 4)

Ghasiram Savaldas is a poor Brahman who comes to Poona for livelihood along with his wife and daughter. Since he gets no dignified employment to suit his caste, he becomes a servant in the house of a courtesan named Gulabi. In addition to the housework that he does for Gulabi, he also sings and dances when people come to enjoy her erotic songs and dance. One day, Nana visits Gulabi and hurts his ankle while dancing. Ghashiram appreciates him and Nana feels so flattered that he offers him a necklace of pearls. However, Gulabi snatches the necklace from him and drives him out with the help of her thugs.

This unexpected turn of events in his life crushes Ghasiram's very spirit. No doubt he was poor but it didn't mean that he had no reputation in the society. And it is not his poverty but his loss of reputation that suffers him more. He tries to explain the mob that he was not a thief but a Brahman from Kanauj, new to Poona, but nobody pays any attention to know his sincere clarification. His conversation with the Sutradhar reveals the trauma of his mind. Ghashiram goes out. He feels tired and hungry. Peshwa has arranged a great feast in honor of Brahmans, and Ghasiram wants to be there. But the soldiers do not allow him. Moreover, on the charge of theft the soldiers beat Ghashiram severely. And this humiliation generates in him a powerful feeling of revenge:

> [...] I'll come back to Poona. I'll show my strength. It will cost you! Your good days are gone! I am a Kanauj Brahman, but I've become a Shudra, a criminal, a useless animal. There is no one to stop me now, to mock me, to make me bend, to cheat me. Now I am a devil. You've made me an animal; I'll be a devil inside. I'll come back like a boar and I'll stay as a devil. I'll make pigs of all of you. I'll make this Poona a kingdom of pigs. Then I'll be Ghashiram again, the son of Salavdas once more. (17)

As it was difficult for a new person to get settled in a new city like Poona and satisfy his hunger for revenge, he hatches a plot of temptation in order to take revenge. He uses his daughter as a manipulation part of taking revenge, and he decides to take help of Nana Phadnavis, the most powerful person of Poona.

Ghasiram offers his own daughter Gauri to Nana and in return gets appointed as the Kotwal of Poona. And hence, the play deals with the technicalities of power. As Vinita Bhatnagar comments:

> Gauri has few lines in the play and certainly none that hint at her own perception of her experience. But Ghashiram's guilt is voiced at various parts of the dramatic text. Thus even in the triumphant celebration of his power, Ghashiram worries over the fate of his daughter. (Bhatnagar 146)

After becoming the Kotwal, Ghashiram interferes with every aspect of people's life with a very strict iron control. On the surface it appears that he is trying to maintain discipline, decorum and decency in the city. But in reality, he is making life even in their own homes difficult in the city of Poona He knocks a door in the midnights, suspects the morality of the house holders and wakes up the neighbours to give testimony against one and others. A tight control even on the celebration of festivals is also imposed. Not only these, there were ordered all manners of rules and regulation even on performing the last rites of death. And Ghashiram's reign thus becomes one of complete terror and dictatorship which takes away people's joy of living. In fact, Ghashiram begins to take revenge on the people of Poona by enforcing the law strictly. He demands permit for everything:

> To kill a pig, to do an abortion, to be pimp, to commit a misdemeanor, to steal, to live with divorced wife, to remarry if one's husband is alive, to hide one's caste, to use counterfeit coins, to commit suicide, without a permit is a sin. A good woman may not prostate herself; a Brahman may not sin without a permit. (26)

He throws his own morality to winds so that he can make city Poona completely immoral. The Sutradhar says:

> Behind Ghashiram Kotwal is Nana's power. If you lay a hand on Ghashiram, Nana will smash you. If you don't, then Ghashiram will get you anyway. (31)

However, with the passing of time, it seems that Ghasiram's desire for revenge is subsided and he thinks of his daughter's marriage. He thinks that he can use his power to get his daughter married to a proper man. He meditates:

> I've got the Kotwali and I've got Poona straightened out! All these proud Brahmans are as soft as cotton now. No one dares to look at Ghashiram straight in the eye! Now once I find a fitting husband for my darling daughter that piece of my heart named Lalitha Gauri and get married, then everything will be the way I want it. (37)

However, his daughter has already become a victim of the corrupt power game. Nana enjoys sexual pleasure with her. She becomes pregnant and at the time of abortion she dies. Ghashiram visits Nana to inquire about the whereabout of his daughter Lalita Gauri whom he had not seen for ten days. In response to the inquiry Nana gave very casual answers. When Ghashiram insisted, Nana told him even more casually that she had been send to Chandra, the midwife. Ghashiram was shocked by this information. Ghashiram visits to Chandra. The midwife makes him realized that his daughter had died. He regretted whatever had happened in his blind desire of revenge through unlimited power and authority. However, he is not prepared to take responsibility and blame for whatever had gone wrong.This is his cowardice. He puts the entire blame for his daughter's death on Nana and wants to take further revenge for the lost of his daughter.

Ghashiram forgets his limits of authority as a Kotwal and tries to overpower Nana. The conflict between them begins after the death of his daughter. This conflict is nothing but the conflict of power and powerlessness. Nana is powerless in front of his lust for Gauri. The power equation changes after the death of Gauri. Gauri's death made Ghashiram furious. Ghashiram tries to overthrow the power and the authority of Nana by not bowing in front of him. Nana tames Ghashiram and overpowers him by making him bow in front of him. He orders:

> Ghashya, how much more will you grieve? Now be calm. What ever happened, protocol should not be forgetton. Don't forget whom do you stand before? First you must bow. Now –bow. (43).

After this incident, Ghashiram realizes that his power is meaningless in front of Nana. Ghashiram acquired power that made him corrupt and arrogant. He forgot the responsibility of his authority as a Kotwal. He tried to overpower over Nana Phadnavis. He had forgotten that Nana was the Chief Minister of Peshwa.

The play ends with the rebellion of the Brahmans against the Kotwal. Nana ends the oppressive use of power and declares a three day celebration for the end of stigma on society:

> Nana. Ladies and gentlemen. Citizens of Poona. A threat to the great city of Poona has been ended today. (*The crowd cheers*). A disease has been controlled. The demon Ghashya Kotwal, who plagued all of us, has met his death. Everything has happened according to the wishes of the gods. The mercy of the gods is with us always.
>
> (*He nudges the corpse of Ghashiram with his walking stick.*)
>
> Let the corpse of sinful Ghashya rot. Let the wolves and dogs have it. Let the worms have it. Whoever attempts to take away this corpse will be punished. Whoever mourns for him will be hanged. All the living relatives of Ghashya Salavdas will be found, bound, and expelled from the city. We have ordered that from this day forward, not a word, not a stone relating to the sinner shall survive. We have commanded that there be festivities for three days to mark this happy occasion.
>
> (*The crowd shouts. Cheers. ...Cymbals. Red Powder. Festivity*). (65-66)

This is how Nana uses Ghashiram Kotwal to reaffirm his own dominating regime over the public of Poona, otherwise his rule was in a declining state. Ghashiram's sorrow and inspiration is a lesson to the audience going against to extremes for achieving unlimited power and authority. It is a demonstration of sorrow and suffering that awaited a person who had achieved through the wrong means. The play is a social satire. It projects the society that defends corrupts Nana and punishes the Ghashiram. Thus the play is a powerful satire on the power politics. Tendulkar depicts that the play was not written to recreate the history or the historical figures but it was a reaction of an artist to contemporary political scenario.

Bibliography

Bhatnagar, Vinita. "Theatre as Translation: A Performance based Reading of *Ghashiram Kotwal*", *Dramatic Theory and Practices: Indian and Western,* ed. M.S. Kushwaha, New Delhi: Creative, 2000.

Tendulkar,Vijay. *Ghahiram Kotwal,* trans Jayant Karve and Eleanor Zelliot, Calcutta: Seagull,1986, (All the quotations are from this edition.)

11

Socio-cultural Oppression of Women- A Crime Against Nature: Ecofeminist Reading of Vijay Tendulkar's *Silence! the Court is in Session*

Arindam Ghosh

Ecofeminism identifies a common logic in the exploitation of women and the devastation wrought on nature by man; and thereby criticizes the mutual subordination of women and nature through patriarchy and anthropocentric (also androcentric) scientific technological advancement. The conjoined term ('ecology' and 'feminism') while exploring the real nature of domination and subordination points out that the anthropocentric dualism of humanity/nature and the phallocentric binary opposition of man/woman are at the root of the subjugation of women and the source of anti-nature beliefs. V. Davion argues that "Women have been associated with nature, the material, the emotional and the particular, while men have been associated with culture, the non-material, the rational, and the abstract" (qtd. in Garrard 23); and this helps us to draw a parallel between the ethics of the feminists and the ecologists and to understand the common space shared by 'woman-identified movement (Mies & Shiva 14) and environmentalism. Vandana Shiva and Maria Mies in the book *Ecofeminism* have criticized modern science and capitalist economy for their patriarchal tendency of homogenizing and universalizing: scientific rationality considered as essentially male property [we are reminded of Plumwood's critique of gender-biased reason/emotion dualism: "reason has so often been called upon to hyperseperate both men from women and humans from animal" (Garrard 25)] is shown to be insufficient in its reductionist and automatized paradigm which fails to consider women and earth as active participants; thereby masculine and patriarchal tropes have led to the marginalization of women and our alienation from external nature. Hence radical ecofeminists demand that 'ecology consciousness is traditional women consciousness' (qtd. in Garrard 24). Although the movement has often been accused of 'essentialism' and 'anti-scienticism'[1] (Griffin's term), it approaches, as Garrard observes, the logic of "discrimination and oppression on grounds of race, sexual orientation and class as well as species and gender" (26); and thereby it attempts to deconstruct the culturally structured dichotomies and divisions between man and woman which is seen as almost synonymous to that of man and nature. Ecofeminists shout for justice and demand liberation from male "aggression, conquest, possession, control. Of a woman or a land, it makes little difference" (Mies & Shiva 15).

Vijay Tendulkar's plays capture the intricacies of human society and voice concerns for man's existential anguish. More particularly, he exposes the harsh cruelty and injustice towards women which range from physical violence to psychological oppression. He aims to debunk the myth of male hypocritical drive towards power and superiority and hopes to assert for the dignity of women, their right and emancipation. But on another level, we find that he has always displayed awareness of the relationship between human beings and the physical environment which encompasses them from birth to death. He reevaluates the position of man in the face of an ecological and cultural crisis and finds that man's morbidity, self-destructive ways and psychological trauma are due to his lack of communication with nature and also because of his arrogance to go against the rules of nature. We are actually trapped into a kind of limbo ('living in death')– this boredom, emptiness and claustrophobia had been beautifully pictured by T. S. Eliot in *The Waste Land*. Now, when Tendulkar comes to relocate the position of women amid this hollowness, the existential crisis is doubled: for, besides facing the general hazards, the women have to counter and tolerate the socially imposed patriarchal dictates; they must go by the constructed codes of womanhood. They are robbed of their right to spontaneous self-expression; they are exploited physically through coercive force and through ideology. Many of Tendulkar's plays equate this subjugation of women with the man-led cultural pressures on external nature: industrialization, globalization and urbanization had adverse effects on human health, both physical and mental but it had more deteriorating impact on the lives of women and non-human beings (such as flora and fauna). The economic gain by dominating nature which is at the root of a capitalist, materialist technology-driven civilized society has compelled us to see that "the relationship of exploitative dominance between man and nature ... and the exploitative and oppressive relationship between men and women ... were closely connected" (Mies & Shiva 3).

With increasing interest for the conservation of human values and women's rights Tendulkar's plays combine environmental ethics in that: activities of the human world has been interpreted through natural imagery; the legitimization of sexual, gender and racial preconditions is depicted through reassessing natural laws; and in his plays there are constant meditation over the nature/culture and emotion/reason dualisms. Cultural consciousness surfaces in the play *A Friend's Story* which presents a society that considers homosexuality as 'unnatural', inviting us to brood over what is 'natural'.[2] In *Gashiram Kotwal* the female character Gauri becomes 'frightened deer', 'running mice', chased by 'wolf' (male lust); the play uses the idea of 'place' as an ecocritical trope and shows the distinction between culturally polished urban complexity and 'raw untouched nature' and thereby aims to capture the transition from nature to culture and their consequent separation. This aspect has been more effectively dealt with in the play *Kamala* which also reveals the exploitation of women for commercial benefits. A culturally equipped social reformer and renowned journalist, Jai Singh in the name of women empowerment buys a tribal woman and keeps her without bathing and food before presenting her to the media; he commits the crime of displacing the tribal woman from her natural habitats and takes advantage of her 'natural endurance'.

Silence! The Court is in Session, as Ram Sharma points out, 'presents a metaphorical trial between the humanists and the anti-humanists' (Prasad & Barbuddhe 125). The play brings out the hypocrisies of a patriarchal society that castigates women and leaves men unquestioned for the same offence. The play presents the mock-trial of a spinster school teacher Miss Leela Benare who is accused of infanticide and unmarried motherhood. She is cross examined and all the character present drag up her personal life by manufacturing tales of her illegitimate relationship with Prof. Damle in the name of Just 'a game'. As the trial goes on all of them turn inimical towards Benare and claim her dismissal from the job as an immoral woman. Finally, the forcefully silenced Benare is given a chance to defend herself through a long soliloquy: which reveals the plight of a single woman 'trapped' within a patriarchal society. As it is stated earlier, ecofeminism claims that patriarchy tries to justify its position through certain categorical binaries which are conducive for the hierarchical domination: such as, mind/body, male/ female, human/non-human, spirit/matter, culture/nature. In the play we find that the oppressive social system of abusive patriarchy operates through reestablishing the assumptions of these dualisms. The persons who condemn Benare appear to be the embodiment of the culturally progressive face of patriarchy and the sacred keeper of the systematic moral code of conduct: they corner Benare by their androcentric assertions and Benare's helplessness becomes the cry of the whole nature, trampled under the one-dimensional technology driven process of progress.

At the outset the play is about the restrictive powers of a male-centric society which limits the role of a woman through its masculinist strategies. Leela's independent attitude, her devotion towards her profession, her popularity among the students undermine and transcend the parochial domestic role that women are assigned; hence her clash with the representatives of the value-laden social system. She must become a meek and docile woman that society wants her to be; she must surrender her spontaneous vitality and slip into a kind of role play. Judith Plant showed how mechanized 'cultural constraints' (Plant 234) enabled man to perceive nature as resources for his own use and this further appropriated the role of the dominator in exploiting women. Here, patriarchal metaphor forces Benare to revoke her assertive declaration of free will: 'I'll do what I like with myself and my life!' (SC 5); and she is, we are shown, merely a 'hen' (feminine, soft and easy prey of male desire, chased by 'dogs'). G.P. Desponde observes regarding this: Benare "is represented as 'a hen', a symbol of innocence and feminity and fellow companions as 'dogs', a symbol of cruelty, dual personality and masculinity. So, the pursuit of the hen by dogs symbolically reflects Miss Benare's inhuman exploitation by her male fellow companions" (15). These images also help us to understand the ideological impact of dualisms (Griffin's concept) in which the superior one terrorises the inferior other so as to maintain his dominance over the other.

Now, if we concentrate on the figure of Benare we find that there is a natural lust for life and forbearance, an audacity for ignoring social stringency: initially she was like a free bird with her carefree attitude and throughout she behaves or speaks in such a manner which reflects the effortless process of nature.

Her entrapment and exploitation in the patriarchal system is hence the destruction and deterioration of the non-human life on planet earth through 'producer-consumer networks' (Mies & Shiva 3). Tendulkar attempts to foreground female cause by using natural images: 'a toy parrot made of green cloth' symbolically suggests the gentleness and sweetness of Samant; on another level it points to the existential crisis that Miss Beanre faces – she is a mere plaything in the hands of the fellow persons (figuratively it highlights Nature's slavery to man); the image also confirms sexist demarcation and hierarchisation among species. Then Benare's 'finger' is caught 'in the bolt' which speaks of her curtailed existence: she is forced to carry out a half-fulfilled life – her elanvital is suppressed under social dictation and moral inhibitions. This is a crime against human nature and therefore against Mother Nature. Sometimes latter Benare generally comments on human nature that – children are 'so much better than adults' (SC 4). And the speech that follows objectifies the fact that culture corrupts – that it has a 'scratching' (ibid.) effect on children and women; ecofeminists suggest that this cultural consciousness (of which an adult male boasts of) makes us interpret these inequalities as inherent; and we are compelled to meditate upon the fundamental concerns for survival and preservation of life on this planet – that includes not only women, but children and the vast diversity of species. It may not be coincidental that the original theme of the performance chosen by the troupe was – 'A Case against President Johnson for Producing Atomic Weapons' (7). Here it is worthy of mention that the first anti-nuclear power movement was organized by the peasant women of Germany; it makes evident the fact that the crime against nature hurts women more than their male counterparts. Naturally we see that Ponkshe appears to be more comfortable with this 'scientific age' than Benare.

The play undoubtedly voices feminist concerns for it exposes the hypocrisies of a preeminently male-biased society which obstructs women in their quest for self knowledge and self realization. But we must not forget that the dominant theme of the play is that of a serious social problem of 'unmarried motherhood' (SC 71) and men's attitude to that mother. And in that it is worth remembering that the ability of producing a child has been bequeathed to women by nature; so any discourse on motherhood must be considered as a fitting subject of nature. The patriarchal pavilion eulogizes motherhood and somewhat godifies her image in a religious manner: 'Motherhood must be sacred and pure' (75). By imposing holiness on motherhood they can easily disregard the biological demands of a woman and so accuse Benare: "The woman ... has made a heinous blot on the sacred brow of motherhood" (70). Motherhood is a boon without which life becomes 'bare, bare' (6). Sukhatme's conception of motherhood and his high flying Sanskrit proverbs fail to recognize that a mother is afterall a woman with all worldly longings and he even remains oblivious (or pretends to be so) of the organic process of the biological childbirth that equates a mother with nature herself. Again Karnik and Sukhatme debates over the definition of a mother ['one who gives birth' (36)] and their ultimate conclusion – "who says only humans can be mothers and not dogs" (ibid.) – dissolves the boundaries between the human and the non-human; in other words the issue of giving birth to a child helps us to perceive an integrated view of the natural world which includes humanity; and in which 'pups' and 'human child' both have same 'ecological niche'.[3] Later on Benare has addressed the offspring in her womb as 'a tender little bud' (75) and 'the fruit of that love' (63) – these vegetable imageries highlight the nurturing and caring aspect of a mother and of Mother Nature which androcentric attitudes chose not to recognize.

Maria Mies while commenting on 'total commercialization and industrialization of reproduction' (Mies & Shiva 205) in the book *Ecofeminism* observes that "women ... do not yet handle their bodies – or parts of their bodies – in a rational way ... they do not yet deal with their bodies as marketable, and hence profit-generating property" (205-06). When we examine Benare's case thoroughly we find that she is assertive about her body but did not use her body (rather being used) to achieve material goals. At the age of barely fourteen her 'body' becomes an easy target of male lust when she is deflowered by her own maternal uncle; again her body is used by Prof. Damle and the impact of this on her was that of tearing of 'flesh'. Her body, infact, becomes like 'an imaginative landscape marked by sexuality and violence' (Prasad & Barbuddhe); social cruelty towards her body appears to be like environmental injustice. Helpless Benare is depicted as 'a trapped animal'; - caging of animal point to the heinous human crime of displacing species from its natural habitat and thereby restricting it from participating into the energy circulation among the species. Here, Benare too is ensnared by the vile human designs (Mrs. Kashikar even physically forces her to come to the witness box). Benare's metamorphosis from instinctual vitality to a 'half-dead', 'silent like a statue' (SC 51) state metaphorically is then the general outcome of the condition of the weak and the marginalized under the predominating masculine culture. Mrs. Kashikar, however, equates the celebration of the body with sexual liberation and promiscuity. Again, cultural formulations and prejudices surface in Ponkshe's quoted words which invite us to reconsider the age-old binaries – emotion/intellect, body/mind. Prof. Damle's intellectualism attracts emotional Benare; Benare offered him both her body and mind but Damle was only glad to accept the physical part of it and thus contributed in her victimization. Moreover, Benare's chauvinistic oppression in an urbanized, industrialized milieu provides us another interesting point of view: it is widely accepted that in the physical conflict man had genuine edge over women but the newer realm of technological advancements had shown the tendency of forcing women out of the centrality of action. So, Benare's losing of her job is no incident to be judged in isolation; infact it is a post-industrial condition which is striving towards – 'the destruction of their (nature, women, female nature) survival base' (Mies & Shiva 7).

In order to understand the imbalanced power structure and the biased mechanisms of the hierarchical divisions (which includes God, man, woman, non-human and baser nature) we must spare some space for discussing the songs (imbued with nature images) assigned to Miss Benare. Along with imparting dramatic significance the short ballad like verses bring forth the extreme pain and existential crisis that a woman (also read nature) must face in order to survive the abusive torture of patriarchy. Regarding the songs, Shibu Simon comments: "The 'parrot' is suggestive of Samant and 'nest' may refer to Benare's chastity which she is deprived of by Professor Damle" (Prasad & Barbuddhe 186). Through bird images the dramatist forced a common natural phenomenon to convey deeper meanings for human society which in turn will heighten humanist as well as environmentalist concerns. A.B. Agarwal rightly observes: "the pair of 'crow/sparrow' and the act of stealing away sparrow's nest by crow show the mechanism of patriarchal social system" (198). In another instance Benare's possessiveness towards her books has been expressed through everlasting natural images ['The grass is green/The rose is red' (SC 9)] which by contrast serve to heighten the transitoriness of human experience. That Benare, a woman is closer to Nature is suggested through that she is thinking in terms of floral images; and further – 'Sending it deep inside you' (ibid.) and 'it must mingle with your blood', (ibid.) which are suggestive of an organic, biological process, mark her attempt of creating an invisible spiritual bonding with nature. Hence, we are reminded of Charlene Spretnak similarly embodying spirituality in female biology which is 'comprised of the truths of naturalism and the holistic proclivities of women' (qtd. in Garrard 24). Then Benare recites another poem depicting man's existential questions in front of a violent cosmic force, aided by the operation of the elements (air, water, earth and fire); symbolically the poem represent Benare's own plight within a radical, gender-biased society.

Ram Sharma again observes that "Leela's argument against body and its mechanical connections and her discourse of emotion saves her from dehumanization" (Prasad & Barbuddhe 127). Benare's final monologue is infact, what can be termed as 'collective mindscape' (ibid.) of a group of women who try to resist through 'verbal reasoning' (ibid) enslavement under phallocentric strategies. In the true spirit of individualism she manages to leave aside all the setbacks ('burden') and discovers 'how wonderful every moment is' (SC 72)! In each and every single little trifle incident of life she can sniff elevated romantic joy, for they serve to enlighten us about 'natural interdependences' of each cell in the social and cultural ecosphere, moreover the feelings connect her immediate personal space with the physical, the social and the global:

> The sky, birds, clouds, the branch of a dried-up tree that gently bends in, the curtain moving at the window, the silence all around – all sorts of distant, little noises, even the strong smell of medicines in a hospital even that seems, full to bursting with life. Life seems to sing for you! (SC 73)

Benare's meditation on life/death in the pervasive atmosphere of human cruelty turns out to be the eternal conflict of vitality and death in the realm of nature. She was somewhat able to energetically triumph over morbidity – "I taught them (the students) beauty. I taught them purity. I cried inside, and I made them laugh" (ibid.). Carolyn Merchant pointed out how 'the organic cosmology' delayed ecological catastrophe, persistently evoked by scientific and cultural revolutions. Here Benare seems be advocating both for women and nature when she directly attacks and consequently exposes the hollowness of the male-centric capitalist society obsessed with 'progress': "These are the mortal remains of some cultured men of the twentieth century. And their bellies are full of unsatisfied desires" (74).

In the end Tendulkar's 'gyno-centric' approach to the socio-cultural events in the play has left him the scope to approach the marginalized objects in the society with a serious concern for environmental degradation. He seems to suggest that exploitation of women in the hierarchical system of society is analogous to that of the ruthless torture that man had piled on nature. Thus he tried to imbibe the case of Benare's illegitimate pregnancy with ecological consciousness above the concerns of moral and social indictments – for afterall, "There's nothing like the experience (to a woman) of one's belly growing into a mountain"[4] (qtd. in Garrard 24). Benare's condition can be viewed as 'a political subject' (Prasad &Barbuddhe 184) for she demands liberation from the dominant establishment. But the way he adopted to incite the noble aspirations (despite all hecklings) of a woman's life [that '... my son – my whole existence! I want my body now for him – for him alone (SC 75)] becomes a significant attempt 'to resuscitate and nurture the impulse and determination to survive, inherent in all living things' (Mies & Shiva 3). Now, taking for granted that "the liberation of women cannot be achieved in isolation, but only as part of a larger struggle for the preservation of life on this planet" (16) and assuming that Benare's exaltation of body over spirit is her surrender to orgasmic bliss [which gave her 'a moment so beautiful, so blissful, so near to heaven' (SC 75)], it would be proper to conclude with Maria Mies' and Vandana Shiva's observations:

> The desire to recover, to regenerate this wisdom (achieved through close kinship with nature) as a means to liberate women and nature from patriarchal destruction also motivated ... turning towards spirituality ... spirituality is largely identical to women's sensuality, their sexual energy, their most precious life force, which links them to each other, to other life forms and the elements. It is the energy

> that enables women to love and to celebrate life. This sensual or sexual spirituality, rather than 'other worldly' is centered on and thus abolishes the opposition between spirit and matter, transcendence and immanence. (17)

References:

1. That all the gender demarcations are socially constructed and that radically preferring emotion over reason has led to anti-rational stance.
2. For cultural manipulation forced into us the idea that everything outside the general heterosexuality (e.g. – lesbianism, homosexuality, transgendered or third sex) are abnormal, marginal– hence unnatural.
3. Ecological niche is the specific space occupied by each species in the physical ecosphere.
4. Radical Ecofeminists tried to establish physical connections between the body of a woman and natural processes. That they can experience fusion with the nature through physical experience has been pointed out by Sharon Doubiago through those above words.

Bibliography

Agarwal, A. B. "Dramatic Technique of Vijay Tendulkar's Plays". The Plays of Vijay Tendulkar: Critical Explorations. Eds. by A. N. Prasad & S. Barbuddhe. New Delhi: Sarup & Sons, 2008. Print.Garrard, Greg. Ecocriticism: the New CriticalIdiom. London: Routledge, 2004.

Mies, Maria & Vandana Shiva. Ecofeminism. New Delhi: Rawat Pub., 1993.

Plant, Judith. "Women and Nature". Reweaving the World: The Emergence of Ecofeminism. Eds. by I. Diamond & G. F. Orenstein. Sanfrancisco: S C B, 1990.

12

Pseudo-liberalism in a Postcolonial Setting: Breaking the Myth in Vijay Tendulkar's *Kanyadaan*

Nitai Saha

Vijay Tendulkar has got wide spread popularity and appreciation as a pioneer of experimental theatre movement not just in Marathi but Indian theatre as a whole. He is ranked with great playwrights like Badal Sirkar, Girish Karnad and Mohan Rakesh. In the 'Preface' to his Collection of '*Six One Act Plays Raatra*', he has mentioned:

> Recently, my name has been repeatedly counted amongst the followers of the new drama sect. I have felt no great urge thus, far to determine which sect I belong to, nor do I expect to feel the need to do so in the future. I have written on any theme that has occupied my mind over time, stubbornly insisting that I write on in which ever form I thought best... It is wrong to support that everything different from the establishment is bad, childish and irrelevant. It is equally wrong to think that only which is different is good, true or valuable. Personally, despite being counted amongst the new dramatist, I love to lose myself in the best of Deval, Gadkari, Khadikar and Warekar... (Tendulkar 197)

Vijay Tendulkar has powerfully articulated the socio-political situations in his plays. He has expressed it by saying:

> As an individual or rather as a social being, I feel deeply involved in the existing state of my society and in my way brood over it. Once in a way I even do something to relieve myself of the tension and anxiety and agitation produced by this brooding, I participated in a protest meeting or dharna or a fast or morcha or a satyagragh I align myself with some civil liberty organisation...As a social being I am against all exploitation and I passionately feel that all exploitation must end...As a writer, I feel fascinated by the violent exploiter and exploited relationship and obsessively delve deep into it instead of taking a position against it. That takes me to a point where I feel that the relationship is external fact of life however cruel, will never end. Not that, I relish this thought while it grips me but I cannot shake it off. (Tendulkar 92)

Tendulkar's stance has come in for critical review. As Gawri Ramnarayan sums his contibution:

> He has been criticized for exaggerating 'the spiritual bankruptcy of the degenerate socio-cultural milieu in which we live'. He has been accused of neo-realistic projections of squalor, poverty, crime, disorder, and mental perversions to titillate the viewer/reader, and worse, of promoting defeatist apathy. But he has also been acclaimed as one of India's best living playwrights. (Interview 168)

With criticism and appreciation, Tendulkar reveals the realistic world in his creations. He perceives the realities of human society without any pre-conceived notions, reacts to them as a sensitive and sensible human being and writes about them in his plays as a responsible writer. In his 'Afterwards' to the English version of *Kanyadaan,* he confesses how he goes about writing his plays:

> I have written about my own experiences and about what I have seen in others around me. I have been true to all this and have not cheated my generation... they contain my

> perception of society and its value and I cannot write what I do not perceive. (71)

Published in 1983, *Kanyadaan* is his most complex creation about the cultural and emotional upheavals of a family. It dwells on an extremely sensitive conflict between upper class and Dalit caste that is still prevalent in several parts of India. Despite sixty years of Independence, Dalits continue to suffer abject misery and ill-treatment in the hands of upper castes. Politicians instead of trying to uproot this evil, seem to capitalize on it. An authentic playwright that he is, Tendulkar opens his reader-audience's eyes to a social problem that continues to evade easy solutions.

Kanyadaan focuses on the controversial and problematic postcolonial dalit sensibility with the contrapuntal question of facade upper castes' liberal attitude in the light of Homi-Bhaba's definition of postcolonialism. The term 'postcolonial' refers to the writings, culture of nations and people who were once colonized by European powers. Therefore all Post-colonial theories look at the feminization, marginalization and dehumanization of the native. They exhibit the psychological effects of colonialism on both the colonizer and colonized. Homi Bhaba defines 'postcolonial' as:

> That form of social criticism that bears fitness to those unequal and uneven processes of representation by which the historical experience of the once colonized Third world comes to be framed in the West. (Qtd. By Nayan 164)

Thus post colonized seeks to understand how oppression, resistance and adaptation had occurred during the colonial rule. It analyses specific strategies of power, domination, hegemony and oppression utilized by the colonizer in the colony. Therefore, postcolonial studies uncovers the ideological subtexts of differences, discrimination and unequal power relations. This ideology of postcolonialism has become central motif in exploring the dichotomy between the notion of Castism and that of the so-called liberalism as displayed by the upper castes in *Kanyadaan.*

In *Kanyadaan* Jyoti, the protagonist, has been placed as a site, a battleground on which the clash between the upper class and Dalit class takes shape. She becomes the vessel in which the conflicting caste ideologies pour their aspirations. In the play inter-caste marriage has been offered as a solution to the caste problem for which Tendulkar has been criticized that he is flogging the dead horse of inter-caste marriage. The title *Kanyadaan* – giving away of the daughter – is very suggestive since it revolves round an unusual marriage of Jyoti, a Brahmin girl who comes from a politically and socially active family. Her father, Nath Devlalikar, is an M.L.A. and her mother Seva, is a busy social worker. Her brother Jayaprakash is an M. Sc. student, while Jyoti is an educated working woman. Theirs is an urban middle class family. Brought up in such a progressive minded and so-called liberal family, Jyoti decides to marry Arun Athavale, a Dalit youth from a village whom she had known only for two months. Arun, a B.A. student, is poor but talented. He writes poetry. Jyoti puts forward her decision to marry Arun before her parents and brother. Nath and Seva are socialists and work hard for Dalits for a long time. Nath is very happy and says, "but if my daughter decided to marry into high caste it would have not pleased me much" (8) since he considered the boy's background and profession irrelevant. But Seva's response to this news displayed a gap between theory and practice. She does not give her consent to this uneven union and finds one excuse after another to prevent the marriage. When Jyoti expresses her 'trust' in Arun and her faith in his poems and biography which inspired her, Seva warns Jyoti for her hasty decision. Although she is self-righteous enough to say that she is not opposed to inter-caste marriages:

> My anxiety is not over his being a Dalit. You know very well that Nath and I have been fighting untouchability tooth

> and nail ... but your life has been patterned in a certain manner. You have been brought-up in a specific culture... he is different in anyway. You will not be able to handle it. (13)

In fact, Seva's anxiety is perfectly natural and genuine since cultural deformities may foster the problem of identity crisis and become the cause of marital disharmony. Seva here seems more rational and pragmatic than Nath and Jyoti who are in the passion of idealism. But Jyoti fails to see sense in Seva's forewarning and asserts, "I will manage mother" (13). The final decision is postponed till they meet Arun.

In the second scene of the first Act Arun comes to Jyoti's house while she is alone. Arun is dark complexioned and has a harsh face, yet he is good looking. The feelings of inferiority that he has acquired in the Dalit environment imposed by our hierarchized society, surface in his mind and make him uncomfortable in this Brahmin house. Being a Dalit he possesses his own insecurity and unconsciously seeks a fulfillment of it in the company of Jyoti. So he requests Jyoti to be with him. Arun feels quite nervous when she is about to go into the kitchen to make tea for him. We also hear about his phobia of big houses and big people, "I feel uncomfortable in big houses," Jyoti is surprised, Arun continues:

> If you will see my father's hut you will understood. Ten of us big and small, lived in that eight by ten feet. The heat of our bodies to warm us in winter. No clothes on our back no food in our stomach, but we feel very safe. Here, these damn houses of the city people, they're like the bellies of sharks and crocodiles each one alone in them. (16)

The contrast between the soft and protected life in which Jyoti has been brought up and the harsh existence through which Arun has come becomes all the more conspicuous. Arun becomes more eloquent as the conversation developed on the subject of untouchability. His words spit venom. They express the age long hatred for upper caste. He persecutes Jyoti to avenge the oppressions of Dalits by upper class people. He asks Jyoti:

Surely we cannot fit in your unwrinkled Tinopal world. How can there be any give and take between our ways and your fragrant, ghee spread, wheat bread culture...

> Will you marry me and eat stinking bread with spoilt Dal in my father's hut without vomiting? Tell me, Jyoti, can you shit every day in our slum's village toilet like my mother?" (17)

Jyoti is unable to bear such rebellious talks and covers her face with her hand. She starts crying on hearing Arun. Yet Arun goes on relentlessly, "And you thought of marrying me. Our life is not the socialist service camp. It is hell. And I mean hell. A hell named life." (18) At Jyoti's cries, Arun shows his apologies on his rude speech. He realizes that he is causing Jyoti a great pain by his bursting out due to his inferiority. He asks her to forgive his mood as they arise out of his feeling of injustice, frustration, inner desire for revenge and his utter helplessness. This pleases Jyoti and she takes her hand off her face and smiles. Arun in his excitement chants a rhyme, "it is jolly game; caught a Brahmin dame." Hearing this Jyoti's self is knocked. She asserts that she is not a sophisticated girl. Arun suddenly twists her arm violently. Jyoti is painfully hurt, more so because of this sudden change in Arun's manic behaviour. Here we can establish that Jyoti first plays the role of Rescuer while Arun plays the victim. Her role prevents her from perceiving the reality. Her rescuing, at first, makes him behave more helplessly and then triggers his feelings of inferiority and insecurity. It brings a philosophical guilt in the psyche of Arun all through marginalized suppression. Consequently Arun shifts to the role of persecutor in order to feel powerful and becomes violent towards Jyoti.

Further, Seva, vis-a-vis with her proposed son-in-law, asks about his future prospects of job so as to ensure economic security as it is essential for running any household. As Seva puts her finger on Arun's raw nerve, Arun feels cribbed by this gesture. He retorts giving her the answer that, "We shall be brewing illicit liquor." (21)

Arun goes on cataloguing the advantages of the trade of brewing illicit liquor even in the presence of Jyoti and Jayaprakash, and when Jyoti tries to pacify the situation and calm down the flayed feelings, Arun shouts at her to shut-up. Nath's entry at this juncture eases the situation. Unaware about the brewing storm, Nath is overjoyed with the prospective marriage. As a mouthpiece of liberal ideology, he reveals his high ideals on intercaste marriage:

> Seva until today, 'Break the caste system' was a mere slogan for us. I have attended many intercaste marriages and made speeches. But today I have broken the caste barrier in real sense. My home has become Indian in the real sense of the term. I am happy today, very happy... (23)

After sometime Arun leaves caring without even touching the tea that Jyoti brings for him. Seva and Jayaprakash then complain about Arun's vile behaviour but Nath ignores their accusation and defends him:

> Not only is he a middle class man, he is a Dalit. He has been brought up in the midst of poverty and hatred. These people's psychological make- up is all together different... We must understand him and that is extremely difficult. (27)

Nath makes a plea for compassion and sympathetic understanding. The rough edges of Arun's character are justified by him on the name of social justice. Here, like Jyoti, Nath also plays the role of the rescuer and in rescuing Arun he tries to get a change from Arun's behaviour. He does not consider him like a similar human being. He wants to be 'catalyst in the transformation' and tries to make 'a difficult experiment'. (31) With the difference of opinion, the decision is left to Jyoti.

Unresponsive to her mental confusion and fed on the diet of her father's liberal ideals, Jyoti marries Arun. The marriage is expected to be the meeting of two cultures rather than coming together of two persons in flesh and blood. It is on this high liberal, moral and idealistic note that the first act ends, as the stage direction indicates that the darkness descends at the end of Nath's speech that foreshadows the future storm in which the family is going to be engulfed after this marriage of two ideologies.

Passing months put Arun and Jyoti's post-marital relationship in deep trouble. Jyoti returned home, crushed and tired. She is a 'beaten' figure in every sense of the term. Seva's fears come true. Arun has no room of his own hence the couple has to spend their nights to some friends or the another's. Every night Arun comes back and beats Jyoti. She comes home with the determination not to return to Arun. Nath is firm on his resolution not to break the relationship; "... Seva, let not this experiment fail." (41) He finds out a solution of Arun's frustration and offers that Arun and Jyoti should stay with them rather than wandering. He condones Arun's ill-treatment of Jyoti as a result of the harsh environment in which he has been brought up: if he gets a better surrounding, such as Jyoti's maternal home, he will definitely mend his ways. Then, Arun appears in defence of his attributed errors. He not only rings up but again comes to apologize for his behaviour. In a perverse conduct, he takes out a knife saying that he is going to cut off his arm with which he beats Jyoti. Sensitive to his histrionic act, Jayaprakash snatches away the knife. To Seva's question why he beats Jyoti he responds:

> Arun What am I but a son of scavengers. We don't know the non-violent ways of brahmins like you. We drink and beat our wifes ... We make love to them ... but the beating is what get publicized.
>
> Seva: Drunk or sober, wife-beating is called barbarism.

> Arun: I am a barbarian, a barbarian by birth. When have I claimed any white collar culture? (44)

The rage expressed in the above lines exposes Arun's psychological state of polarized mind that is suffering with the deformities of the society. His behaviour towards Jyoti cannot be taken as an individual torturing his wife but this is due to the age-long suppressions and subjugations out of which he wants to declare war against upper caste. To be a persecutor, he keeps himself on the above scale to overcome his inferiority and makes use of his power as a typical husband and continues:

> I am what I am ... and shall remain exactly that. And your Jyoti knew what I was even before she married me. In spite of that she married me. She did it out of her own free will. (44)

Jyoti, to prevent the further embarrassment to her parents and brother surrenders to the situation and leaves the house with Arun forever. In rescuing Arun, Jyoti intensifies his feeling of inferiority. Seva is aghast but Nath is delighted; as a spokesman of liberalism, he seeks his aspirations in Jyoti.

> Jyoti I feel so proud of you. The training I gave you has not been in vain. (Suddenly dejected). If only I believed in God, then Jyoti this is the moment I'd go down on my knees and pray for you.

With pride and anguish Nath wishes that his daughter would lead a happy married life. Yet he is surrounded by unknown fears. Between the first and second scenes few months pass by. Arun publishes his autobiography which receives a good acclaim. Nath praises it, "Such a powerful autobiography. Hats off to Arun Rao." (46) At the same time, Seva returns from the hospital since pregnant Jyoti has been brutally beaten and kicked by Arun in the belly. Nath fails to understand Arun's behaviour. He sits completely baffled and wonders as to how a person who himself has gone through so much suffering can inflict pain on others.

> Nath: Such behaviour towards a pregnant wife! ... Here in these pages he describes the humiliations he has gone through with extraordinary sensitivity... and the same man kicks his pregnant wife on her belly? How ... ?" (47)

Seva cannot control herself any longer and bursts before.

> Seva: The truth is that your Dalit son-in-law who can write such a wonderful autobiography and many lovely poems wants to remain an idler. He wants his wife to work. And with her money he wants to drown himself in drinks and have a hell of time with his friends. On top of that, for entertainment, he wants to kick his wife in the belly. (47-48).

Later, Jayaprakash joins the discussion by quoting the news item that the Jews who were once persecuted have now become the merciless murderers of Palestinians. This helps to put Arun's behaviour in a perspective that Nath can understand.

> Jayaprakash: But I remember that some years ago, Hitler's Nazi troops had inhumanly decimated the Jews.... And today the Jews have become the murderers of Palestinian women and children.
>
> Nath: Perhaps they believe that this is necessary as defence strategy.
>
> Jayaprakash: Perhaps. It's possible that guning down women and children is essential for one's defence. But this means that very victim of violence may go on to perpetrate the same brutal violence upon others, perhaps they get a peculiar enjoyment out of it.

In other words, 'yesterday's victim is today's victimizer.' Therefore there is no hope of man's gaining nobility through experience; he can only become a greater devil. Jayaprakash infers at the persecution of Jyoti, a Brahmin lady by Arun, a Dalit.

Tendulkar's firm belief that violence is an innate part of human nature, is seen throughout and most of the liberalists and idealists like Nath fail because they do not take into account this innateness of evil and violence. Nath then confesses that he too feels anger for what Arun says and does after all he is no Mahatma. To put Nath's ideology to further test, Arun visits him with his two friends. He requests Nath to talk about his book in the meeting. When Nath politely refuses, he blackmails him saying that, as his name has been included in the list of speakers, people will say, "The rise of Dalit son-in-law to the literary heights caused heart-burn in the upper caste socialist father-in-law" (55) if he does not speak. Seva, thus, advises him to concede to Arun's request because she fears "If we go against his wishes, it will mean more suffering for Jyoti." (57-58)

In the final scene we see Nath returning home after chairing the discussion on Arun's *Autobiography*. As he comes home he is tormented by his conscience. He blames himself for the misery of his daughter.

> If she has committed any crime, it is this; she took his father's words for gospel truth. She adopted her father's value. (62)

At this juncture Jyoti enters, the encounter between Nath and Jyoti is a great exercise by Tendulkar. Through the discussion he completely demolishes the school of thought that regards man as innately good and violence is merely a matter of environment with the change in circumstances. Jyoti rebukes his father for his liberal and ideal notions, "Your speech today was not only lousy, it was a hireling's speech." (66) Referring to her own life, Jyoti raised the question how to separate the evil Arun from the good Arun, for both are inextricably twined up with each other; Arun is both the passionate lover and her evil tormentor. She has to accept him in total. She expresses:

> I grew up listening to such talk day in and day out ... No man is fundamentally evil, he is good. He has certain propensities towards evil. They must be transformed ... It is essential to awaken the god slumbering within him. .... The truth is you know very well that man and his inherent nature are never really two different things. Both are one and inseparable. And either you accept it in totality, or you reject it if you can... Putting man's beastliness to sleep and awakening the godhead within him is an absurd notion. You made me waste twenty years of my life before I could discover this. I had to learn it on the strength of my own experience... (67)

In the beginning, she was feeling herself helpless but now she realizes that she can handle the situation leaving aside her pre-conceived liberalistic notion by accepting Arun in his totality. She tells Nath how he had made her mentally crippled and how Arun is better than he,

> Jyoti : "... tell me where is that beast I should drag out and destroy, where is that God I should rouse from his sleep? Tell me ... Arun is made of all these things bound together and I have to accept him as he is, because I cannot reject him. (68)

When Nath proposes him to comeback, she brilliantly checkmates him by one of his favourite ideas on his face.

> Jyoti : It will not happen, Bhai because you yourself have taught us that one must not turn one's back upon the battle field ... This drug ... has entered and mingled with our blood. (69)

As a married daughter she reminds her father:

> Jyoti : (harshly) I have my husband. I am not a widow. Even if I become one I shan't knock at your door. I am not Jyoti. Yadunath Devlalikar now. I am Arun Athavale, a scavenger. (70)

Jyoti firmly disassociates herself from her family and forbids them to visit her out of charity. It is through the assertion of Jyoti of her right as a woman and as a wife; she becomes an instrument to break the barriers of marginality and to establish the identity of Arun in the 'centre' as a responsible human being and considerate husband beyond the treachery of caste barriers.

Bibliography

Nayar, Pramod K. *Literary Theory Today*, New Delhi: Asia Book Club, 2006.

Interview, Vijay Tendulkar in conversation with Gawri Ramnarayan', *Vijay Tendulkar's Plays, An Anthology of Recent Criticism*, V.M. Madge, Delhi: Pencraft International, 2007.

Tendulkar, Vijay. *'Afterword' Kanyadaan,* Delhi: Oxford University Press, 1996.

-- *Kanyadaan*' Bombay, Oxford University Press, 2006.

-- Preface to Raatra Ani Itar Ekankika, 2nd Ed. Pune, Continental Publication, 1994.

-- 'A Testament' in Indian Literature, No.147, Jan-Feb.

13

Can the 'Kamala's Speak?: Violence and Subaltern Agency in Vijay Tendulkar's *Kamala*

Pathik Roy

Any critical engagement with Vijay Tendulkar's dramatic oeuvre leaves us deeply entrenched in the ethical concerns and social critiques that find reiterated articulation in play after play. For Arundhati Banerjee, Tendulkar is concerned with 'the middle class individual set against the backdrop of a hostile society'. (Banerjee,1992: vii) Indeed Tendulkar portrays with consummate artistic finesse the alienation of the modern 'little, big man' caught in a vortex of ever shifting, unceasing power play inscribed by a discourses seemingly beyond their control. Critics like M.S. Dharan have explored the 'gyno-centricism' of plays like *Silence! The Court is in Session* and *Kamala*.(Dharan,1999: 28-59) His focus has been on the plight of women and the delineation of their characters in a social milieu that is predominantly phallocentric. Obviously such gyno-centric approaches cannot be innocent of the politics of the man-women relationship obtained within the traditionally hallowed institution of marriage. For instance, in *Kamala*, the husband-wife relation degenerating into a 'master-slave' relation in metropolitan domestic spaces is a standard critical approach. P.D. Dubbe in 'The Theme of Flesh Trade in Vijay Tendulkar's *Kamala*' says, 'Kamala's slavery is narrated directly in the play.... Sarita is a symbol of slavery in family system.' (Dubbe, 1993-94: 96)

However all such critical readings are haunted by an absence of an engagement with the nuanced ambivalent polyphonies that resound in Tendulkar's works. Samik Bandyopadhyay suggests that 'exploring and critiquing the relations of power in all their complex ramification is the hub around which Tendulkar's major plays evolve'. (Bandyopadhyay, 2003: xli) But the exercise of power automatically activates resistance. In *The History of Sexuality*, Foucault sums it up neatly, 'where there is power, there is resistance'. (Foucault,1990: 95) Since power is exercised only over subjects whose conduct or action exists within a field of possibilities, the network of power relations is paralleled by a multiplicity of forms of resistance. Barry Smart puts it thus, '[A] relationship of power has as one of its limits a relationship of confrontation by which it may be displaced or undermined. The corollary also holds, namely that a relationship of confrontation has as its limits the establishment of power relationship ...'.(Smart, 2002: 134) It would be a profitable exercise to re-read Tendulkar's *Kamala* in view of the Foucauldian paradigm of power and resistance. This would involve the issue of violence, the question of agency through resistance and Spivak's idea of the 'silenced' subaltern who can only be 'spoken for'.(Spivak, 1988: 271-313)

Tendulkar had a life long obsession with violence in the socio-cultural life. Indeed his idea of violence partakes of Foucault's concept of 'coercive force' and Gramsci's idea of 'hegemony'. Consequently all discourses that activate an oppressor-oppressed binary is 'violent' in that sense. Explaining his stance he says; 'As a writer I feel fascinated by the violent exploited-exploiter relationship and obsessively delve deep into it instead of taking a position against it. That takes me to a point where I feel that this relationship is eternal, a fact of life however cruel, and will never end' (Tendulkar,1992). Consequently violence must be accepted as a fact of life, a part of the human situation.

Kamala produced in 1981 is a site of violence – coercive, hegemonic and institutional. And yet paradoxically it is this violence that engenders agency and subjectivity. It is a play based on a real life incident – the Indian Express exposé of trafficking of women by Ashwin Sarin, a journalist, who had purchased a woman for some two thousand odd rupees to establish the extent of flesh trade in India. In a series of articles Ashwin Sarin brought into the public domain the nexus between the police and political bigwigs in the prostitution racket. This was however just a topical inspiration that Tendulkar appropriated in his own artistic way to right the play.

Let us first consider the ambivalent position of the media as obtained in the play. The play activates a binary between two kinds of journalism represented by Jaisingh and Kakasaheb. According to Arundhuti Banerjee, 'Tendulkar makes a jibe at the modern concept of journalism that stresses the sensational' (Banerjee, 1992: xvii). On one hand we have Jaisingh, a product of the fast track consumerist society, whose only motivation is personal and professional aggrandizement. For him Kamala is not a human being who deserves respect and basic human dignity. She is a tool to be used and thrown away once the purpose is served. On the other end of the spectrum is Kakasaheb who is projected as a Gandhain and for whom journalism is not merely informative but reformative too.

> Kakasaheb: Why does he have to? My dear, it's not the facts of an occurrence that are important. But the topic is. Discuss that. Comment on it. Suggest a way to stop it– suggest that. After all any murder, rape or arson is like any other. What difference can there be? Why waste our country's time, and ours, writing accounts of them? What sort of journalism is it that smacks its lips as it writes blood-thirsty descriptions instead of commentary? Its business isn't news - it is bloodshed.

However Kakasaheb's type of journalism runs the risk of generalizations at the expense of specificities. Contingencies, difference and specificities are indispensable for the articulation of an issue. An over arching idea of journalism for nation building without local imputs runs the risk of homogenization and subsequent erasure of alternatives. Consequently if Jaisingh's career-driven journalism is scripted with the violence of a dehumanizing agenda Kakasaheb's vernacular journalism that negates individual specificities results in erasures that are equally violent. To say that all things sensational are devoid of any virtue would be simplifying matters to the extreme. After all Kamala's appearance at the Press Conference did create public awareness. Why else would Jaisingh be sacked with such peremptory alacrity? Therefore the media as an institution is inscribed with a dehumanizing violence of a consumerist/voyeuristic society but at the same time the marginalized deprived of agency by other power structures find some degree of visibility through it. Thousands of 'Kamalas' are bought and sold invisibly but a single press conference with one Kamala can make people sit up:

> Jain : His mistake was to cross the path of the wrong people. He jeopardized the wrong friendships.

Jaisingh's dismissal from the job may be looked upon as his nemesis. Jaisingh used Kamala as a stepping stone to success and dispensed of her immediately after. Similarly Seth Singhnia uses Jaisingh as long as it suits him and fires him as soon as he becomes a liability to his socio-political credibility:

> Kakasaheb: Why was he dismissed?
>
> Jain: There have been pressures on the proprietor. Ilearn that some very big people are involved in this flesh racket.
>
> Kakasaheb: But a man who's doing such a wonderful job – his proprietor's paper has become famous and respected because of it.
>
> Jain: A big paper doesn't recognize respect and all that, Kakasaheb–it only knows about circulation and advertisements, and profit and loss.

Kamala is robbed of her agency by discourses of power in society of which one manifestation is Jaisingh and his journalism. However Jaisingh too is a victim of the self same power structure.

Moving from the macrocosm to the microcosm of the domestic space we are confronted with similar institutional power equations for the personal is after all political. In a sense *Kamala* traces the trajectory of Sarita's evolution from a disempowered non-entity to a self aware human being. Sarita's subservient erasure in the beginning of the play is in stark contrast to her gradual assertiveness and achievement of agency as the play progresses. The Sage Dictionary of Cultural Studies defines agency as 'the socially determined capability to act or make a difference'.(Barker,2004:4). Agency has commonly been associated with the notions of freedom, free will, action, originality and the possibility of change brought about through the actions of sovereign individuals. Sarita's agency or ability to act is seriously inhibited by the phallocentric discourse that marginalizes her in all spheres. However as the play progress she attains a capacity to act. This points to the Foucauldian paradigm of power/resistance. No erasure is complete, no silence is absolute. To that extent *Kamala* may be considered as a series of cumulatively enhancing resistances that results in Sarita attaining her selfhood.

The trajectory of Sarita's evolution is gradual and inevitable and we get hints of the imminent change right from the beginning. In a conversation right at the beginning Kakasaheb voices his concern for Sarita's plight by saying that they did not '*give*' her to Jaisingh to take her back as a widow. Sarita's reply to this is significant:

> "But you did *give* me away, didn't you? Then that's that.'

In so far as language constructs our world-view, the use of the word 'give' carries with it the implication of the commodification of women. We are also reminded of the Laws of Manu, the ancient Hindu law giver which talks of the woman changing hands from father to husband and finally to the son. However such linguistic subversions of patriarchal structures remain somewhat muted in the beginning. By and large we find Sarita carefully fulfilling the roles that patriarchy has assigned her as an Indian wife. The internalization of her marginalization is almost complete. She is a domestic housekeeper, a graceful social companion and a sexual consort of her husband.

As someone in charge of Jaisingh's domestic comfort she makes meticulous arrangements for his return from the Bihar trip:

> Sarita: Kamalabai ! Sahib is just coming. Make a curry from that cauliflower in the fridge. See if those mangoes in the basket Kakasaheb brought are ripe. If they are, put out six or seven, See if there's any beer. If there isn't send Rambev to get some. Is last night's biryani still good?

Jaisingh too is an unabashed recipient of these attentions because the patriarchal ideology of which he is an agent has made this natural. Therefore in a most matter-of-fact way he tells Sarita:

> 'Oh and also bring some tea. And that suitcase has four days' worth of dirty clothes in it. Take them out and give them for the wash. But hold your nose while you do it. They must be stinking'.

The lopsidedness of this relationship becomes evident when we take into account that Jaisingh considers it to be his right to disappear for several days without telling his wife of his whereabouts. Though Sarita is not entitled to know about Jaisingh's activities, she is expected to receive every single phone call that comes for Jaisingh and jot down the details.

> Sarita – I have to write down each phone call.
>
> ....

> Sarita – Thats the way you see it. My husband sees it differently. If I say they didn't tell me their names he gets angry with me for not asking.

Though Sarita seems to have assimilated herself into the roles that patriarchy demands of her there are instances in the text that speak of ruptures on the smooth surface of her subservience. For instance Jain calls Sarita a 'lovely bonded labourer'.

> Jain: Hi Bhabhiji, I mean an English 'hi' to him and a Marathi 'hai' to you. This warrior against exploitation in the country is exploiting you. He's made a drudge out of a horse-riding independent girl from a princely house.

Though said half in jest, such conversations activate a counter-discourse and pave the way for Sarita's eventual empowerment.

In many ways, Kamala is the catalyst who jolts Sarita out of her uncritical compliance to patriarchy. She is stunned at the possibility of buying and selling of women as narrated by Jaisingh. However she refuses to accept Jaisingh's logic that he had to buy Kamala to redress this issue and initiate a public debate regarding prostitution. She has the courage to take up a position against Jaisingh and there is a great mental resistance to Jaisingh's spurious logic when she says:

> 'And for that did you have to buy a woman?'

This initial non-acceptance of Jaisingh's phallocentric logic gradually gains momentum till we find Sarita assessing and articulating her position in the 'Jaisingh-centric' domestic space in unambiguous terms much before the provocatively ironic exchange between Sarita and Kamala in Act II. Sarita has an instinctive understanding of Kamala's absolute erasure and disempowerment. Consequently her concern that Kamala should have a bath and proper clothes is a bold and significant step towards evaluating things in her own terms. Quite predictably she is not allowed to have her way by Jaisingh.

> Sarita: But I am asking you.
>
> Jaisingh: That's exactly what I'm telling you. She will come to the Press Conference in the same clothes she's wearing now.
>
> Sarita: She's a women ,after all and her sari is torn.

Sarita's identification with Kamala as a woman is at its incipient stage here mediated by the social registers of caste and class. Nevertheless Sarita is time and again disturbed by Jaisingh's casual appropriation of Kamala for his vested interests and his equally indifferent attitude to her future. When Jaisingh says that they have given a lot of thought to the plan Sarita asks him a disturbing question: 'Did you give any thought to her (Kamala)?'

However it is only after the Press Conference that we find Sarita interrogating and dispensing with the roles that patriarchy demands of her. In their drunken exuberance Jain and Jaisingh regale themselves with the ribaldry that went on in the guise of a Press Conference. It becomes evident that Kamala is stripped of all her dignity as a human being and made the butt of ribald jokes by a pack of insensitive and unfeeling journalists. Both Kakasaheb and Sarita are shocked by the description and Sarita's disgust is evident when she says:

> 'So while they were asking her those terrible questions and making fun of her – you just sat and watched, did you?

Sarita cannot reconcile herself to a scheme of affairs that strips a woman of her dignity, uses her and discards her when the purpose is served. This engenders in her a profound aversion which gets manifested as she progressively rejects the roles of a domestic housekeeper, social companion and sexual consort.

Immediately after the drinking spree is over Jaisingh hungers for physical intimacy with his wife:

> Jaisingh: You must tell me. I must know. Don't I have a right to have my wife when I feel like it? Don't I? I'm hungry for that too. I've been hungry for six days. Is it a crime to ask for it? Answer me!'

In 'heartfelt aversion', Sarita disengages herself and leaves. What Sarita contests over here is the patriarchal discourse that inscribes the woman's body as its domain. The effacement of the rights of the woman over her body is being legitimized through the institution of marriage when Jaisingh says, 'I'm your husband, after all.' Sarita refuses to make herself available to Jaisingh just because he happens to be her husband. She wants her body back.

Very soon we find her declining to fulfil the role of a social companion for Jaisingh. Jaisingh wants her to accompany him to a party that is rather important for him professionally. He takes it as a given fact that Sarita would accompany him and does not even bother to ask her:

> Jaisingh: You don't want to come? Why?
>
> Sarita: That's my will.
>
> Jaisingh: Your will?
>
> Sarita: Aren't I allowed to have a will of my own?
>
> Jaisingh: [Sarcastically] Never noticed any sign of it before. If you didn't want to come, you could at least have told me earlier. Then I wouldn't have accepted for both of us.
>
> Sarita: Did you ask me?
>
> Jaisingh: Of course! I left a message with Kamalabai
>
> Sarita: That isn't called asking

Both the tone and content of this exchange show that Sarita has achieved agency, however limited, over her actions. Jaisingh is ill prepared for this. He had taken it for granted that Sarita would put on the saree that he had bought for her from

Trivandrum and act out the role of a graceful, pretty wife at his side. Sarita resists the patriarchal politics that commodifes the wife to a pretty object by the husband's side. Jaisingh's emphasis on Sarita's dressing up properly for the occasion reflects this consciousness. His pretty, well dressed, amiable wife would be yet another avenue for societal visibility.

Sarita's dialogue with Kamala in Act II is laced with heavy irony and it is a turning point in her evolution as a sovereign self. She tells Kakasheb how Kamala shook her out of her disempowering slumber.

> Sarita: I was asleep. I was unconscious even when I was awake. Kamala woke me up. With a shock. Kamala showed me everything. Because of her I suddenly saw things clearly. I saw that the man I thought my partner was the master of a slave. I have no rights at all in this house.

The fact that she had looked upon Jaisingh as a 'partner' indicates that she was aware, however dimly of an alternative paradigm of a husband-wife relationship based on mutual respect, responsibility and decision-making. After all though marginalized by gender, Sarita is an educated lady from a middle-class, upwardly mobile family.

The one-liner climax of the play is reached when Kamala asks Sarita – 'How much did he buy you for?' It is a moment of epiphany for Sarita. Her identification with Kamala is complete. If Kamala is auctioned in the Luhardaga Bazar in Bihar, she has been auctioned in the larger bazaar of matrimony that has stripped her of all rights and agency. Kamala's further plan to divide the work between the two of them so that they can keep the 'master' happy further clarifies her position in the household.

> Kamala: Memsaheb, if you won't misunderstand, I'll tell you. The master bought you; he bought me, too.... We'll keep the master happy... I'll do the hard work, and bring

> forth the children. You are an educated woman. You keep the accounts and run the house. Put on lovely clothes and make merry with the master.... Fifteen days of the month, you sleep with the master; the other fifteen, I'll sleep with him. Agreed?

It is interesting that Kamala who is rendered absolutely invisible by multiple marginalizations should come up with such a plan. Within her limits she is not ready to forego what she considers her 'rights'. Therefore though 'silenced', Kamala is not absolutely inarticulate. Earlier in the play, Jaisingh has a tough time convincing her to go to the Press Conference. It is only when he takes recourse to the dynamics of a master-slave relation that she capitulates. Thus though the marginalization is internalized, there are ruptures that resists total merger. Spivak talks of the voiceless subaltern who is paradoxically 'silenced' by benevolent intellectual representations in her essay, *'Can the Subaltern Speak?'* Kamala's 'silence' however is not an inarticulate erasure. How else would she be the agent of Sarita's self-realization?

Kakasaheb is the sounding board against which Sarita's evolution is recorded. Initially it is a passionate and vociferous negation of her peripheral existence. Jaisingh has told her in no uncertain terms that it is he who takes decisions in his house and no one else. Reeling under the impact she cries out:

> 'Listen to the story of how he bought the slave Kamala and made use of her. The other slave he got for free – not just free – the slave's father shelled out the money – a big sum'.

There is the pang of betrayal and anger in this. It is a passionate denunciation of her slavery. But Sarita must go further. Self realization must bring in its wake composure and firm resolve. Sarita's concern for the fallen Jaisingh at the end marks the birth of a new self. She stands by him firmly not as a 'slave' but as an equal extending a supportive hand to a man in distress.

Her action is a freely chosen one rendered without physical or institutional coercion. The firmness of her resolve is evident when she says – 'But a day will come, Kakasaheb, when I will stop bring a slave' Sarita can never unlearn what she has learnt. The subaltern Sarita is finally no longer without agency amidst the 'violence' that is institutionalized by the myriad societal discourses of power.

(Note: All textual references are taken from *Kamala*, translated by Priya Adarkar, in Five Plays. Vijay Tendulkar (Bombay: OUP, 1992).

Bibliography

Bandyopadhyay, Samik. (2003) 'Introduction', *Collected Plays in Translation*, Oxford University Press.

Banerjee, Arundhati. (1992) 'Introduction', *Five Plays*. Vijay Tendulkar, Bombay: Oxford University Press.

Barker, Chris. (2004) *The Sage Dictionary of Cultural Studies*, London: Sage Publications.

Dharan, N.S. (1999) '*The Plays of Vijay Tendulkar*', Creative Books.

Dubbe, P.D. (1993-94) 'The Theme of Flesh Trade in Vijay Tendulkar's *Kamala*', in *The Commonwealth Review* (ISCS), Vol V, No. 1, pp. 94-96.

Foucault, Michel. (1990) '*The History of Sexuality*', Vol.I: An Introduction, trans, Robert Harley, London: Vintage Books.

Smart, Barry. (2002)'*Michel Foucault*', London and New York: Routledge.

Spivak, Gayatri Chakravorty. (1988) '*Can the Subaltern Speak*?' in Cary Nelson and Lawrence Grossberg (eds) 'Marxism and the Interpretation of Culture', London: Macmillan, pp, 271-313.

Tendulkar, Vijay. (1992) '*A Testament' in Indian Literature*, No. 147, January-February, 1992.

14

When Caste Comes Calling: A Study of Caste Conflict in Vijay Tendulkar's *Kanyadaan*

Susan Lobo

Dipankar Gupta tells us that caste issues are never confined to the boundaries of villages in India, but "... act and interact in a nexus beyond the village" (ix). Caste identities actually get greater scope to play themselves out once they break out of the confines of the village. Gupta argues that urban spaces simply provide greater freedom for caste identities to give uninhibited expression to the caste factor. He goes on to explain how caste issues have undergone a transformation in modern India:

> "untouchable castes that were once considered supine and docile are now militant, aggressive and fully conscious of their power and rights in a democratic polity. No matter which way one looks at caste, the system such as it was supposed to have been, has clearly collapsed. Where there was once a seeming tranquillity of caste relations ordered by a status hierarchy (howsoever localised in character) we now have a plethora of assertive caste identities each privileging an angular hierarchy of its own." (x)

Tendulkar's play *Kanyadaan* foregrounds the complexities of caste as it plays itself out in a Brahmin family when the daughter of the family decides to marry a Dalit. We see Arun, who plays a stereotypical lower class brute, unapologetic about his Dalit identity, resisting every effort at being integrated into the Nath family, determined to give his prospective Brahmin bride a taste of what Dalits have suffered through generations. The play is set in a middle-class colony where the ideology of the Nath household is underscored by photographs of Mahatma Gandhi, Acharya Narendra Dev, Yusuf Meherali and Sane Guruji hanging on the walls of the living room. Nath Devlalikar, nearing 60, is a Member of the State Legislative Council. Disillusioned with the way things have turned out politically after independence, he continues to remain an idealist and visionary. His wife, aptly named Seva, is also actively involved in social welfare activities, and offers a counterpoint to her husband with her realistic approach to issues familial and socio-political. Nath's daughter, Jyoti, is 29, idealistic like her father while his son Jayprakash is more realistic like his mother. Nath plays the benevolent patriarch of a progressive minded family where members are given space to follow their dreams, while simultaneously working for the progress of the nation. Nath proudly proclaims "We have a democracy in this house and we are proud of it. Democracy outside and dictatorship in the home, we don't know these two-timing tricks." (4) However, while Nath's idealism and progressive ideas may be an asset in politics, they lead to disastrous consequences for his family, for Jyoti in particular.

Nath's idealism is infectious; and Jyoti, being young, impressionable and highly influenced by her father is unable to resist the temptation to marry this angry, young, budding writer and poet she has just met. Nath himself is so excited himself about the prospect of his daughter marrying a Dalit that he actively dissuades her from taking time to know the man better. While for Nath, Arun's Dalit identity is attractive, for Jyoti, it is Arun's writing that does the trick. Her only clearly articulated statement about why she has already decided to marry a man she has known for less than two months is "His poems and his autobiography have inspired me with complete faith in him"(10). It is clear that she has fallen in love with the persona Arun projects through his writing than with the man himself.

Jyoti's agenda in deciding to marry Arun is as political/ socialist as it is romantic – she hasn't really fallen head over heels in love with him but thinks she can heal the wounds of this angry, young man by marrying him; she believes she can set things right because she is different from other upper-caste girls: "I am not one of those delicate touch-me-not creatures. I belong to the Seva Dal tradition." (15) And what are Arun's reasons for marrying Jyoti? Even he doesn't seem to have fallen madly in love with her. On the contrary, he conveniently detaches himself from the decision, telling Jyoti at one point: "No loss to me. It's your marriage which will fizzle out. That okay by you?"(18). It seems that Arun's agenda in marrying Jyoti is not marital bliss but revenge: what better way to avenge Dalits than to marry a Brahmin girl and make her live the hellish life Dalits have had to live because of the Brahmins? If for Nath, this inter-caste marriage was a kind of experiment, then so it was for Arun as well, except that in his case, the experiment entailed testing Jyoti to prove his belief that even those who champion the Dalit cause are shams.

Arun, unfortunately, fails to put himself to the test. In trying desperately to expose the Nath family, he becomes a hypocrite himself. Even his desperate apologies for beating Jyoti while she is pregnant, his proclamations of love, his threat to cut off his hands as a just punishment for beating his wife, are mere theatrics, and for once, even his normally obtuse father-in-law can see through the pretence. By projecting the negative stereotype of Dalits onto himself, Arun becomes what Dalits have always been made out to be. Constructing his image in the stereotypical image that upper-caste society has through generations imposed on Dalits gives him the freedom to ill-treat Jyoti and insult her family. In Arun's own mind, he is a Dalit above all else and Jyoti is a Brahmin above all else. His oversensitivity to his caste identity overrides other aspects of his personality, and precludes any hope of a positive relationship with Jyoti and her family. His inability to see beyond his caste becomes his fatal flaw.

While Arun's anger at the suffering of the Dalit community cannot be denied or downplayed, the question is, how much of his behaviour can be attributed to his Dalit background? How many of his bestial and manipulative acts can be excused on the basis of the argument that that's how he is because he is a Dalit, and because of the righteous rage that comes with that consciousness? Is wife-beating the prerogative of Dalit men? While on the one hand Arun's neighbours inform Seva that when Arun hits Jyoti he is often heard cursing her parents, on the other, Arun himself admits that his father regularly beat up his mother, using it as a justification for abusing his wife. Doesn't this fact clearly show that Arun is merely using his Dalit background to condone his crimes? After all, his mother was not a Brahmin like Jyoti. What excuse did his father have for beating her? Also, it is a common truth that domestic violence goes beyond caste/class boundaries, and that even rich, educated men abuse their wives. If we consider the fact that Arun is a graduate, and a poet for good measure, shouldn't his education have taught him better? If he perpetuates the same cycle of violence, the least he could do is not blame it on his Dalit upbringing: domestic abuse and caste are two separate issues, and the former cannot be condoned on the basis of the latter. As Seva rightly puts it, beating up one's wife is called barbarism. There may be a vast cultural divide between the upper and lower castes but by making abuse of women a natural part of Dalit culture, and suggesting that because he does not come from a white-collar culture he does not know any better, Arun is using caste as a convenient excuse to not only justify but also endorse caste distinctions based on violence against women.

Arundhati Roy points out in one of her interviews that expressing politically radical views in the public arena is one thing, and practising those ideals in one's personal life is quite another. She asks, "…how many Gandhian/Maoist/Marxist Brahmins or upper-caste Hindus would be happy if their children married Dalits or Muslims, or declared themselves to be gay?" (Roy 190). To give credit to Nath, he seems to be making a sincere attempt to practise what he preaches. Then why is Arun so sceptical? Why does he resist Nath's attempts to welcome him into his family? Is it because he is able to see through the façade of the liberal family that believes in an egalitarian ideal? Because Nath's attempts to integrate him into his household and into respectable society smack of condescension, and because he, Arun, has too much self-respect to be treated thus? It would seem so.

It becomes apparent from the outset that Nath is blind to the contradictions in his ideology of equality. He deludes himself, denying the fact that he, like the rest of upper-caste society, is not yet ready to accept Dalits as equals. While he overtly expresses ideas of equality, ironically, the very statements made in defence of Arun most clearly expose his hidden prejudices. On the one hand, he gets excited not in spite of the fact that his prospective son-in-law is a Dalit but *because* he is one. When Jayprakash calls Arun a bastard, a furious Nath reprimands him with these words: "You have been brought up with certain values! And you! It is wrong to show disrespect to anyone, under any circumstances. We are cultured and civilised."(Tendukar 52). By implication, Dalits like Arun are perceived to be uncultured and uncivilised. When Seva reprimands Jyoti on her hasty decision, Nath intervenes with the words "Right now we haven't even seen if the boy is dark or fair…"(12). When Jyoti informs them that Arun's family has debts, and that his brothers do nothing, Nath's response is a glib "A typical picture of those people. What is so special about that?"(9). Nath's use of the phrase "those people" highlights the ideological and cultural divide that separates the Brahmin, urban, middle-class, liberal, socialist 'we' from the lower class, rural, often uneducated and backward Dalit 'they'. Nath's statement about Arun's background being "typical" illustrates the prerogative of the describing subject to generalise about the objectified other, and the typical tendency of the speaking subject to negate individual differences and specificities of the spoken of object.

Like her husband, Seva, too, is riddled with prejudices about Dalits, except that she is more honest about it. But Arun can see through her as well as he can see through her husband, and is irked by her attitude towards him. When he visits them the first time, Seva, who has clearly seen him twisting Jyoti's arm, refuses to confront either of them about what happened. Instead, while she makes no attempt to conceal her displeasure, she welcomes him, urging him to sit down, and reprimands Jyoti for not having served him tea. Seva's subtle way of showing Arun that, unlike Dalits like him, they are cultured and civilised people who are well versed with conventions of social etiquette is not lost on him. When she begins to grill him about his education and plans for the future like any prospective mother-in-law, she reveals how conventional rather than liberal she really is. Arun is quick to catch on and can see how Seva's questions are designed to belittle him as suitable husband material for a daughter of this house, which only fuels his anger and provokes him to cleverly, though tactlessly, turn the tables on her by telling her that he and Jyoti can always survive by brewing illicit liquor!

While commenting on the employability of Dalits, Arundhati Roy states: "Dalits, adivasis and other dispossessed people should realise that they can't bank on the politics of compassion." (180) Arun seems to have arrived at a similar conclusion, and manages to beat the system at every turn. His coup de etat comes when he corners Nath into attending a function to celebrate his autobiography. Arun has understood Nath better than Nath himself, and has him exactly where he wants him. Nath refuses to give in under his blackmailing tactics because it would mean endorsing an autobiography he knows from personal experience is blatantly false. But Arun attacks Nath's vulnerable spot, his image as a liberal socialist leader:

> "These people believed you were a well-wisher of the dalit community. That you championed the cause of 'A well in every village for the dalit'. You launched a satyagrah for that cause. You deliver socialist addresses at the State assembly. With the trumpet call of idealism, you got your daughter married to a dalit. Therefore, they thought you would surely come to this discussion." (Tendulkar 56)

Arun makes Nath choose between his public image as a progressive political leader and his protective instincts as a father. In defeating Nath by his underhand games, Arun extracts his greatest revenge against the system that victimised his kind. By twisting the facts in his autobiography, and combining falsehood with his beautiful prose to achieve fame as a writer, he notches up another victory against the caste system. Mainstream Marathi literature is summarily dismissed by Arun, who arrogantly asserts his place in the Bhakti tradition: "All Maratha literature is stuffed with the petty bourgeois outlook and with soppy romanticism. I am the only one after the saint poets- who else is there?"(55). To give him credit, Arun has used the power of language to establish himself as the son-in-law of a respectable Brahmin family (remember, it is his writing that attracted Jyoti, and even Nath cannot deny the beauty of his writing) so that in spite of abusing the daughter of that family, he goes on to achieve respect and fame in society at large. Arun has won the battle and the war- or has he? Earning the wrath of his in-laws and the bitter resignation of his wife to a miserable life as his wife cannot be considered a success story by any standards.

Arun 's only saving grace is perhaps that he is not blind to his flaws; if anything, he takes perverse pleasure in deliberately drawing attention to them, indeed, flaunting them at every opportunity. Arun's tragedy is that he sees himself more as he is seen by the Brahmin, upper-class/caste other. The struggle before him is to reconcile the contradictions in his personality: the uncouth brute with a "scavenger's manner" vs. a bright young man with potential; the abusive lover/husband vs. the sensitive writer. It is a battle he loses miserably, even as he seems to have got on top of the system by marrying a Brahmin girl, and by establishing himself as a successful writer by falsifying the truth in his autobiography.

> By the time Jyoti realises that the two selves that reside in her husband cannot be isolated and dealt with separately, and that they co-exist, however uneasily, within the same man, it is wisdom that comes too late: "Arun is both the beast and the lover. Arun is the demon, and also the poet [...] Tell me, where is the beast I should drag out and destroy, where is that god I should rouse from his sleep? Tell me...Arun is made of all these things bound together and I have to accept him as he is, because I cannot reject him."(68)

But this is where Jyoti is wrong. She did have a choice and could easily have rejected Arun especially when she had the support of her family. Trapped at the intersection between caste and gender, she makes the tough choice of abiding by her marriage instead of exercising the easier option of escaping to her maternal home, thereby signalling her transition from a naïve, young girl to a woman of substance.

The term 'kanyadaan' evokes the idea of a woman as an object or a piece of property that is handed over to her husband and his family. It also entails an understanding that once a woman is married she is not to return to her maternal home no matter what trauma she may have to endure as wife and/or daughter-in-law. By deciding to live with her brutal husband instead of returning to her parents, Jyoti has not resigned herself to the patriarchal code; instead, her decision is calculated to punish the father who failed to live up to his own espoused ideals.. It is a double tragedy for Nath - to be rejected by both, his son-in-law and his daughter, as a cheat and a hypocrite. It is a blow from which he will never recover.

Critics have often blamed the tragedy of the play on Nath's idealism. Randhawa, for instance, explains: "In his maniacal urge to uproot casteism and caste distinctions, Nath makes his daughter serve as a guinea- pig for his 'lovely experiment'. Obsessed with his fixation of translating his ideology into a practice he uses his daughter as a scapegoat of his social commitment to ratify his socialist agenda…" (81). While this is true to some extent, I believe that it is Jyoti and Arun who must take the lion's share of the blame. In deciding to marry Arun, Jyoti exhibits a certain naïveté which is typical of many young women in love, who are firmly convinced that they can change their partners after marriage, or that their partners will change for love of them. One can't say that Arun deceived her; if anything, he went all out to give her a foretaste of what her marital life would be like. He dismisses her request to chat with her in the kitchen while she makes tea because only men who are pansies do that; he twists her arm for no reason, and insults her in front of her family. He himself describes his behaviour as a scavenger's manner. Moreover, Jyoti was explicitly warned by her mother and brother against marrying Arun. It seems to me, therefore, that the failure of their marriage cannot be blamed on caste factors alone, and that a more personal reason lies at its root. Even relationships where partners come from similar backgrounds are wracked by conflicts, but conflicts have a chance of being resolved if the foundation of the relationship is love, trust and faith. In the absence of these, caste factors only serve to aggravate the problems between that Jyoti and Arun, but caste cannot be made out to be the primary reason for the failure of their marriage because their marriage didn't stand a chance from the beginning. To illustrate, I would like to make a comparison with Karnad's *The Fire and the Rain* which has the love story of Aravasu, a Brahmin, and Nittilai, a tribal girl, at its heart. In sharp contrast to Arun and Jyoti, for Aravasu and Nittilai, their respective caste backgrounds do not impinge on their consciousness; it is love which forms the basis of their relationship. It is love that makes Nittilai run to Aravasu's rescue after her wedding, knowing that by doing this she is signing her death warrant, as indeed happens when her throat is slit by her brother and husband for dishonouring their community. It is Aravasu's love for Nittilai that so pleases Lord Indra that he grants Aravasu the boon to ask for whatever he wants; and, ironically, it is this very love for Nittilai that makes Aravasu take back his initial request to have the dead Nittilai brought back to life, and ask instead for the release of the Brahma Rakshasa's soul. It is in recognition of this kind of redeeming, self-sacrificing love that the gods finally send the rains the seven-year long fire sacrifice was being conducted for. In sharp contrast to Aravasu and Nittilai, for Jyoti and Arun, love does not triumph over caste because love was never the foundation of their relationship, which is most probably why Arun does not allow Jyoti to prove him wrong, to dissipate his anger, and to heal his wounds with love.

The point is that successful inter-caste marriages can work, but like any other dream, the precondition is that the dreamers must first have faith in their own dream. When Arun himself doubts the possibility of their marriage succeeding, the dream has failed before it has even begun. What chance does their marriage have when Arun himself challenges the grounds on which it can work?:

> "Generation after generation, their stomachs used to the stale, stinking bread they have begged! Our tongues always tasting the flesh of dead animals, and with relish! Surely we can't fit into your unwrinkled Tinopal world. How can there be any give and take between our ways and your fragrant, ghee spread, wheat bread culture?" (Tendulkar 17)

Dipankar Gupta elaborates on what it will take to eradicate or minimise caste-based conflicts in modern India:

> "To be able to go beyond caste identities is not something that either democratic politics or market economics can accomplish with ease. To disarticulate caste, endogamy has to be surmounted. Only urbanisation and its logic of anonymity can accomplish this task. True metropolitan experience, as Salman Rushdie once said, is when it is impossible to determine who one's neighbour is going to be. What is true for neighbours can easily be extended to sons-in-law as well." (Gupta xx)

In the context of this play, however, Tendulkar has highlighted how an inter-caste marriage culminates in tragedy all around, suggesting that inter-caste marriages can do very little to ease caste-based conflicts. Instead, he indicates that any kind of violence, once inflicted upon a people, only serves to perpetuate more violence. In spite of his experience, Nath's belief that all Dalits need not be like Arun; his conviction that they will instead be sensitive to the sufferings of others because of the suffering they have experienced, is in direct opposition to Jayprakash's observation on the Jews who were once victims of Nazi atrocities, but are now victimising Palestinians in the Middle East. From his reading of historical events, Jayprakash deduces that "... the moment one gets a chance one becomes a greater tyrant... one persecutes others with a vengeance, because one exults in doing that.", and concludes that: "Therefore, there is no hope of a man's gaining nobility through experience, he can only become a greater devil." (Tendulkar 51). It is this dystopian view that gains credence through Arun's behaviour and which is borne out by history, but such a world view also negates human capacity to forgive, and to rise above tit-for-tat strategies. How else can by the vicious cycle of violence be broken? While Tendulkar may have given us a complex and realistic view of the caste problem in India, and raised several pertinent questions that need to be addressed, the play presents a dismal picture and precludes any hope of eliminating caste discrimination. The absence of any resolution or a ray of hope makes *Kanyadaan* one of his most disturbing plays.

Tendulkar once explained in an acceptance speech that he was part of a generation that had fought for freedom, had lived the freedom movement but then found that the new world was a disturbing, confusing place that gave rise to more questions than it answered, with the result that they grew up to be a confused generation, a generation that preferred to escape from the issues that needed to be confronted. With regard to *Kanyadaan* he stated that it was a play that was related to that generation and era. He added that "It is not the story of any victory; it is an admission of defeat and intellectual confusion. It gives expression to a deep rooted malaise and its pains" (Chowdhury and Rajan 35). Perhaps that is why the play first earned him a slipper in the face and then the prestigious Saraswati Samman literary award!

Bibliography

Choudhary, Shoma & Rajan, Gita (eds). *Vijay Tendulkar*, New Delhi: Katha, 2001.

Gupta, Dipankar (ed), "Introduction: The Certitudes of Caste: When identity trumps hierarchy" in *Caste in Question: Identity or Hierarchy?* New Delhi: Sage, 2004, ix-xxi.

Randhawa, Harbir Singh, *Dalit Literature: Contents, Trends and Concerns*, New Delhi: Sarup Book Publishers Pvt Ltd, 2010.

Roy, Arundhati, *The Shape of the Beast: Conversations with Arundhati Roy*, India: Penguin Books, 2008.

Tendulkar, Vijay, *Kanyadaan*, New Delhi: OUP, 1996.

15 Pawns in the Game of Chess: A Study of the Gendered Slaves in Vijay Tendulkar's *Kamala*

Supriya Debnath

The Resurgence of the Modern Indian Drama in English during the 1960s is actually a collective attempt of four dramatists from different regions in India, writing in their regional languages – Girish Karnad in Kannada, Mohan Rakesh in Hindi, Vijay Tendulkar in Marathi and Badal Sircar in Bengali. With their innovative and experimental work of contemporary relevance, "they were said to have ushered modernity into the sphere of Indian drama" (Banerjee xviii). Drifting from the ideological canons of philosophical drama nurtured by Tagore and Aurobindo, they seek to eliminate the disparity between the page and stage enabling theatre as the instrumentation in articulating the discourses of cultural deformities of Indian society. Their cumulative efforts to deal with the problematic of contemporary Indian subjectivity on the various axes of power, gender, sexuality, politics, history, tradition, class and socio-cultural change expanded new horizons in the field of Indian English drama.

Vijay Tendulkar has been in the vanguard of not just Marathi but Indian theatre for almost forty years. As a prolific playwright, he has authored twenty-eight full length dramas, twenty-four one-act plays, and eleven plays for children. His experimentation both with the themes and techniques of drama has given Indian theatre a rich and challenging repertoire and laid the foundation of a distinctive tradition in the history of world theatre. He represents the new awareness and attempts of Indian dramatists of the post independence phase to depict the agonies, suffocations and cries of man, focusing on the middle class society. A keen observer Indian reality, Tendulkar perceives the cultural, social and moral degeneration of the contemporary society revealed in terms of gender discriminations, power politics, caste mechanism, oddities of personal relationships, isolation of the individual and his confrontation with the hostile surroundings, and, as a committed writer, he makes conscientious efforts to surface those issues, making them an integral part of his dramatic credo –

> "I have written about my own experiences and about what I have seen in others around me. I have been true to all this and have not cheated my generation. I did not attempt to simplify matters and issues for the audience when presenting my plays, though that would have been easier occupation .... My plays ... contain my perceptions of society and its value and I cannot write what I do not perceive" (Vijay Tendulkar 'Afterword', *Kanyadaan 71*).

As a devout humanist, Tendulkar delves deep on the depiction of the suffering and subjugation of those, who, still today, dare not to voice their pains and problems. Moved by social ailments and maladies, he strives to evolve theatre as a potent medium to articulate the voices of the subaltern, with a view to relocating their space and redefining their identities in the social order:

> As an Individual or rather as a social being, I feel deeply involved in the existing state of my society (because I am affected by it though not immediately in some cases or not as much as some others are) and in my way brood over it. Once in a way I even do something to relieve myself of the tension and anxiety and agitation produced by this brooding. I participated in a protest meeting or dharna or a fast or morcha or a satyagraha I align myself with some

> civil liberty organization... As a writer, I find myself persistently inquisitive, non conformist, ruthless, cold and brutal as compared to the other committed and human ... As a social being, I am against all exploitation and I passionately feel that all exploitation must end... As a writer, I feel fascinated by the violent exploiter and exploited relationship and obsessively delve deep into it instead of taking a position against it. That takes me to a point where I feel that the relationship is external fact of life however cruel, will never end. Not that, I relish this thought while it grips me but I cannot shake it off. (Tendulkar : "A Testament", 92)

Tendulkar possesses an exceptional sensibility for the victims of gender discrimination. Gender has been defined by the patriarchal fathers as a social construct. While sex is a biological phenomenon, the attributes of the masculine and feminine are constructed through gender paradigms which is to give a sense of identity to the individual in a society. Gender and power are inevitably interrelated in a society that witnesses a constant battle for aggrandizement. Women in our society, as Foucault opines, fall into "an extremely complex system of relations" based on "a highly intricate mosaic" of man-woman relationship (Foucault 62). The gender division in a game is marked by the response to power. The male pursues it, the female submits to it. Since power lies in the hands of men in a patriarchal society, women are relegated into the position of the 'other'– both in their home and the world. Though not a self-acknowledged feminist, Tendulkar examines the power relations in our patriarchal social system and delineates how women are exploited by men irrespective of their relation to them – a daughter in *Ghasiram* Kotwal, a sister in *Vultures*, a colleague in *Silence! The Court is in Session*, a wife in *Kamala* and a concubine in *Sakharam Binder*. Spivak's study of the unhappy condition of the subalterns– "If ... the subaltern has no history and cannot speak, the subaltern as female is even more deeply in shadow"–

is testimonial to Tendulkar's female subalterns who undergo all sorts of tortures – physical, mental and emotional, and are often deprived of most of human rights, relative to life and the dignity of the individual(Spivak:1997:28). Silence is a symbol of oppression, a characteristic of the subaltern condition, while speech signifies self-expression and liberation. The very word 'silence' of the title of the play, *Silence! The Court is in Session,* indicates the silence imposed on women in Indian society and brings out effectively the recurrent theme of gender deformities comprehensively exemplified in most of the plays of Tendulkar. Infact, the realisation of the discriminations based on gender, transformed in the form of resistance and retaliation, constitutes the cardinal core of the dramatic art of Tendulkar.

Written in naturalistic vein, *Kamala* (1981) was based on the first-hand experience of Ashwin Sarin, the then correspondent of the *Indian Express*, who bought a tribal woman for Rs. 2300 and wrote a number of articles with a view to exposing the ghastly flesh trade and the involvement of large scale politicians in it during the early 1981. By giving a glimpse of this real life incident, Tendukar "raises certain cardinal questions regarding the value system of a modern success-oriented generation which is ready to sacrifice human values in the name of humanity itself"(Banerjee : xvi). Besides making a jibe at the modern concept of journalism which stresses the sensational and the business- oriented and capital– dominated social structure, the playwright explores, as in his most of the other plays, the exploitation of women in contemporary Indian society. The idea of gender dis–crimination has been projected through the suffering of two women– an illiterate tribal woman sold away in the flesh market and a so-called happy housewife married to a well-known journalist, both of whom are used as mere springboards in a man's quest for power and pelf. The play thus exposes the exploitive power politics of the patriarchal society designed to reduce women to mere 'gendered slaves' both in home and the world. I seek to focus on this point in my paper.

The play opens with an impression that Jaisingh Jadav is an agile and adventurous journalist associated with an English daily published by Seth Singhania, a press baron. He exposes different scandals risking even his life and feeds the sophisticated daily with sensational news. His works widens the circulation of the daily and simultaneously attains for him promotion and higher salary as well as recognition in professional field. But this initial impression gradually dwindles as the play progresses and he is exposed to be an insensible pursuer of fame and name. To get an eye-witness for the inhuman flesh trade running on in the later half of the twentieth century, he goes to Luhardaga beyond Ranchi in Bihar and buys Kamala, an Adivasi woman, for two hundred and fifty rupees. Thus ironically enough, Jaisingh himself commits the crime he intends to expose. His defence of his inhuman act of buying Kamala reflects his sheer hypocrisy and innate self-deception:

> Jai Singh: Because when I first wrote about it, I didn't have any definite facts. But I could smell something wrong. The police, as usual, washed their hands of it. The Home Minister put his hands over his ears. They made the false charge that news-papermen tell lies. So it fell on me to put the noose round the right neck– with evidence (Act one15).

He deliberately plans to present Kamala at a surprise press conference as an object of evidence that such flesh trade scoop still happens in modern democratic India. Far from being a noble venture, his mission is simply motivated by personal interests. He does not have any motive to reform Kamala's life. Instead, he seeks to capitalize on it in order to succeed in his professional life without caring, in the least, for the victim of the immoral trade. He is thus ready to sacrifice human values in the name of humanity itself.

Jaisingh returns home with Kamala and keeps it secret from others except Sarita, his wife, Kakasaheb (Sarita's uncle) and Kamalabai, the maid. He tells about Kamala to Sarita only after giving her a warning to keep the secret intact till the press conference is over. He never cares for her as a human being and treats her simply as a 'performing machine'. With savage selfishness he does not let her bathe before the press conference, whereas he enjoys a luxury bath after the tedious journey and prohibits Sarita even from offering a decent dress to her, so that she would look natural and the press conference would gets its hype. It has aptly been attributed, "there is a cruelty in the heart of man. Even though man is a civilized being now, there is still the savageness of primitive man in him" (Devi: 143).That he has no sympathy or sense of respect for women gets reinforced when he tells his wife of the way he bought Kamala:

> Sarita: They auction--women?
>
> Jai Singh: Yes, women. Can't believe it, can you? The men who want to bid--handle the women to inspect them. Whether they are firm or flabby. Young or old. Healthy or diseased. How they feel in the in breast, in their waist, in their thighs and.....
>
> Sarita: Enough. (Act One 14)

To quote Beena Agarwal, "The implicit crudity in this observation makes Sarita petrified. She shudders at the thought of the auction of women in the flesh market. The excitement of Jaisingh and nervousness of Sarita makes a strong dramatic situation to expose the horrors of gender discrimination". Jadav is infact a representative of the male-dominated society which pays scant regard to women and utilize them simply as an object to attain pelf and power. Smita Paul aptly comments in this context: "He has bought Kamala not as a human being but as a bundle of flesh. His torture is therefore more piercing than the traditional customers in the flesh market. Here we can compare Jaisingh with Sakharam in *Sakharam Binder*, another dealer in flesh market."

Jaisingh is eager to create a sensation in the press conference as he says to Sarita, "See how we'll blast out this shameful affair. There'll be high drama at today's press conference. It'll create an uproar"(Act One15). He is least bothered about what will happen to Kamala after the press meet. As an insensitive opportunist, Jaisingh meticulously executes his plan and attains the desired success in exposing the inhuman trade at the cost of the victim herself. The press conference itself assumes a form of exploitation of Kamala as she was asked a number of abusive questions there and made a laughing stock. Sarita came to know it later from Jain:

> Jain: Where are you off to, *Bhabhiji?* Wait. The best bit is still to come, *kya re?* [*Jaisingh, drinking, shakes his head.*]

Some of us are absolute donkeys. But some of us are brilliant. They are a match for anyone who comes in front of them. There was one question- if there is free sex among you, what do you do with the illegitimate children?

> Jai Singh: He thought all adivasis indulged in free sex day and night. What nonsense!
>
> Jain: With that, another one began to itch to ask a question. He asked, you must be having free sex too. How many men have you slept with?
>
> Sarita: [*She can't help it*]. Weren't they ashamed to ask such questions?
>
> Jain: If they had any shame, they would be.
>
> Jai Singh: [*Drinking*] But listen--there's more.
>
> [*Sarita has sprung to her feet. Kakasaheb makes her sit down again].* (Act Two 29)

Kamala being illiterate fails to discern those sheer sensational queries. But Sarita feels ashamed of the vulgarity of the Press Meet that reduces Kamala to a commodity. Despite this, it should be admitted that the conference sheds light on the subjugation of women in democratic India even in the later half of the 20th century. In the Adivasi society, women, after being exploited, are sold by their masters like the cattle in the market place.

Jaisingh represents a sophisticated type of those masters of the Adivasi society. Prior to the Press Meet, he never gives her an inkling of his motive behind purchasing her and encourages her to nurture hopes of a handsome husband, a palace like house and children, by asking her to think of his house as hers:

> Jai Singh: ...Kamala, how do you like here?
>
> Kamala: [Not emerging from the veil] It's nice. Such a big house! Like a royal palace.
>
> Jai Singh: (Winking at Sarita) Would you like to stay here always, Kamala?
>
> Kamala: [Nodding her head delightedly]. Yes! (Act One 13).

P.D. Dubbe aptly says, "He duped Kamala who had come prepared to become his bonded keep with all the associated feeling of sex, motherhood and living" (Dubbe: 44). Jadav has no moral scruple in utilizing Kamala as his pawn in the game of chess. He 'sold a woman–that poor and illiterate woman' to the pressmen only for his personal interest. As Smita Paul opines, "Buying and selling may be called a dominant metaphor in the play. Kamala is brought from the flesh market and she is sold to the market of male politics." Had she been bought by a regular customer in the auction, she would have to sell her body, but now she is at a loss and loses both her dignity and emotional balance. As soon as his purpose is over, Jaisingh disposes of her as a wasteful commodity and discards her in an orphanage of poor women.

If Kamala is an object of professional success of Jaisingh in the outside world, Sarita is a symbol of slavery in family system. To quote Arundhati Banerjee, "Like Kamala, Sarita is also an object in Jadav's life, an object that provides physical enjoyment, social companionship and domestic comfort" (Banerjee: xvii). She survives within the confinement of four domestic walls the garb of silence and submission. Like a subordinate, she has to take note of all the phone calls during her husband's absence. Kakasaheb, her uncle, tells her that she need not ask the names of the callers; if necessary, they themselves will give their names. Sarita replies naively that her husband sees it differently, and if she doesn't inquire of it, he would get angry with her:

> Sarita: I have to write down each phone call.
>
> Kakasaheb: Well, I've just taken at least three. How many are you going to write down? If it's anyone important, they'll tell you their names. If they don't, you can happily assume they're not important.
>
> Sarita: That's the way you see it. My husband sees it differently. If I say they didn't tell me their names he gets angry with me for not asking. (Act One 3)

Sarita thus remains obsessed with the authority of her husband and leads a life of drudgery. We find her busy preparing her husband's necessary things after she receives a message of his expected return. She at once becomes alert and hastens preparation to receive him. She asks Kamalabai, the maid, to cook a curry for him and to get beer for him and also enquires whether his clothes have been brought back from the dhobi. All these she does in such a way as if a guest of honour, not her husband, is coming back.

Contrary to it, Jaisingh, the so called saviour of the society, cares little for the feelings of his wife. He goes off anywhere, comes back at any odd hour and never thinks it necessary to intimate her about it. Sarita has to lead a life of anxieties due to his reckless behaviour and irregular activities. Jadav, on the other hand, shows least concern for her. Even on his return after a week's home away, he utters not a single word of compassion to her. Rather, he demands comforts for himself:

> Jai Singh : Well, who were all the people who phoned me? [*Sarita hands him the notebook.*] Ask someone to heat up water for my bath. ... Oh, and also bring some tea. And that suitcase has four days' worth of dirty clothes in it. Take them out and give them for the wash. (Act One 8)

For Jaisingh, Sarita, like Kamala, is thus a mere performing machine. She has to perform her role as the male ego wants it. She has to do all the household works, accompany her husband at parties and satisfy his carnal desires, without asking for anything in return. After the press conference is over, Jaisingh being drunk wants her physically. And at this point when Sarita refuses, he bursts in violent anger:

> Jai Singh: You must tell me. I must know. Don't I have the right to have my wife when I feel like it? Don't I? I'm hungry for that too--I've been hungry for six days. Is it a crime to ask for it? Answer me! (Act Two 32)

It is evident that she has to live only as the shadow of her husband:

> Jai Singh: [*Handling the bundle to Kamala, says to Sarita*]. It's I who takes decisions in this house, and no one else. Do you understand? (Act Two 42)

What Simon de Beauvoir says about the modern men applies to Jaisingh here: "the men of today show certain a duplicity of attitude which is painfully lacerating to women; they are willing on the whole to accept women as a fellow being, an equal but they require her to remain the inessential" (Parshley: 291). Jaisingh is unkind and inconsiderate to the maid-servant Kamalabai, too. He bosses over her rudely, gives her orders after orders and never cares for her troubles. He often rebukes her even for the slightest breach of her duties. Thus the saviour of the slaves makes slaves of his family.

Kamala's entry in the household reveals to Sarita the egoistic and deceitful nature of her husband and the utter insignificance of her existence in the house. As Beena Agarwal points out, "The interchange of personal feelings between Sarita and Kamala after the press conference comes up as a turning point in the play. Tendulkar develops a chemistry of common feminine sensibility to prove that woman can have better realization of their fellow woman". Kamala, in spite of her poverty and illiteracy, does not fail to understand that Sarita had no belongingness in family. Her innocent question– "How much did he buy you for?"(Act Two 34) enlightens Sarita on her position in the family. Tendulkar himself has admitted the authenticity of the query in his article, *Kamala vs Indian Express*:

> "I distinctly remember that the article contained a paragraph where the tribal girl innocently questions a well-educated and liberated housewife as to what amount she has been bought for by her master. This was what inspired me to make the play *Kamala* (italics added) which sought to depict the slavish condition of Indian women in marriage."

Though Jaisingh took a handsome dowry in marriage, Sarita replies, "Seven Hundred". Kamala innocently remarks, "It was an expensive bargain, memsahib" (Act Two 31). Thus "Kamala, the silent subaltern", as Smita Paul opines, "metaphorically becomes vocal to Sarita, the childless woman". She makes her shockingly realise that the auction of an illiterate rural woman is quite similar with the marriage transaction of an educated urban woman, as both are bought: "The master bought you; he bought me, too. He spent a lot of money on the two of us" (Act Two 35). Her radical suggestion to Sarita of the common sharing of Jaisingh's household as well as his sexual life is thus an 'epiphanic' revelation to Sarita:

> Kamala: ... so, memsahib, both of us must stay here like sisters. We'll keep the master happy... the master will have children... I'll bring them up. You keep the accounts and run the house...Fifteen days of the month, you sleep with

> the master; the other fifteen, I'll sleep with him. Agreed? (Act Two 35)

At this, Sarita painfully realises that she too, like Kamala, is a mere pawn in Jadav's game of chess:

> Kakasaheb: Kamala is just a pawn in his game of chess.
>
> Sarita: Not just Kamala, Kakasaheb. Me too, me too (Act Two 43).

The long conversation between Sarita and Kakasaheb demonstrates that the exploitation of women is a perpetual process in Indian society. Kakasaheb confesses to Sarita that he himself behaved ruthlessly with his wife:

> Kakasaheb: ... I gave your aunt a lot of trouble. As if it was my right. I didn't care what she felt at all ... (Act Two 47)

As a male chauvinist, he made her follow him dumbly because it is her 'duty' as a married woman:

> Kakasaheb: It may be unpleasant, but it's true. If the world is to go on, marriage must go on. And it will go on like this. (Act 47)

The play is thus a scathing critique of the institution of marriage. Though marriage is considered as the holiest of all ceremonies, it actually operates on a master-slave relationship in our society. "Tendulkar imbibes a postcolonial bias in revealing the fact that women are still mere slaves to their male masters. All the three female characters in the play are in one way or the other subjected by the dominant male character Jaisingh Jadav , who is placed at the focal point of the play." (Paul)

As Sarita sees herself in the light of a slave, she undergoes a great change, and becomes an assertive woman who has finally discovered her identity:

> Sarita: I was asleep ... Kamala woke me up with a shock. Kamala showed me everything ... I saw that the man I thought my partner was the master of a slave. I have no rights at all in this house.Because I'm a slave. Slaves don't have rights... Dance to their master's whim. Laugh, when he says, laugh. Cry, when he says, cry. When he says pick up the phone, they must pick it up. (Act Two 46)

"The vision of Kamala becomes the strength of Sarita. It stirs her consciousness to make protest against her slave-like position in Jaisingh's house" (Agarwal).Her suppressed self demands autonomy for it and consequently, her fear transforms into retaliation:

> Jai Singh: Do you want to come to the party?
>
> Sarita: No.
>
> Jai Singh: You don't want to come. Why?
>
> Sarita: That's my will.
>
> Jai Singh:[*Rather surprised*] your will.
>
> Sarita: Aren't I allowed to have a will of my own?
>
> (Act Two, P.45-46)

She masters her courage to retaliate her oppressor and proposes to hold a press conference to expose the tyranny of her husband:

> Sarita: I am going to present a man who in the year 1982 still keeps a slave, right here in Delhi. I am going to say this man's great advocate of freedom. And he brings home a slave and exploits her ... Listen to the story of how he brought home the slave Kamala and made use of her. The other slave he got free–not just free–the slave's father shelled out the money–a big sum. (Act Two 46)

When Kakasaheb, in spite of his disgust for Jaisingh, defends him and identifies all the external forces of power as masculine and femininity as synonymous with passivity, Sarita breaks into vehement protest and challenges the male hegemony:

> Sarita: Why? Why can't men limp behind? Why aren't women ever the masters? Why can't a woman at least ask to live her life the same way as a man? Why must only a man have the right to be a man? Does he have one extra sense? A woman can do everything a man can. (Act Two 47)

But, in spite of her awakening to her true self, she like other women of Tendulkar, lends her emotional support to her husband when at the close of the play he is treacherously dismissed from his job by the proprietor under the pressure of the 'big people' involved in the flesh market. Here she follows the tradition of an Indian woman who always stands by her husband. Shanta Gokhale in her essay "Tendulkar on his Own Terms" considers Sarita to be Ibsen's Nora:

> Sarita is a Nora who has stopped short of the final breaking out. Though she does not make a dramatic exit at the end of the play, however, she has understood her situation as surely as Nora does. (Gokhale: 93)

But Tendulkar makes a faint suggestion that she cannot unlearn what she has come to realise. At the end of the play, she hopes to attain independence sometime in future:

> Sarita: I'll go on feeling it. But at present I'm going to lock all that up in a corner of my mind and forget about it. But a day will come, Kakasaheb, when I will stop being a slave. I'll do what I wish, and no one will rule over me. That day has to come. And I'll pay whatever price I have to pay for it. (Act Two 52)

To sum up, power structured gender politics and the question of survival for women amidst the dominant male culture gains a new momentum in the postcolonial literature. Vijay Tendulkar has undeniably brought out a new significance, new light and the new theory for gender politics for the identity of women in the Indian context. Most of his plays "have highlighted a new concept to the perennially profound issues confronting man in the metaphysical, cultural, social, economic, emotional, intellectual and political spheres" (Sundari).

Bibliography

Primary Sources

Tendulkar, Vijay. *Collected Plays in Translation.* New Delhi: OUP, 2008. All quotations from *Kamala* are from this edition from which only Acts and page numbers are cited.

Tendulkar, Vijay. "Afterword", *Kanyadaan.* Delhi: Oxford University Press, 1966.

-- "A Testament". *Indian Literature.* No. 147, January – February, 1992.

Secondary Sources

Banerjee, Arundhati. "Introduction", *Vijay Tendulkar: Five Plays.* New Delhi: Oxford University Press, 1992.

Dass, Veena Noble. "Women Characters in the plays of Vijay Tendulkar". *New Directions in Indian Drama.* New Delhi: Prestige, 1994.

Devi, P. Pramila. "Vijay Tendulkar's Kamala: The Theatre of Cruelty". *Studies in Indian Drama in English,* (ed) A.N. Prasad, Bareilly: Prakash Book Depot, 2003.

Dubbe, P.D. "The Theme of Flesh Trade in Vijay Tendulkar's Kamala". *The Commonwealth Review (ISCS),* Vol.V, No.-1, 1993-94.

Foucault, Michel. *Power/Knowledge: Selected Interviews and Other Writings 1972-1977,* Ed. Colin Gordon. New York: Pantheon Books, 1977.

Gokhale, Shanta. "Tendulkar on His Own Terms" Vijay Tendulkar, Eds. Shoma Choudhury and Gita Rajan, New Delhi: Katha, 2001.

Gokhale, Vikram. "*On Kamala*". *Vijay Tendulkar's Plays: An Anthology of Recent Criticism,* (ed) V. M. Madge, Delhi: Pencraft International, 2009.

Iyengar, K.R. Srinivasa. *Drama in Modern India*, Bombay: The P.E.N. All India Centre, 1961.

Loomba, Ania. *Colonialism/Postcolonialism,* London: Routledge, 1998.

Parshley, H.M. *The Second Sex, trans.* New York: Penguin, 1972.

Ramnarayan, Gowri. "An Interview with Vijay Tendulkar", *Frontline*, March 27, 1992.

Rangacharya, Adya. *The Indian Theatre,* New Delhi: National Book Trust, 1971.

Renuka, E. "*Silencing Women's Voice: A Study of Vijay Tendulkar's Silence! The Court is in Session*. Kakatiya Journal of English Studies, Volume 15, December 1995.

Spivak, Gayatri Chakravorty. *"Can the Subaltern Speak?" The Post-Colonial Studies Reader,* (eds) Bill Ashcroft, Gareth Griffiths and Helen Tiffin, London: Routledge, 1997.

Online Sources

Agarwal, Beena. *Tendulkar's Kamala: Resistance and Reversal of Gender Colonialism.* www. *sparkejournal.com.*

Joseph, S. John Peter. The Playwright as a Social Critic: A Critical Study of Vijay Tendulkar's Silence! The Court is in Session. www.tjells.com.

Pandey, Pramila. Vijay Tendulkar's Kamala: A Symbol of Slavery. *www.*languageinindia.com

Paul, Smita. *Vijay Tendulkar's Kamala: Subjugation of Women in Home and the World.* www.msacademic.net.

Sundari, A. Gender Politics in Vijay Tendulkar's Silence! *colleges.papyrusclubs.com.*

Tendulkar, Vijay. *"Kamla' Vs Indian Express."* www.cscsarchive.org.

16

Marginalia Fights Back: Resistance Against Violence in Mahesh Dattani's Selected Plays

Tapashree Ghosh

The Indian Nation State was born on 15th August 1947 after India gained Independence from colonial rule. The architects of Indian Independence had envisioned a new beginning for India. On the eve of Indian Independence Jawaharlal Nehru, the first Prime minister of Independent India, in his famous 'Tryst with Destiny' speech declared:

> At the stroke of the midnight hour, when the world sleeps, India will awake to life and freedom. A moment comes, which comes but rarely in history, when we step out from the old to the new, when an age ends and when the soul of a nation, long suppressed, finds utterance.... We have to build the noble mansion of free India where all her children may dwell.

In the post Independence era the vision of free India where all the children of the nation happily dwell remains an unattainable goal. Between the dream/vision of building new destinies for the nation and the reality of its broken image fell the shadow of violence? Violence against the marginalized sections of society continues even today. Perhaps freedom in the true sense of the term may be achieved in a Post – Postcolonial world where boundaries are blurred-not only boundaries between nations but boundaries of the mind.

The present paper analyses Dattani's selected plays from a Postcolonial feminist perspective to bring out the manner in which victims of discrimination and violence resist patriarchy, marginality and thereby assert their selfhood. The paper also attempts to study the ways in which Dattani deviates from the western paradigm.

Feminism is not a monolithic discourse. There is not one but many feminisms because experiences of women are region, culture, race, color, education, economy and religion – specific. Postcolonial feminists such as Gayatri Chakraborty Spivak, Chandra Talpade Mohanty, Trinh T. Minh-na are critical of Western Feminists as they have for long ignored the voices of non-white, non-Western women by universalizing the realities of white, western women. Postcolonial feminists see the parallels between recently decolonized nations and the state of women within patriarchy-both take the perspective of a socially marginalized sub-group in their relationship to the dominant culture. Postcolonial Feminism is altering/reshaping the configurations of both postcolonial and feminist studies. To quote Rajeswari Rajan;

> Postcolonial feminism cannot be regarded simply as a subject of postcolonial studies or, alternatively, as another variety of feminism. Rather it is an intervention that is changing the configurations of both postcolonial and feminist studies. Postcolonial feminism is an exploration of and at the intersections of colonialism and neocolonialism with gender, nation, class, race and sexualities and rights. (53)

Mahesh Dattani's plays are set in contemporary India and mostly deal with the middle classes of Indian society. Contemporary Indian middle classes lead a hybrid existence. They are constantly adjusting and readjusting with the claims of east and west (Loomba, 173). Their identities are fluid as the parameters which determine their identities are continually changing. Their experiences are unique to them. Western theoretical frameworks cannot justly explain the Indian realities as the West tends to view matters through their own culturally determined perspectives. Western perspectives differ from the eastern perspectives due to differences of race, culture, location, ethnicity, class and caste. In order to foreground the realities of postcolonial Indian women a new lens must be used. A shift of gaze is essential.

According to Dattani, "Theatre is a reflection of what you observe" (Interview with Anita Nair). Using the medium of theatre, Dattani foregrounds "invisible" issues (interview with Erin B. Mee. "Invisible Issues: An interview with Mahesh Dattani" Cri. Pers. 157) - issues which exist in Indian society but are pushed to the periphery and never made part of mainstream discourse. Dattani brings those closet issues centre stage, makes the audience confront those issues so that once the curtain falls and the audiences move out of the world of the play to the world outside they can act as agents of change.

Family is the smallest unit of society. Through his plays Dattani dissects family life to reveal contemporary social reality. Indian society is gender, biased. It privileges the masculine. Power dynamics within a family are so structured that women face patriarchal oppression, subjugation and control within the framework of the family. Home becomes site of violence (thereby subverting conventional associations of warmth, intimacy, security and protection).

At this juncture it is essential to note that there are various forms of violence- domestic, marital, social, physical, sexual and psychological violence. Patriarchal society uses violence as a tool/ weapon to subjugate women and thereby perpetuates patriarchal domination. To quote the views of Dr Manik Chakraborty;

> From womb to tomb, a woman is under the constant fear of violence. She may be subjected to it at any place ...

> even within the safe confines of her mother's womb. (*Gender Justice*, 94)

The Constitution of India guarantees Right to Equality, Right against Exploitation to all its citizens but merely creating laws cannot prevent violence and ensure justice to the victims. Issues of violence are mostly unreported as women fear social stigma and public disgrace. Women must stand for their rights. Again broadening of social temperament, enlargement of social perceptions is also essential. However, in Dattani's plays, marginalia, in spite of being victims of violence, fight back and thereby assert their identities.

Issues of gender discrimination and violation of rights of women recur in Dattani's plays. In *Tara* Bharati's decision to give Chandan "the third leg" cripples Tara forever. Without consulting her husband Bharati and her father-in-law decided Tara's fate. Mr. Patel reveals this horrifying truth to the children:

> A scan showed that a major part of the blood supply to the third leg was provided by the girl.... The chances were slightly better that the leg would survive... on the girl. Your grandfather and your mother...would risk giving both legs to the boy.... Chandan had two legs for two days...the leg was amputed. A piece of dead flesh which could have-might have-been Tara. (Dattani, CP 378)

Tara faces discrimination even after her death as Chandan makes her tragedy his tragedy:

> Forgive me, Tara. Forgive me, for making it my tragedy (Dattani, CP 380)

Thus her story is violated by her Siamese twin.

In *Seven Steps around the Fire* Dattani brings the margin to the centre and lets the subaltern speak. Using the format of whodunit structure Dattani reveals how society discriminates against the third gender. The play reveals the manner in which the most important right – the right to live is violated. The marriage pyre becomes the funeral pyre of Kamla as she dared to enter into the holy alliance of matrimony with Subbu, a member of mainstream society. The physical and sexual tortures Anarkali faces within the four walls of the prison reveal how years of social conditioning have made us cruel and insensitive towards the plight of marginalized. Hizras the Eunachs are treated as animals both inside and outside the prison. Society refuses to regard hizras as human beings with human needs, desires and rights.

While dealing with the issue of violence faced by the marginalized sections of society Dattani not only focuses on the issue of gender but also focuses on issues of race, social position, class, ethnic origin, religion, identity, history and economy. The nature of violence faced by the hizra community in *Seven Steps around the Fire* is different from the nature of violence faced by Dolly, Daksha, Alka and Baa in *Bravely Fought the Queen* which again differs from the nature of violence Shanta and Mala face in *Thirty Days in September*.

There can be no homogeneous understanding of postcolonialism or feminism. A pluralist approach is essential to penetrate the silences. The polyphonic voices of third world women must be heard. Dattani uses the medium of theatre to do the same. In the *Preface* to his *Collected Plays* Dattani wrote, "I am certain that my plays are a true reflection of my time, place and socio – economic background" (CP, xv). Living at a time where male-female ratios in certain parts of the country are alarming; cases of female foeticide, female infanticide, deaths related to dowry are often reported in the newspaper; crime against women, rape cases are increasing, Dattani's plays are relevant and close to life.

In *Bravely Fought the Queen*, Dattani, as Michael Walling suggests, makes use of the "play" to "play" with the idea of gender and gender related roles (Cri. Pers. 71). In the Trivedi household power runs along the lines of age and gender. Women here are as isolated as the "twin houses" of the Trivedis', situated in the middle of nowhere (Dattani, CP 238). Trapped in unhappy marriages, economically dependent on their insensitive husbands, women have "nowhere" to go. They are forced to abide by the dictates of the men folk (Chaudhuri, 84).

Baa is the power centre of the household. Though bedridden she rules with the "weapon of her wealth" (TPMD 84). Dattani keeps her room centre stage to suggest her centrality in the household. Baa asserts her position and presence as the mother-in -law by constantly ringing the loud, annoying bell. Like the shrill sound of the bell her presence cannot be ignored.

The play opens and we see Dolly dressing up for a party that has already been cancelled by the brothers-Jiten and Nitin Trivedi. Dolly and Alka are unaware of the cancellation of the party thereby pointing the communication gap in their married lives. Alka's request to move out with her husband is turned down by Nitin who reminds her of her socially assigned role as the dutiful daughter-in -law who must give "company" to her "lonely" mother-in-law (Dattani, CP 241). Alka's desire for love, companionship, pleasures of marital life and motherhood remain unfulfilled as Nitin is a homosexual who has married only to pass off as a heterosexual man.

The lives of the two sisters are equally void and hollow. They try to hide the miserable truths of their lives by using fabricated stories. They lead a masked existence constantly hiding reality from the gaze of society. Thus, truths like Nitin's homosexuality, Daksha's abnormality are carefully shoved off beneath the glitter of make-up and glamour of society parties.

In the Trivedi family expectations of women are brutally murdered. For Jiten female body is either an object of desire or of control. Once he crosses the threshold of the Trivedi family he visits prostitutes, at office he plans to use female body to titillate his customers and thereby market his products. At home he subjugates women by using either direct force or patriarchal ideologies.

In *Bravely Fought the Queen* women are victims of violence. Their rights are constantly violated. This has a deep rooted effect on their body, mind and soul. Three generations of Trivedi women- Baa, Dolly, Alka and Daksha are victims of physical and domestic violence. In case of Alka, physical violence was a part of her life even before marriage:

> He [Praful] burnt my hair. I can still smell my hair on fire. (Dattani, CP 257)

> Marriage to her brother's homosexual partner increased her agony. Jiten physically tortured pregnant Dolly which leads to Daksha's premature birth and abnormality. The incident scarred her forever. Daksha was subjected to violence even before she was born. This ruined Daksha's life. Her mental and physical growth got stunted. Memories of marital abuse haunt Baa as well. In her delirium, she relieves the physical violence faced years ago. To quote Miruna George, "The play explores the psychological damage caused to the women in the Trivedi household by the privileged men who signify patriarchy." (Cri. Pers 149)

When pressures of reality become unbearable both Dolly and Alka temporarily escape from the clutches of reality. Alka drinks excessively to forget all pains while Dolly fantasies about Kanhaiya, her ideal lover and emotional anchor. Narrating her encounter with Kanhaiya Dolly says,

> The thumri plays. And it ends. Another one plays. I forget when that ends and a new one begins! All I'm aware of are two powerful black arms around me and the beautiful sound of the heartbeat of a warm, gentle soul. The voice of Naina Devi comes back. It is the most beautiful song I've ever heard in my life! (Dattani, CP 262)

Her entire being participates in the spirit of the love song. Sexuality has been a taboo word for the women especially in the Indian context. But, Dattani understands and represents the physical and emotional needs of a woman. Again, during Alka's rain dance Dattani presents a sensual picture of Alka dancing in the rain, brandishing her imaginary sword. It symbolizes her rebellion against stereotyped notions of patriarchy. Dolly and Alka identify themselves with Lakshmi Bai and Naina Devi- women who transgressed stereotyped notions of women, gender and gender roles.

Dolly and Alka subvert gender roles. Like the historical queen who fought India's first battle for Independence, they tear open the masks to reveal the reality of their lives. Alka exposes Nitin's sexual orientation thereby revealing the hollowness of their marriage. Dolly publicly exposes Jiten by revealing the truth regarding Daksha's birth:

> Daksha was born-two months premature. With the cord around her neck! (Dattani, CP 312)

Sexual politics that is prevalent in society prevents the development of a woman as a woman. In the Trivedi family, women are financially dependent on their husbands. Their identity is with respect to their respective husbands. They have nowhere to go. This makes them vulnerable to torture. They do not legally terminate their marriages but fight back within the framework of their marriages. This, in a sense, may be called their emancipation. Having achieved emancipation of the mind they can resist marginality, fight back domination, subvert gender roles, voice their long suppressed opinions, expose falsehood and challenge the tyrannical rule of patriarchy. Their situations, the complexities and paradoxes of their lives are typical of India. Dattani foregrounds their realities and personal battles.

The play *Thirty Days in September* deals with the serious issue of child abuse and its deep rooted psychological impact on the life of the innocent victim. In fact sexual violence has a long term effect on the character, perceptions and psyche of the child abused. In her note on the play, Lillete Dubey describes *Thirty Days in September* as a "sensitive" and "powerful" play which "manages to bring home the horror and the pain[of abuse] within the framework of a very identifiable mother-daughter relationship" (CPII, 4).

The play traces Mala's psychological journey of self-discovery as she comes out of her abusive, guilt ridden and shameful past. In her first meeting with the counselor she blames herself for her abusive past. Her affairs last only for thirty days:

> It has to end in a month's time. In fact I like it best when I can time it so that it lasts for thirty days. I even mark it on my calendar. After that, I have to- move on...it is no longer satisfying to me and I don't mean the physical part of it, although that is usually the main attraction for me... not that I actually enjoy it when they are doing it to me... I think I like it... when they sort-of-you know-use me... The only person who can, who could have prevented all this is my mother (Dattani, CPII 18).

Mala does not emotionally participate in these casual affairs. She does not enjoy the physical aspect either. She keeps the memories of her past alive through these acts of sexual intercourse with older men. Again she feels betrayed by her mother. Shanta silently witnessed her daughter's suffering and thereby added to Mala's psychological turmoil.

It is ironical that Shanta uses prayers to Sri Krishna as an excuse to avoid facing the horrors of reality. She wants Mala to forget her past and marry Deepak who is in love with her. She dismisses her past as "bad dreams" (Dattani, CPII 25). Child abuse cannot be dismissed as nightmares. It is the most horrifying reality. In order to compel Shanta to face reality Mala throws away the portrait of Sri Krishna. As the glass covering the portrait breaks,

Shanta breaks her silence and blames Mala for tempting her uncle and cousins. Shanta thinks marriage is the only way she can mend her nature. She seems to believe in the conventional mindset that marriage is the cure for wayward sexual behavior. Old fears resurface and overwhelm Mala as her uncle comes to stay with them. Using split – stage technique Dattani reveals the drama happening within Mala's psychological space.

Mala revisits the abuse she faced as a child and hears the voice of the man ordering her to touch him. She relives her seventh birthday (the day Vinay molested her and claimed it to be a birthday gift). He had ordered her to sing nursery rhymes until he finished molesting her. During the process of molestation Vinay had said, "Nobody will tell you how ugly you are. But, you are good only for this...only for this" (Dattani, CPII 44). Mala covers her head in shame as she remembers the words of her uncle:

> You like it! You enjoy it! After four years you have become a whore! (Dattani, CPII 44).

Thus uncle Vinay had legitimized his crime by blaming Mala for the abuse she faced. He also suggested that conventional standards of morality do not apply for her. Mala starts believing that she is good only for abuse. This gives rise to her sexually promiscuous nature.

In the final confrontation between the mother and the daughter Mala blames Shanta for ruining her life with her silence. She also reject Deepak's proposal to marry her as feelings of love has no significance in her life. Mala's accusations trigger Shanta's emotional outburst. She reveals how she too was subjected to sexual abuse by Vinay. Years of sexual abuse has made her submissive. Overwhelmed with guilt, humiliation and self-hatred she has lost the voice to protest against injustice:

> But my tongue is cut off...I cannot shout for help...Uh,eh,oo aa aa,aaaaaaaaaaa...Aaaaa, ooo, eee, oooo, aaeeeeeeee, aaaaaaaaaaaaaaaaeeeeeeeee!

Hence, she failed to save her daughter from abuse. Shanta punishes herself by jabbing a sharp piece of glass in her mouth. She begs forgiveness from Mala who holds her protectively.

> Mala declares February29th as her "Freedom Day". (Dattani, CPII 57) During the process of molestation Vinay had asked her to recite "Thirty Days has September, April, June and November. February has twenty-eight. All the rest have thirty-one!" (Dattani, CPII 57). Hence Mala declares February 29th-the only date free from memory of abuse as her "Freedom Day". She begins to enjoy the pleasures of life:

I can smile again. I can be a little girl again. Not again, but for the first time.... And for the first time I enjoyed sex.... And for once I could look at Deepak in the eyes and say 'I love you' to him and believe it when he says the same to me (Dattani, CPII 34).

Free from the trauma of abuse Mala is confident of herself and her identity. She has won her personal battle. She has achieved emancipation from her guilt ridden past.

Thus, in Mahesh Dattani's plays women though victimized fight back violence, oppression, discrimination and marginality. They do not uproot themselves from their socio-cultural background but assert themselves within the ambit of their lives. Dattani defines the concept of freedom for Indian omen in the Indian socio-cultural value system. Dattani thus deviates from the Western paradigm to represent Indian women not through western eyes but through eastern, Indian eyes.

Bibliography

Agarwal, Beena. *Mahesh Dattani's Plays: A New Horizon in Indian Theatre*, Jaipur: Book Enclave, 2008.

Chakrabarti, Nirmal Kanti and Shachi Chakraborty, eds. *Gender Justice*, Kolkata: R. Cambray and Co. Pvt Ltd, 2006.

Chaudhuri, Asha Kuthari. *Mahesh Dattani: An Introduction,* New Delhi: Foundation, 2005.

Dattani, Mahesh. *Collected Plays,* New Delhi: Penguin Publishers, 2000.This book is mentioned in the text as CP.

- -. *Collected Plays,* Vol.2, New Delhi: Penguin Publishers, 2005. This book is mentioned in the text as CPII.

Dattani, Mahesh. Preface, *Collected Plays,* by Dattani, New Delhi: Penguin Publishers, 2000, xi-xv.

Dattani, Mahesh. "Mahesh Dattani_The Invisible Observer_ A profile by Anita Nair", 17 Mar. 2012 http://www.anitanair.net/profiles/profile_.mahesh_dattani.htm.

Dhawan, R.K. and Tanu Pant, eds. *The Plays of Mahesh Dattani: A Critical Response,* New Delhi: Prestige, 2005. This book is mentioned in the text as TPMD.

Dubey, Lillete. "A Note on the Play" *Thirty Days in September. Collected Plays.* Vol.2. New Delhi: Penguin book, 2005.

Loomba, Ania. *Colonialism/ Postcolonialism.* London: Routledge, 1998.

Mohanty, Chandra Talpade. "Under Western Eyes: Feminist Scholarship and Colonial Discourses", *Feminist Review 30, Autumn, 1988.*

Multani, Angelie, ed. *Mahesh Dattani's Plays: Critical Perspectives,* New Delhi: Pencraft International, 2007. This book is mentioned in the text as Cri.Pers.

Nehru, Jawaherlal "Tryst with Destiny". India, 14 Aug. 1947. Speech, http://en.wikipedia.org/wiki/Tryst_with_destiny.

Sunder Rajan, Rajeswari. *Real and Imagined Women: Gender, Culture and Post-colonialism,* London: Roultedge, 1993.

17

Race, Gender and Disability: Problematising Physical and Mental Disability in Mahesh Dattani's *Tara* and *Bravely Fought the Queen*

Swati Roy Chowdhury

Disability, both physical and psychological, in the Indian context is a much neglected issue and when the question is about negotiating the problems faced by such challenged Indian female the attention paid is even less. Anita Ghai's comments best sums up this attitude:

> "If disability affects them (boys and girls) in almost identical fashions, but then it's a patriarchal society. The birth of sons is always celebrated; the birth of a girl is never celebrated. And the birth of a disabled girl – they say, 'a girl', and on top it off disabled!"[1]

Curiously enough, though the Disability Rights Movement has been most often viewed as a trajectory of feminist movements in India, even the feminist practitioners in India overlook such a delicate issue as if it is of little consequence. Still less is the participation of the academicians or the artists against discrimination faced by this unfortunate margin of the Indian society.

In spite of the lack of attention paid to females with disabilities in academics and literature there are certain instances where they indeed occupy some space – Mahesh Dattani's *Tara* and *Bravely Fought the Queen* being two such examples where the playwright tacitly draws attention to the agonies of two girls namely Tara and Daksha in *Tara* and *Bravely Fought the Queen* respectively who are ill-fated enough to be born as females in a patriarchal society, their despondency being increased manifold because they are born with certain deformities beyond their control. However, differences between the two characters in question can be easily located since Tara being the central character manages to grab much limelight while Daksha with her unseen presence is a more poignant example of exclusion of disabled girl child from the society. Moreover while Tara's impairment is physical Daksha presents a more complicated case of mental retardation. The purpose of this paper is not to focus solely on the private sufferings of the two characters already mentioned but to see them as a collective trope in investigating and asserting the position of underprivileged physically and mentally challenged female population in India and therefore the two characters offer a more expansive view of the inequality that is inherent in Indian social structures.

Indian societies in general are essentially and traditionally patriarchal and, thus, like any other male dominated society the conventions of patriarchy are viewed here as natural and normal. Ironically, therefore, even the women are taught to believe in male supremacy as God's law. This has a serious connection with the destiny of many of the sufferers born with physical or psychological disabilities especially the female ones. Sources say that a majority of mothers of children born with any variation of disability suffer one kind of violence or other during their pregnancy. Apart from that other forms of violence against children can also lead to a disability and the violence increases manifold if the child is of feminine gender. Such sources also assert that many of the causes of disability are preventable by providing expecting mothers with better prenatal and post natal care. But in a country like India where traditionally the role of a wife is chiefly as an instrument in giving birth to only boy children[2] such basic pathological and psychological needs are more often than not ignored. Daksha, the spastic daughter of Dolly and Jiten in Dattani's *Bravely Fought the Queen*, in spite of being a fictitious character in a popular contemporary drama, exposes to us the horrible truth of chauvinistic exploitation of women even when the latter pass through most vulnerable health conditions. Her spasticity is not because of any eugenic defect but is an accidental machination of an angry husband, Jiten, who ends in beating up his wife Dolly in her mature days of pregnancy. Dolly recalls the entire event with heart-rending pathos and resentment:

> "They were your [Jiten's] hands hitting me! Your feet kicking me! It's in your blood!" [3]

What is worth observation in Dolly's angry accusation is the trend of exploitation that has been perpetuating in Indian households through ages. Dolly's reference to Jiten's 'bad blood' directly connects him to his equally torturous father that Baa, Jiten's mother, confirms elsewhere in the play. However, one feels that perhaps Jiten surpasses his cruel father in this respect because the man in question at least spared his children with healthy lives which poor Daksha is denied because she is born premature with severe bodily and psychological abnormalities beyond the scope of being completely cured.

If Daksha is a prey to chauvinist maltreatment Tara, in Dattani's other famous eponymous play is a victim of choice that is guided by patriarchal conventions. In a rare eugenic condition Tara and her brother Chandan are born as conjoined twins such that only one may have the privilege of having a normal life. The two children being of opposite sex, the chief factor that operates in the parental choice is that of the biological identity of the child. Erin Mee writes in the note of the play:

> "*Tara* centres on the emotional separation that grows between two conjoined twins following the discovery that their physical

> separation was manipulated by their mother and grandfather to favour the boy (Chandan) over the girl (Tara)."[4]

In spite of her slightly more biologically favoured chances of survival and in spite of being smarter than her brother, Tara is denied better chances, physically–the second leg.

As has been already indicated patriarchy penetrates deep into the roots of Indian cultural and social ethos as normal and desirable. Consequently even the female population learn to believe in the efficacy of patriarchy as social and cultural determinant and that is reflected in their actions and behaviours. Research reports indicate that many of the cases of violence inflicted upon women are either contrived by women or directly machinated by them. Thus there is Baa in *Bravely Fought the Queen* who unwillingly acts as a major stimulation behind Daksha's impairment and there is Mrs. Bharati Patel, Tara's mother, who is least hesitant to gift life to her son depriving her own daughter Tara of normal sustenance. The point that is salient here is that the bias that Daksha and Tara face from their family members including other women in the family is the consequence of the latter's being unable to break the barriers of their collective unconscious that has been long nurtured in a patriarchal set up. Baa, thus, justifies the battering of pregnant Dolly in the hands of her drunken son Jiten on account of the illegitimacy of the daughter- in- law's birth and Bharati cannot even dare to think of a healthy daughter at the expense of a crippled boy. The reality that the discrimination against Tara is carried out by the victim's own mother whose preference is the male child or Daksha meets her undue sufferings to certain extent because of her own grandmother make the plays more potent documents against gender discriminations compounded by disabilities suggesting that it is women who play equally important roles in perpetuating the chain of injustice.

Apart from the roles played by families in pushing disabled females to the verge of waste, economic and cultural factors have also been responsible for the antipathy against and inferiorization of the girl child and the fates of girl children born with deformities are even more pathetic. In fact it is more relevant to consider these factors not as discrete but as definitely interlinked with each other such that both Economics and Culture play prominent functions in determining the family's attitude towards a malformed girl child. As in most other aspects of our society, the economic factor lies at the core of discrimination against the girl child and especially physically and mentally challenged girl child. Viewed as economic burden to families, Indian girls are often relegated to a life of limitation. The necessity to find apposite life partners for daughters in a system where arranged marriage is the tradition, as also the requirement to raise dowry, adds to the so called "burden" on parents even amongst the urban middle-class. Naturally, a boy is viewed as an asset by the parents who can stay with them and provide them with better dividends in future while the girls would be away with their in-laws. Boys are future earners and girls merely depend on them all through their lives. In the words of Manu, the powerful Indian sage:

> "In childhood must a female be dependent on her father, in youth on her husband; her lord being dead, on her sons: a woman must never seek independence".[5]

Unsurprisingly, therefore, when the choice is between a boy and a girl, the former stands a good chance of being the chosen one even if other factors point out that the girl should be preferred. Hence Chandan's preference over Tara (who is not only a girl but to complicate the matter still a girl born with physical deformities) is justified in this economic framework grossly drafted by patriarchal customs. The worldly-wise grandfather of Tara and Chandan conforms to this tradition of discrimination by refusing Tara a single paisa of his immense wealth and making Chandan, his grandson, his heir to an enormous amount of money though both of them legally have equal claims over his property. Even Tara's father Mr. Patel is keener on taking his son to the office to prepare Chandan for his future and unenthusiastic about Tara's economic empowerment though Chandan admits that she is the better among the two as far as competence in conducting business is concerned. Tara realizes this and accepts her rejection with an aggravated disinclination by refusing another step towards her empowerment i.e. by being admitted to the college:

> "There's no point in my going to college if I have to drop halfway through or stay away for days not knowing when ...No!"[6]

Tara's physical deformity coupled with her gender makes her existence pathetic but one does not find her silently weeping for her misery; instead she vents her disgust by refusing opportunities that come to her:

> Tara: "Oh, what a waste! A waste of money. Why spend all the money to keep me alive? It cannot matter whether I live or die".[7]

However, not all are as talented and eloquent as Tara. In Daksha, for instance, one discovers a muted subaltern. One never comes to hear a word from her but forms an opinion about her depending only on others' reflections. Her spasticity is a disgrace to the family and that must be carefully concealed. The Trivedi family does exactly that by sending her to a distant school and thus the audience in the play is denied from Daksha's own version of her sufferings.

The question that may arise now is whether it is justified to include Daksha in the same category as Tara especially when the latter is disowned from property while the former is left with an ancestral house of valuation one and a half crore rupees by her grandmother? The answer is intriguingly affirmative and it requires a deeper probe into the complexities of human psyche. Firstly, Baa decides to hand over her ancestral house to Daksha because in her two sons she discovers shadows of defiance- Jiten, her elder son resembles his father and hence by association is not the mother's chosen one; Nitin, in spite of being her favourite, defies her in not throwing out his wife even if the latter challenges her matriarchy. Thus, excluding her sons as her prospective heirs leaves her with only one alternative- Daksha- because apart from Jiten and Nitin she is the only surviving member in Baa's bloodline. More importantly in doing so Baa takes a compensatory stance by trying to make up for all the harm done to Daksha by her by ensuring financial security for the disabled child, just as Bharati Patel does by mollycoddling Tara for all the injustice she has inflicted on her daughter, by trying to empower her with a career and by her willingness to donate kidney to Tara so that the daughter lives a few years more. In spite of all these, one realizes that they are only poor reparations for much greater losses. Baa, therefore, measures Daksha's distress in economic terms and tries for a barter reinforcing the notion that a spastic girl child in an Indian family is a subhuman entity whose emotions, feelings, aspirations and even life can be commodified.

Surveys indicate that such discrimination based on gender and disability factors are more likely to occur in rural and poor settings. Lack of availability of education, lesser access to scientific techniques and poverty that are part and parcel of rural lives in India are often held responsible for gender bias in India; but in the two given instances, we find that both the victims belong to upper or upper middle class urban family with fairly ample access to education. What then, may be the possible reason behind Tara and Daksha's unfortunate lives? The answer lies in Indian societies' cultural rootedness in patriarchy which pushes women with abnormalities to the margin of the society as 'nobody'. This is significant because in the Indian scenario where women are comfortably considered as 'Others' women with deformities are equally conveniently rejected as non existent. While access to education considerably changes such perspective, the rudimentary belief in supremacy of the male governs much of such prejudiced stances even among the urban elites. Baa, Prafull and Jiten may shed tears for the unfortunate Daksha; Mr. Patel, his wife and her father may spend lots of money and shower loads of affection on Tara to give her a comfortable life but those at their best are affordable reimbursements for humanity denied.

If the family is the microcosm then the society we live in may be safely regarded as the macrocosm. The callousness displayed towards disabled women/girls in the family is, therefore, magnified at the level of the society. Subjects to inhuman jittering and – though it may sound like an oxymoron– inhuman sympathy the already ailing individuals gradually recoil into an alien domain. Daksha is thus strategically moved to a special school away from her family in a distant place the name of which even her mother refuses to remember. The family rarely mentions her in their efforts to ward off their own prick of conscience. Tara, on the other hand, shows antipathy to the so called normal girls in her surroundings since they ogle at her amputated limb as some sign of an alien. She rarely makes friends with her peers at school or in her neighbourhood in spite of her mother's frantic effort to bring her back to the mainstream society:

> Bharati: She... she must make more friends... She can be very good company". [8]

Hence her question to young Roopa "You will be her friend?" comes with the promise of adequate reward:

> Bharati: "If you promise to be her best friend- what I mean is if you would like to be her friend- I will be most grateful to you and I will show it...in whatever way you want me to". [9]

But Roopa's declaration to her best friends betrays the real nature of society's disapproval of a physically or mentally challenged girl:

> Roopa: "...Oh, my God! Guess what? I went to her house! Yes. Right inside! ...She is a real freak of nature...Oh God! I'll never go there again".[10]

All these factors combine to create a social system in which the girl child has to live and die. Tara is killed by social system- just as Daksha is forced to live the life of an alien- which controls the minds and actions of the people. And what is the reason of their sadly similar predicament? The answer to this pathetic question is obvious in India. Tara is not wanted and nor is Daksha. Girls are not wanted and restriction to their entries in the society becomes even more vehement if they are deformed in some way or other.

References:

1. Excerpts from an interview with Dr. Anita Ghai, one of India's advocates for rights of the disabled women by Laura Hershley in the *Disability World.* Quoted in "Disability in India Issues and Concerns", Leni Chaudhuri, 19 March, 2012, <http://www.apangutkarsh.com/pdf/disabilityinindia.pdf.>.
2. The presence of a woman in a man's social life is necessary solely for procreation, that too to give birth to male offspring only – *putrarthe kriyate varya* (wife to beget male children).
3. Mahesh Dattani, *Bravely Fought the Queen* in *Collected Plays,* (New Delhi: Penguin, 2000), p.312.
4. Erin Mee, A Note in the Play, *Collected Plays*, Mahesh Dattani, (New Delhi: Penguin, 2000), p.319.
5. Manu; *Institutes of Hindu law: or, The Ordinances of Menu (sic), according to the gloss of Culluca: comprising the Indian system of duties, religious and civil.* Chapter. V, 147. Trans Sir William Jones, (London: W.H Allen & Co. 1869), p.113, *Google Books.* 20. March.2010.
6. Mahesh Dattani, *Tara* in *Collected Plays,* (New Delhi: Penguin, 2000), pp.360-361.
7. Ibid. p.370.

8. Ibid. p.340.
9. Ibid. p.341.
10. Ibid. p.343.

Bibliography

Chaudhuri, Leni. "Disability in India Issues and Concerns". 19 March, 2012. <http://www.apangutkarsh.com/pdf/disabilityinindia.pdf>

Dattani, Mahesh. *Collected Plays,* New Delhi: Penguin, 2000.

Dhawan, R.K and Pant, Tanu, Eds. *The Plays of Mahesh Dattani: A Critical Response,* New Delhi: Prestige Books, 2005.

Manu. *Institutes of Hindu law: or, The Ordinances of Menu (sic), according to the gloss of Culluca: comprising the Indian system of duties, religious and civil.* Trans Sir William Jones, London: W.H. Allen & Co., 1869, *Google Books,* 20 March, 2010.

18

Picturing India From Colonial Past to Postcolonial Paradigms: A Critical Analysis of Selected Plays of Indian Women Dramatists

Bolla Jyothsnaphanija

Women dramatists in India have architected their presence in the cannon with their creative literary devices of magic realism, innovative characters in rewriting myths, and language of fire in the colonial context, and postcolonial praxsis. Issues of women's problems in Mahesh Dattani's writing, translating silence of oppressed women in Vijay Tendulkar's dramas, reconstructing Indian myths in Girish Karnad's plays are revisited in Indian women's dramas. Their traverse from colonial home studio scape towards modern theater is arduous endeavor. This paper highlights the colonial ideologies in the plays of pre Indian independence, and perceptible shift towards postcolonial themes in contemporary women's plays. This paper purports new challenges to theater culture over mail gaze. Identifying gender in terms of visual representation is one aspect of this paper. How women playwrights dissolve the cultural, linguistic, religious, social differences in writing their plays? How the new playwrights define gender? would be underscored in this paper.

In the colonial India women have taken themes of widow re marriage, Sati, and colonial impact on the country. Women at that time, mostly confined to domestic space, moreover folklore was considered as women's artistic expression. Drama was considered as public space, male gaze oriented, women limited their innovative skills in writing plays. At this tough time, Swarnakumari Devi's voice was assertive, and creative. She was widely reputed as the eldest sister of Rabindranath Tagore. In her play *The Wedding Tangle* (1904) concerns about mistress/ servant relation, widow re marriage, dowry system, killing women's identity. Soshi the young widow, as wellas the faithful servant is projected as silent revolutionary in this play. The mistress's character is typical of Indian woman who is helpless, trivialized by her family members, who is highly dependent on the others. In writing colonial India, Swarnakumari Devi shifts her focus constantly in metaphorising domestic space for colonized country. In her play *Princess Kalyani*, she presents clear picture of ancient beliefs in religion, and womanhood. It is the story of conquering evil the by virtue. In a Historiographic metafictionistic sense, Devagiri's princess's role was entangled. S. Janaki also skillfully employs this literary device in writing the history of Rajputs being defeated in the war with Mughals in her play *The Siege of Chitor*. In emphasizing the compassion of Akbar the mughal ruler, her portraiture is controversial, her language is mysterious.

Few women had the privilege of accessing colonizer's language to use extensively for exhibiting their resistance over our traditions. Rasheed Jahan's *Woman* (1937) is one such play, where patriarchy is challenged with the protagonist Fatima who is courageous, revolutionary. As a childless woman she suffers constant threat of her husband getting remarried. This play marks burgeoning modernity in colonial India, Westernized medicine for Indian patients, dowry system disprivillaging women. Both the plays are not composed to give proper stage directions. Both the plays having home as setting, portray the plight of colonized women in realistic tendency.

Bharati Sarabhai presented Indian religious beliefs in new perspective. Her two plays, *The Well of the People* and *Two Women,* written in poetic prose, preached philosophy on religion, interlinking Gandhiji's views on casteism, and national movement. Both the plays present courageous women rare to that period. In her play *Two Women*, Sarabai's language is lyrical but powerful. Anuradha in that play says, "Sometimes I feel like one of our fields, starved of rain and water from the well, driven by the ploughs of society and the family. I am a field that everyone has fed from and that no one has bothered about, to see that it is rested, renewed, kept green for their future crops. I have become dry. I am now barren." (22) These words reflect the long rooted emptiness in one's life who is reduced to nothing by the family, society, culture and religion. Mrinalini Sarabhai's voice was the most powerful in critiquing policemen in the freedom struggle. In her play *Captive Soil* the intensity of freedom struggle was accounted.

In men's narratives, women's voices were hushed persistently. Few women playwrights have retold the ancient myths from women's perspective. Indira Devi's co-authored *The Beggar Princess* tells the story of Meera who devoted her life for the love of lord Krishna. In rewriting the ancient stories, the women playwrights have used the language of their own where sensuous representation of women's body, for instance in Kalidasa's works, was replaced. K. B. Thakur's play *Mother and Child* tells the pain of mother Kunti who was unable to connect with her son Karna. The play beautifully portrays the relation of mother and son. The helplessness of a mother who has to uphold societal conventions was portrayed in this play. Shanta Rama Rao's play *A Passage to India* critiques colonization. As a dramatized version of E. M. Foster's novel bearing the same title, she employs new technique of dramatizing the novel form. It is more over, a native version of that novel. In representing colonial India, few women playwrights have even come out of the domestic setting, feminine sensitive language, and natural setting. They have historicized the real events, recorded injustice done to the country and the women, re-written age old myths which were set in submissing women's identity. Their language became powerful, themes were based on political upheaval, and celebrated the tragedy of the art.

In the postcolonial India, women playwrights retell the history in the fictionistic sense. J.M. Billimoria's *My Sons* (1963) retells Indo Pakistan war in Historiographic metafictionistic sense. She proposes the idea that, even in the postcolonial India, the citizens of India have no freedom. War and different sorts of violence are killing their identities, lifes. The play focuses on five students of Bombay University who share unbreakable bondage inspite of their religious, cultural, linguistic differences. Dina Mehta's *Tiger Tiger* (1978) is a significant play in telling the story of Tipu Sultan. Uma Parameswaran also used historical aspects for her plays. In most of her plays, she recounts sufferings of women in India's partition. Her play *Sons Must Die* focalizes tragic experiences of three mothers who lost their sons in the war at Kashmir. The women playwrights in the postcolonial India besides musing over the present globalized country also contemplated on its previous historical roots.

Though women's position is raised in the postcolonial context, still number of problems suppress their identity. Few women playwrights have dealt with extreme sensitive situations. Dina Mehta's *Getting Away with Murder* focuses on child sexual abuse, which has became a serious threat in the present situation. In this play, Mehta clarifies that even educated women also do not enjoy independence. Sonali the educated woman wants to abort her child, if it is a girl. Mehta purports gender based violence which starts before actually the girl child is born. Her another play *Brides Are Not for Burning* replicates domestic violence against women. Laxmi the bright student has to drop out her studies to take care of her younger brother and sister. After marriage, she has to experience harsh treatment from her in-laws. As a childless woman she has to face humiliations from her in-laws. Tormented by her mother-in-law's words she locks herself in kitchen, and burns herself with Kerosene till death. Tara the neighbour who witnesses this injustice, remains silent after being physically abused by her husband. Through this play, Mehta indicates brides are not for burning, they have to have the life of their own. Mehta portrays silent sufferings of women. In her play *The Myth-Makers,* Mehta introduces lonely actress Pramila who is dependent on her unfaithful lover. In most of the women's plays, new version of what was unheard previously was composed. Shri Devi Singh's *Purple-Braided People* (1970) as the title indicates, very delicate composition and poetic in nature. With her extremely sensitive language, Singh pictures the events. P. Sengupta is the other playwright who sensitizes her audience about violence towards women. Her play *Mangalam* presents strong themes pervading unbearable violence at women's home spaces. Manjula padmanabhan's *Lights Out* is also heart rendering story which describes rape traumatisation of a woman. She points at the irresponsibility of the neighbors, on lookers who hesitate to help the woman. The title is symbolic of conveying how the people live in darkness without visioning injustice. The language is more powerful, and the plot is moving. Taking the plot from a realistic incident where a woman was subjected to gang rape in Mumbai, she points at crime and sexual violence against women in the metropolitan cities.

Even in the Independent India, poverty remains the same. Still, poverty and hunger are threatening many lives in this country. Manjula Padmanabhan takes this situation and portrays in her play *Harvest.* It is the story of Om Prakash who mortgages his body for scientific experimentation. He does this for getting money as his family lives in utter poverty. Population explosion is a threatening problem in postcolonial India, which she portrays in this play. Mahasweta Devi portrays life of the subalterns in her plays. She voices the experiences of the marginalized. In her play *Mother of 1084*, Sujata Chatterjee was portrayed as upper middle class woman who learns life when her son is killed by the police for his involvement in the Naxalite movement. She learns that she didn't know her son's revolutionary ideas before. She finds her husband's hypocrisy after her son's death. This play shows how still freedom movements emerge against exploitation in the Independent India. Another contrasting character to Sujata is Nandini who was also from Naxalite movement which was raising in West Bengal in 1960s. Dibyanath Chatterjee Sujata's husband is typical of male chauvinism who never lets his wife to choose the life of her own. He curtails her financial independence with ironhand. But Sujata with her aggressive character tries to be independent. Sujata was transformed as self reliant, politically conscious individual at the end of this play. Mahasweta Devi portrays typical lives of Adivasis in this play. Prostitution, sexual violence towards women, ill treated wives, unwanted daughters, uncared widows, poverty and dissolution towards Adivasis still give the feeling that India is under colonization even at the present. Political upheaval, corruption, injustice were portrayed without any camouflage in this play. This play is perhaps the most powerful narration in relocating women's political consciousness. Mahasweta Devi says, "I felt increasingly that a writer should document his own time and history. The socio-economic history of human development has always fascinated me". In writing about the socially exploited, she never compromises on her plot or language though it may arise controversy. Her play *Aajir* voices the consequences of oppression and slavery. Aajir in Bengali means one who sold himself for money. This play is the story of Paatan whose life is oppressed in slavery. Her portrayal of low caste people in this play is generous. Cultural alienation, family bondage, life of emigrants frame the backdrop of Uma Parameswaran's play *Rootless but Green are the Boulevard Trees* where she emphasizes on Indian cultural roots.

In the postcolonial context also, women playwrights have tried to unveil the good-girl image uphold by myths. In rewriting the Indian myths, these women playwrights have emphasized on psycho analytic perspective of the mythologized characters. In her play *Gandharee and Kaikeyee* Kamala Subramanian imparts significance to the silent struggle of two important figures Gandharee and Kaikeyee of two important ages. Both the women were projected as antagonists in the mail narratives. Subramanian shows that, both the women were influenced by external factors which decided their course of action. Both the women have extreme affection for their sons to ascend the thrown, in troubling the other women Draupadi and Sita. This play is ground breaking in speaking the silence of the antagonists of two Indian classics *Ramayana* and *Maha Bharatha.* Uma Parameswaran also retold major myths of Indian tradition in her plays *Meera* and *Sita's Promise.* In both the plays the playwright employed her own version of story. Meera delineates how she was given three roles of Devaki, Yasoda, and Radha by lord Krishna. *Sita's Promise* introduces the characters of Rama, Sita, and Lakshmana but entirely in the modern imaginative space.

It is rightly pointed out, "The notion of 'femininity' is a fiction created by men, assented to by women, untrained in the rigours of logical thought or conscious of the advantages to be gained by compliance with masculine fantasies". Women writers have travelled out of the fiction, and established their own theater space. From the pre independent period, towards postcolonial context, women playwrights have contributed copiously to the Indian theater. But their significance was not identified. In unveiling social prejudices, in comprehending Indian heroic history, in challenging cultural stances and myths Indian playwrights have attained great success. Their presence in modern Indian theater points at stereotypical male gaze which privileges male authorship of the plays. In the pre independent period their concern was political, historical, and domestic. But in the modern women's theater, those interests are altered with Historiographic metafiction, magic realism, and political allegories. This shift is remarkable in the modern Indian theater which necessiates new challenges, new theories, and new modes of interpretations to the genre itself.

Bibliography

Devi, Mahasweta. *Anthology of Five Plays,* Calcutta: Seagull Books Pvt Ltd, 1997.

Thakur, K. B. *Mother and Child,* Bhavan's Journal, 1960.

Mukherjee, Tutun. *Staging Resistance: Plays by Women in Translation,* New Delhi: Oxford University Press, 2005.

Janaki, S. *The Siege of Chitor,* Bhavan's Journal, 1960.

19

Cruelty Violence Greed and Gender Discrimination:

Reflection of Contemporary Socirty in Mahasweta Devi's *Mother of 1084*

Asit Kanti Sarkar

Contemporary Indian English drama and Indian drama in English translation have been quite successful in manifesting the picture of present India, its multi layered and multi diversified society with boons and maladies ,virtues and vices. These dramas, often under the cloak/reinterpretation of history, legend, myth and folktales, criticise the modern Indian society, its prevailing social norms, approach towards women, hierarchal position of males, sham hypocrisy, greed, cruelty, violence and so on. Girish Karnad, Vijay Tendulkar, Badal Sicar, Mahesh Dattani, Mohan Rakesh, Indira Parthasarathy and of course Mahasweta Devi are some of the noteworthy dramatists to express profound socio-political concerns and other issues human life.

According to Basham "The origin of the Indian theatre is still obscure."(434) But it is certain that India has a long history of dramatic art, and it dates back to Christian era. Indian playwrights have always depended on the vast history, legends and contemporary society of their country for their plot construction. In fact, Indian culture, history and legends are so old and rich and on the other hand Indian society is so varied and unique that it has been an sure/easy choice for the playwrights old or new.

Mahasweta Devi is one of the contemporary playwrights who have based their plays on the modern as well as age-old maladies existing in our society. She tries to reveal heart rendering condition of the down trodden, especially marginalised women, and questions the existing ideals of the "so-called tidy life" *(Deshpande 706).*

Devi was born in the year 1926 in Bengal. Since the young age she began to show keen interest in literature. Her first novel *Nati* was brought out in 1957. Gradually she raised herself to the level of an inspirational activist writer voicing the causes of the marginalised or deprived. Devi has been actively associated with many grass root level social movements and problems. She has remained as a prima facie in the movements around the plight of the farmer and labour class, feudalism in rural politics, indifference of states to the marginalized people which includes communities like untouchables and tribals. Her voice remains never silent at the injustice and inequality of our society. Being a dynamic social activist she has expressed her views on the Naxalite movement, made protest against women domination and even has actively taken part in recent Singur, Nandigram controversy.

Mahasweta Devi has been awarded with many prestigious awards in recognition of her social awareness and literary output. She has been honoured with Padma Vibhushan, Magsaysay and Padmasree awards for her work amongst dispossessed and dominated tribal communities. Besides these, she is the recipient of India's highest literary award Gnanpith Award (1996) and Yashwant Rao Chavan National Award for 2010 for her contribution to national integration, democratic values and the socio-economic development of India. Recognising her work and social activism, the Human Resource Development Ministry has appointed her as National Research Professor for a second term of five years from February, 2011.

Mahasweta Devi does not belong to the writers who believe in the sentence "Art for Art's sake". She writes: "It is my conviction that a story writer should be motivated by a sense of history that would help her readers to understand their ow times.I have never had the capacity nor the urge to create art for art's sake" (Bandyopadhyay XII). She believes in certain purposes of writing and never thinks of her art devoid of purposes, devoid of life. To her literature is "the best medium of protest against injustice and exploitation" (XII). In fact, the main motto of all her writing is "to enable the mass to get rid of their complacency, and gather power to protest against all kinds of oppression" (Chakraborty 9).

The term Naxalites comes from Naxalbari, a small village in West Bengal, where a section of the Communist Party of India (Marxist) led by leaders like Charu Majumdar, Kanu Sanyal and Jangal Santhal initiated a violent uprising in 1967 against the landlords and moneylenders Charu Majumdar, inspired by the doctrines of Mao Zedong, provided ideological leadership for the Naxalbari movement, advocating that Indian peasants and lower class tribals overthrow the government and upper classes by force. A large number of urban elites were also attracted to the ideology. In 1970s, the Naxalites gained a strong presence among the radical sections of the student movement in Calcutta Students left school to join the Naxalites. Naxalites took over Jadavpur University. Their headquarters became Presidency College, Kolkata.The Naxalites found supporters among some of the educated elite, and Delhi's prestigious St. Stephen's College, alma mater of many contemporary Indian leaders and thinkers, became a hotbed of Naxalite activities.

The Naxalite movement of the late 1960s and early 1970s left an indelible mark on Mahasweta Devi's sensitive mind. In an interview, indicates this movement the first major event that inspired in her, "an urge and an obligation to document" (Bandyopadhyay XII).

The play *Mother of 1084*, a translation of her Bengali original "Hajar Churashir Ma" by Samik Bandopadhyay, is a proper documentation of her inner urge, feelings for the marginalized wrath against running evil, corruption, cruelty, power game and patriarchy in contemporary society. Originally written as a story for the periodical Prasad in 1972 and adapted for the stage by the writer herself in 1973, it grew into a full-scale novel a year later in 1974. It is a play about "the awakening of an apolitical mother" - Sujata Chaterjee, a traditional apolitical upper middle class lady, who is awakened one early morning by a phone call and informed with the shocking news of her son Brati, lying dead in the police morgue bearing the corpse no 1084. This leads her to make a post-dated venture to her son's revolutionary activism resulting in her own alienation from the family and the society which, though outwardly complacent, is cruel, violent, hypocritical and bourgeois to the core.

Cruelty, violence, inequality, gender discrimination have been themes of her writings. Most of the protagonists of Mahasweta Devi's works, take the help of violence when they realise that their vocal criticism against this rotten, corrupt society is capable of making any difference. She seems to advocate violence to make a change in this society. In her works violence is given a Marxist interpretation and all her characters come from the marginalized section of the society-women, refugees, outcastes etc. *Mother of 1084* of Mahasweta Devi does stand apart from the rest of her output, in more ways than one. Unlike some of her earlier short narratives such as *Standayini, Draupadi and Gohumni,* which are focalized around the tribal women, this particular play is centred on an upper middle-class, bourgeoisie, "apolitical" woman.

The play is a true reflection of the contemporary society which is rotten to the core. The play is a mixed bag and captures the maladies of our society through the portrayal of different characters who are the products of this society. Violence, gender discrimination, *inequality* cruelty are intertwined in the play like strands in a rope. The diseases are inseparable in the play and runs throughout the play through every character.The title itself is tinged with the colour of cruelty. The title Mother of 1084 hints the sad lot of the mother of someone who is marked with the ignominious number 1084 and denied of basic respect, mere importance of a human being, and being called by the name given by his or her parents.

The play *Mother of 1084* moves around the character of Sujata Chaterjee, a middle-aged woman belonging to a so- called 'bhadralok', bourgeoisie Calcutta family. Born into a conservative, affluent family, Sujata is allowed to do her B.A. so that it helps her marriage prospects, but is ultimately married off to Divyanath Chatterjee, a Chartered Accountant, despite the fact that his financial situation is far from being balanced. In thirty-four years of their married life, Sujata gives birth to four children, two sons (Jyoti and Brati) and two daughters (Nipa and Tuli). When the novel opens, two of her children are already married, Jyoti to Bina and Nipa to Amit. In the eyes of the world, all of them are leading a perfectly happy or at least a complacent life. But as Sujata goes on to discover later, this happiness is only skin-deep like the present condition of our 'all quiet' society. Sujata makes this and several other such discoveries only after the sudden and mysterious death of Brati, her younger son, with whom she had always shared a very special relationship. She discovers that all of thirty-four years of her married life, she has been living a life on lies. Her husband, being an incorrigible philanderer, always cheated on her and worse still, his children's tacit approval. Moreover, it is the discovery of her importancelessness in the family.

Mother of 1084 is a story of Sujata's multiple oppressions within a familial, patriarchal and feudal social order, and rightly it should be read as a story of how Sujata moves out of her cocoon of social respectability and civilized façade, only to discover the little known, primitive, underground world of the Naxalites or that of her son, about whom she knew very little while he was alive. Going beyond, it's also a story of how an "apolitical mother", ultimately pushed over the threshold, is compelled to recognize the basic human need to formulate or re-formulate her moral/political or ideological position in a crass narcissistic, utterly commercial world of 'bhadraloks' such as Chatterjees. If it's any indication of what Mahasweta actually wanted to communicate, I'd like to believe, her position is unambiguously clear. It's only in the process of formulating or defining one's moral/political, ideological position that an individual could possibly hope to heal several inflictions of oppression, or prepare himself/herself to fight the mechanics of 'oppression' at personal or collective level, thus paving the way for self-liberation.

From the beginning to the end, Sujata is treated as an unimportant object. The question in the very beginning of the play, "Dibyanath Chaterjee's house?"(683) marks the age-old dominancy of male over female. The line re-presents and reasserts the well known society where people never think of knowing a family by the name of its female member. The situation becomes complete when the voice over the telephone seeks a male member to betray the news of Brati's Brutal murder. "Is there any male member around?" (683), reflects our typical characteristic of accepting women as tender and unworthy making vital decisions or receiving shocks.

Sujata was neglected in the family by her husband and even by her sons and daughters. The following sentences reveal very clearly how much she was neglected by her husband him:

> Sujata: (uncomprehending, in a panic). What will you hushup? What are you talking about?
>
> Dibyanath: Jyoti, there is no time to waste. He goes out.
>
> Sujata: Jyoti! (Jyoti busy in dialling a number. She does not reply) Jyoti!
>
> (Reproving) Jyoti! What's happened? (684)

Nobody pays a heed to her appeal or even give a minimum response to her quarries.

Her husband bothered to consult his son Jyoti about Brati's death rather than his wife, Sujata. Dibyanath remains oblivious of Sujata's presence, and his comment, "There is no time to waste" is suggestive of the right Sujata enjoys not in her family. Even Jyoti, her son, is hostile in his "Yes" (684) as if forced to reply her mother's minimum and natural quarries on her son's death. Diyanath is not ready to share merely a word with Sujata, but blames her before the Kapadias for spoiling Brati: "Bad company, bad fiends, the mother's influence" (708).

In spite of having a full family Sujata is all alone. She is not asked for a single time when her daughter Tuli's date of engagement was fixed. There is none to take initiative to hospitalise her and her pain of appendix goes unheeded though Dibyanath is promptly sent to yoghurt the moment his masseur left. Nobody take care of her. What everyone takes special care of is pinching her directly or indirectly in Brati's name. Her emotional attachment for Brati is source of embarrassment for other members of the family. Tuli, who is of her own gender and could easily be her 'comrade' threats- "I hope you'll behave normally with Tony's friends." Her realization– "I am all alone" is more than true and reflects the position of women in our society where women remain alone in family throughout her life. In her father's house she is separate as a part time member preparing to go to father-in laws house after marriage. After marriage she becomes an intruder in the family. She must abide by the rules and duties other groom's family. And when she becomes the senior most women in that family; she is treated just as a housemaid without any importance and luxury of minimum right.

Sujata is cornered in the family. She finds a certain relief in meeting Somu's mother or Nandini, in whom she smells the memory of Brati. She comes to understand the ideal Brati was following.Dibyanath, Jyoti, even Tuli, who are the representatives of the rotten society, makes Sujata's surroundings claustrophobic. Each time she visits either her own past or that of Brati, Somu's mother or Nandini, her long-suppressed personal loss, her grief is slowly released into the ever-widening, eddying spirals of collective framework of betrayal, guilt and suffering.

Her insistence on wearing a plain, white sari for the party is also a significant gesture. being physically weak diseased, (for a few years, she had living with a rotten appendix inside her system), and traumatized by her younger son's death and subsequent repression of grief, she simply gives up. Outraged at the manner in which his associates, his immediate family and the state have abandoned the dead Brati, Sujata decides to go, throwing all pretensions ,false social respectability and the fear of public censure to winds .When she screams and collapses into a heap, her husband is quick to speculate that her "appendix" has burst. Whatever the symbolic overtones of his statement, she certainly succumbs to the slow process of inner and outer rot and decay.

Brati, the absent protagonist of the play is Sullenly rebellious, right from his childhood, He had made no secret of his disregard and contempt for the existing social order, his familial code and value-system. Turning his back upon this decadent and defective moral and social order of which families are miniatures, he decided to join the Naxalite movement sweeping through the State of West Bengal in late 1960's and early 1970's.

He is someone who had dared to be different in this rotten world based on greed, cruelty, fraud and betrayal and ultimately fell a victim. Unaware of his secret mission, Sujata was not even able to dissuade her son from taking the 'odd path'. During his period of struggle, he came into contact with a young girl, Nandini, a member of the underground movement and with whom he shared his vision of a new world order. Brati's dream for a new world was left in dream. Being betrayed Aninda , one of his comrades and natural product of our corrupt society, , Brati and three of his close associates, Somu, Partha and Laltu, are brutally murdered by the goons hired by police and divested of his identity as a person, and given another 'dehumanized identity' as corpse number 1084. Brati was no criminal, as his only crime was that he refused to accept the code of a decadent society. As Sujata also realizes that death is the only punishment for those who lose faith in the system.

The play is also a sad tell of Nandini who lives death- in-life burdened with the wound of toture, both physical and mental. Nandini Mitra, daughter of Suryakumar mitra and student of Presidency College is Brati's beloved besides being co-fighter in their mission. Unlike Sujata Nandini from her initial appearance is thoroughly political in her outlook Inspite of belonging to upper strata of the society she could associate with boys like Somu, Laltu and Bijit who belonged to the poor refugee families. Nandini is the representative of the undercurrent violence and cruelty in so called "All's right with the world" society. Sujata's illusion, that remained even after the death of her son, was shattered when she met Nandini, the burning figure of those "thousand young men rot in the prisons without trial" (29-30) and undergo limitless torture. The way she has been tortured by Saroj Pal by putting burning cigarette on her cheek, making her almost blind and many more, as Nandini tells "That was the beginning" and "I won't be able to tell you all that happened after" (P 705), epitomises the ruthless torture and violence one has to face in the police lock up, especially when she is a woman.

Dibyanath Chaterjee, husband of Sujata and father of Brati, is the true representative of the patriarchal society. Though husband, he never loved Sujata; only lusted after her and was willing to impregnate her with child after child, but was never around to own up responsibility for her. Soon after marriage, he had begun to run a secret liaison with a typist in his office, for whom he had later rented out an apartment, too. As a result, all her children were born out of a combination of lust, hatred and self-recrimination.

Dibyanath does not care for Sujata and dismisses her basic importance that she deserves as a mother in the family. He uses his wife for his benefit and to quench his lust. He fixed up a petty bank job for Sujata when Brati was barely three years old; it wasn't out of any consideration for her economic independence, but essentially to help the family tide over a temporary financial mess.

Dibyanath is a true representative of those elite class people who are ready to sacrifice their family bond for their social status and so called name and fame. When he hears the news of Brati's murder not only does he refuse to go, but he also forbids other family members from doing so. He tries to hush up the tragic incident of his son's death and violets the duty of a father by betraying no emotional response when Somu's Father, who belongs to the lower strata of the society that is not dried up of emotion yet, tries to resist her son's death and dies out of shock.

Saraj Pal, Deputy Commissioner of Detective Depatment, is another flag bearer of the rotten society. He represents the police force that could unleash ruthless atrocity on the prisoners in the name of investigation and plot the butchery of revolutionaries without considering the legal action. Anindya, the Judas of the play is symbol of betrayal which is also a characteristic of contemporary society. Tuli, Neepa, Amit, Dhiman, the minor characters of the play are the product of the society. The have adopted themselves with the ways of the rotten world and knows how to enjoy life being opportunist.

The play, though revolves round the police repression of the urban Naxalites in West Bengal, is thus a true representation of the contemporary society. It is a true exposure of the social system and Mahasweta Devi has successfully lays bare the ulcers of our "all-is-well society".

Bibliography

Basham, A.L.: *The Wonder That Was India*, Rupa Co., New Delhi, 1987.

Chakraborty, Kaustav: *Critical Perspective on Mahasweta Devi's Mother of 1084*, Dipali Publishers, Malda, 2007.

Deshpande, G.P.: *Modern Indian Drama: An Anthology*, Delhi, 2009.

Bandyopadhyay, Samik: *Five Plays*, Seagull Books Pvt Ltd, Calcutta, 1986.

20

Conflict of Gender and Power Politics in Parenting: A Feminist Study of Mangalam

Praggnaparamita Biswas

In the mirror of sociological scholarship, the conflicts of gender and the related power politics in parentage appears as a major issue within feminist thought. Gender is a much used and abused concept. The subsequent power politics due to gender role makes enough convolutions in the process of parenting. The patriarchal outlook of father-headed family always takes advantage by replacing the motherly importance. The age-long conflict of relevance for father-mother's impact on children's socialization theorizes the psychological debate of the bonding between parents and children. Poile Sengupta's play *Mangalam* deals with this problem of parenting in which matri-authority is more powerful than patriarchy and due to this reverse subordination masculinity is on the verge of humiliation. The compulsory heterosexuality dramatises a different out look in which male encounters the shame of centrifugality in family affairs due to his penury and tries to get back the authoritative power by means of violence and control on reproductivity of his wife. Thus, the play exemplifies the obnoxious game of power politics caused by gender difference.

However, it is frequently said that gender is a matter of 'social construction' which hub on the ways in which men and women learn to be masculine or feminine that is fabricated by society. More precisely, by using this phase, it refers some norms of society particularized for men and women. From the very childhood, in home, we are trained by elders to what to do as a girl or boy and what are not suitable to them. In brief, the birth of our sexed body immediately fixes a tag along with its entrenched beliefs, code and conduct customs etc. on us. Thus, society formulates a particular criterion before us for playing the exact social role according to our sexual identity. This is the fundamental trait in gender formation. Here, it is important to mention that our acquired biological sex is a stable one, but 'society given' gender is volatile one.

Materialist aspect of feminism pays much attention to the structural features of the social world in which men and women are fitted into distinct societal pattern. It puts emphasis on concrete social relations through work, family, sexuality and so on. Being influenced by the Foucauldian idea of discourse and its dovetailing with feminism, gender theorists try to explore the man-woman encounter in terms of discursive apposition. Materialist feminists give more attention to our gendering position within social institutions and organizations, but ignore gender as an aspect of subjectivity. In materialism, the system of power and control are interrelated to shape the social relations. The goal of materialist feminist is to locate oppression in terms of complex matrix of gender, class, race, ideology etc. and to identify the historical roots of such oppression in order to transform society. Feminist analysis about social relations of gender lies in the fact of women's subordination and inferior position to that of men that causes the exploitative and oppressive gender discussions.

The Marxist concept of class, thus automatically converges with sexual classes in which man and woman figure as distinct social grouping bound together in antagonistic social relationships of gender which have a material basis. This material reality of gender differences give rise to social practices that produce and reproduce gender inequalities. In his prolegomenon to *The Origins of the Family* (1884) Frederick Engels uses the materialist method to underpin the stage of development of labour of female folk: their labour for child bearing and rearing, unpaid domestic chores and sometimes low wages at workplace. All these systems of female body and female sexuality are regulated by the organisation of patriarchy and make a sense of male dominance and women subordination. This kind of compulsion felicitates the proliferation of capitalism, both for the male and the state. Thus, female body and sexuality function as a 'state apparatus' for establishing social institutions and at the same time paves way for gender disparity in society.

In discussing gender and power relation, the complex web of patriarchy is closely associated with it. Marxist feminists describe patriarchy as an ideological and psychological structure in which women's position is a consequential ideas formulated by society and gradually leads to its capitalist organization. Again, socialist feminism views patriarchy as generating its own set of material social relations. French materialist feminist Monique Wittig points out the institution like marriage along with its consequential heterosexuality is the basis of women's oppression. She suggests that 'the category of sex is the product of heterosexual society in which men appropriate for themselves the reproduction and production of women and also their physical persons by means of the marriage contract' (Wittig). But common belief is that in patriarchy woman is pushed to the margins but in matriarchy she belongs to the central of system. In reality, matriarchy has always remained as a theoretical alternative and has never been practiced. Though sometimes we get a few flicks of matriarchy but the family administration has always been monitored by any male from matrilineal side. So, replacing of patriarchy by matriarchy is a mere shifting of the oppressive structure from the margin to core.

Actually gender as a concept has a peculiar relationship with power politics. The one and only condition of patriarchy is male supremacy i.e domination on women. The system of patriarchy accelerates through some existing institutions like family, matrimony and female reproduction. Patriarchy is deeply rooted in men's control of women's productive and reproductive labour. It is necessarily related to power. It necessarily incorporates and sanctions an unequal distribution of power which helps maintain the status quo of oppression. Man is born with a male gender privilege and the organization of patriarchy is locus where he can exude his superiority. In Foucauldian theory, "patriarchy is the name of a global effect of domination made possible by a myriad of power relations at the microlevel of society" (Sawicki: 59, 1991).

Indian woman playwright Poile Sengupta in her play *Mangalam* talks about the problem of gender and sexual difference in the domestic domain. Her invisible female protagonist Mangalam, a dead mother is on trial of family court and unable to escape harsh criticism from her husband who continuously castigates about her pre-marital chastity. Even after pathetic demise, her husband accuses her as a whore. During her lifetime she was an object of repugnance as well as an object of sexual violence because the sadist husband Dorai made her pregnant every year to see her turmoil. He used the sexual violence as a medium of vengeance because of his inability to establish himself as the family suprimo. The problem lies with the fact that due to a gender tag, a woman should be cautious of everything throughout her lifetime, especially about her virginity; while a male is allowed for anything according to his wishes. So, while femininity is a matter of prestigious vigilance on virtuous virginity, masculinity instead is a way of exuding his virility. The question of sexual or gender difference seems prominent when Dorai individually claims all appreciations related to their children but quickly imposes allegations upon his wife in case of wrong deeds by their offspring. It is as if, Dorai as a father does everything alright for bringing up the children while Mangalam as a mother is a negligible one in rearing up them. Dorai just intentionally tries to ignore the spousal contribution of his wife in the process of childbirth and caring. The equation of three 'm' – marriage, mothering and motherhood, turns into an ultimate zero in formulating the marital life of Mangalam. The great irony of her fate is that even death can't provide her a little bit of relief. She is dissected in her family laboratory through the deeds and misdeeds of her children.

Male domination over female body and sexuality is a part of power politics. Power as a dimension of gender, comes central to women's liberation concept of patriarchy. The social analysis like man as a dominant sex class and rape as an assertion of men's power over women depicts female folk as passive. The bureaucratic institutionalization of power relations has been operating through women's sexual history, marital situation, domesticity, child bearing and caring. Exegesis of some scholastic articles provide the argument that patriarchy is concerned with the control of the wife's labour in the family and the wife's sexual fidelity and procreation by practicing the institution of marriage. The concepts of production and reproduction have been closely associated with the labour force, biological reproductivity, sexuality, domestic chores of women in order to give an analysis of how patriarchal society makes grip upon the production of female labour force alongwith its reproduction capacity. By utilizing the advantage of male gender, man like Dorai sucessfully attempts to master on Mangalam's reproductive labour. This is an instant of power politics.

The play *Mangalam* can be interpreted from the point of blasphemous maternity. Mangalam, a dead mother of a south Indian Brahmin family, was a victim of childhood sexual abuse at the hand of her sister-in-law. Her America based intelligent son Sriram is the result of this unintentional blunder. But, through the tricks of her rich father, she then knots the wedlock to an honest but poor Brahmin Dorai. In spite of all sufferings and ill treatments of her life time, she never discloses the name of her abuser which creates a gradual irretrievable rift in their marital relation. While she tries to maintain a grave like silence about the past scandal, Dorai becomes more violent towards her, even criticizes harshly for her whoredom. Being an il/legal father of an intelligent son like Sriram, Dorai feels a filial affection and proud of him, but ashamed of his own daughter Chitra's elopement. He accuses her as the carrier of her mother's genetically impure heredity of prostitution. Mangalam never achieves any recognition and admiration as a mother of Sriram, but easily desecrate as a mother of Chitra. Thus, throughout the play we can visualize the devaluation of maternity and its aftermath in family life. The significant of the play lies in the fact that the teenage sexual violation of Mangalam haunts her dead spirit, even her mothering of a boy-child like Sriram, has failed to trace back her feminine dignity and chastity in the eyes of her clan and society. As a (m)other she is always the victim of 'symbolic' phase. She is the scapegoat of social taboos imposed by patriarchal society.

The womanish journey of Mangalam begins with full of incident and accident. At the very beginning of her puberty, she was the victim of childhood sexual abuse at the hand of her drunkard sister-in-law. The bachelor but pregnant Mangalam has got married to a poor Brahmin Dorai Subramanian for both maintaining the family respect and hide the secret. But the marriage immediately turns into a nightmare for her part. During her life time she never gets any love, respect and affection from her husband who always makes her pressurized for disclosing the name of her abuser. But it is too difficult for a lady to utter the name of abuser relative as it is not only related to her personal shame but also closely associated with her elder sister Thangam's life and above all to her family name and fame. To avoid the individual and collective trouble, she gradually becomes the victim of her masochism and husband's sadism. In the view of Dorai, she was already "*touched...not one decent man would have touched her* (109)... *She come to me after being used, she was somebody else's leavings*" (121). Being a 'touched' one, she is twicely outcast from society. Because of patriarchal background, a lady like Mangalam has easily stigmatized for conceiving the child in out of marriage relationship, while a man is beyond the question of physical purity, even if he has slept with other women out of marital relationship. From Dorai's point of view "*It's different for a man*" (121).

The childhood sexual blunder of Mangalam creates a great impinge upon her spousal life. Dorai's random nagging and curiosity about that particular 'person' creates the situation more critical for Mangalam. But his effort has gone into vain before the adamant nature of her. The thirty-one years of her marriage, she has suffered a lot to hide this person. Her torturous life comes into light through the words of the two witnesses Revathy and Thangam, her daughter-in-law and elder sister respectively. The extreme hatred of Dorai transforms into vulgarity, perversion and vengeance. His strategy of coercive sexuality with Mangalam enhances the suffering to a great level. The continuous agony due to excessive childbirth weakens her both in physically and mentally. "*He gave her children year after year so that he could see her suffer, every night, he made her suffer*" (119). The unhappy marriage of Dorai inspires a malicious sense of power controlling attitude in his psyche. The coercive sexuality or marital rape is the malign version of his personal vengeance upon Mangalam. The somatic need of matrimonial relationship replaces with a vicious sexuality for them. The female body of Mangalam is a site where Dorai exercises his perverted masculinity. The female body politics of sexuality thus appears in bipolarity: the Foucauldian concept in which power is often seen as a possession and the Marxist model through which power denotes simply as a form of oppression or repression. The coalition of these two interrelated 'power' trap manipulates the menace of spousal martyrdom for mangalam. This endemic suffering also includes with wife battering. The nail and hand marks of Dorai upon her body are the proofs of this marital violence. Thus, the enactment of marriage is an utter failure in Mangalam-Dorai relationship. The bitterness of their conjugal life makes him obsessed even after the demise of Mangalam.

Apart from this troublesome marital violence, the mothering also arises a crisis in Mangalam's life. The god gifted motherhood seems as a loop for her. Sriram, her first boy child is a result of unwanted sexual misapprehension; in a word an adulterine in the society. But, being an intelligent and immigrant of America, he is the proud of Subramanian family: his bastardness is overlooked by the clan and society. His intelligence and diasporic inhabitance serve as a social ladder for Dorai's upgrading in his surroundings. By fathering such kind of son like Sriram, Dorai's credit is being estimated in terms of patriarchal criteria. But all these achievements of her son don't make any support for erasing the 'scar' of her 'kiddult' fallacy. Though she bore and breed such a beautiful son, still she remains an unrecognized in society. Her mothering is stigmatized and labeled as a perpetual 'other' by the taboos of patriarchy. It is as if the Karna-Kunti episode repeats in modernized version. The grand mistake of Mangalam is her by-born womanhood and so she must be the subject of subordination. While Sriram flourishes as a prosperous one, all credits go to his father Dorai and it does not matter whether he is legitimate or not. In this business, the motherhood of Mangalam is out of question. This is the irony of our male biased society.

Just opposite picture has been projected in case of mothering a female child. Chitra, the legitimate younger daughter of the spouse Mangalam-Dorai, exemplifies this discrimination. Before completing her college education, she has absconded with a non-Brahmin boy by going against the family decision.

Dorai's expectation nips in bud. His own daughter's elopement and subsequent inter-caste marriage makes him white in anger. In utter frustration, his pent up anger finds a violent outburst: "*My sons are fools and my daughters are prostitute... The whole town is laughing at me. She has thrown mud on me, that wretched girl* (108). Abusing his own daughter as a whore, he degrades himself in the nadir of humanity. It is the ample proof of his inadequacy and inability to maintain the contrivance of family bonding. His escapism tendency to avoid the harsh reality is the provocation to throw the arrows of accusation towards his dead wife Mangalam. The charge of Chitra's elopement goes into Mangalam's responsibility as it is Dorai who bitterly says to Kannan: "*Do you know...from where your sister learnt her whoring? From her mother. From your mother.*" (110). His misogynistic attitude and bias for castism projects him so narrow minded before audience and even he is not ready to accept the newly married bride-groom; rather he pronounces: "*The girl is dead*" (112). It is the interesting aspect of our society that while a boy achieves the name and fame, he easily inherits the stamp of 'father's son', but in case of a daughter, if she tries to free herself by breaking the conventional social norms and chains, she is immediately labeled as her 'mother's daughter'. This is traditional theorization of any patriarchal society. Dorai is not exceptional from it. While the (il)legitimate son Sriram after the foreign settlement cordially becomes '*His son*', but after the elopement of Chitra, his own daughter transforms into '*Her daughter*'. Thus, Dorai always tries to establish his fatherly grandeur by subsiding the essential motherhood of Mangalam.

Actually Dorai is the stereotype representative of patriarchal society. The maternity, maternal feelings etc. don't have any meaning and sensation in his dictionary. As a man, he is too much materialistic in his unconscious. He has almost hypnotized by the perfume of wealth of his father-in-law. He never tries to free himself from this cage, rather involves himself more with it. He stays in dilemma. After getting informed about the pre-marital pregnancy of Mangalam, he has no sympathy, amity or soluble mentality, rather becomes more violent towards her. A sense of deceitfulness broods over his mind. In this mental irresolution, to quell his revenge, he exercises the physical, psychological and sexual torment towards his wife. To her, the frequent childbirth due to excessive ravish emerges as a kind of punishment in guise of maternity because it reflects only the sexual perversion and blind rage of Dorai, not any emotional attachment and intimation of the spousal relationship. His thought of self-entrapment by dint of Mangalam's father's socio-economical status, makes him more inferior to himself. In order to avoid all these complexities, he finds satisfaction in the foul domination of 'sexual body politics'. He never pays any respect to her womanhood, rather criticizes her like this: "*She was a whore...nothing but a whore, a high class prostitute*" (122).

Thus, throughout her life time, Mangalam's childhood abuse haunts her like a ghost. It acts like a mother of all irritation in her marital life. Being impregnated in unmarried condition, she has to marry a person who is just a foil to her personality and social status. Due to this unequal marriage and her personal tragedy, she becomes mentally shattered. Even the mothering of children is not sufficient to recover her lost identity, chastity, and femininity. The blow of regular violation transforms her into a masochist one. She tries to hide all her pangs and silently welcomes the hug of death. She becomes alienated, marginalized Other within her own house. Mother Mangalam turns into an Other Mangalam in her natal-marital family. Her disastrous childhood error dealt the *coup de grace* to her motherhood. Her innocence and ignorance are fatally interrelated for her immature tragic end. Her death brings no lamentation to her husband Dorai, except reminding the past scandal more widely. In spite of a matriarchal ancestry, Mangalam is the social victim of concurrent patriarchy. Here lies the ambience of Indian sociology. Through the characterization of dead mother Mangalam, Sengupta depicts the fate of Indian womenfolk.

The stage version of the first half of the play tries to display what is going to happen in the second act. Here we come to visualize the same kind of power politics but in different version. The dramatic characters of first act are here playing the role of real life family members. In this story we can see the recurrent issues of extra-marital affair, sexual exploitation of which thangam and sumati are the respective victims. While finds the fact that her husband is carrying with someone else, thangam decides to leave him. But unlike her feminist protest or resistance, her daughter seems not so strong to shun off her mental trauma. The fear of loss, deprivation, sexual torture always envelopes her mind as initially she was ditched by her fiancé and eventually she is the victim of molestation. After watching the yester-night drama, the discussion almost takes into action in this household. Only difference is that, here thangam is victim of her husband's fraudulence. So, condition is almost same both for mangalam and thangam. Both of these mothers serve for their husbands, children to run the family, but their ultimate achievement is zero. Both are destined by abandonment of their respective husbands. Patriarchal framework of family only sucks and squeezes them into nothingness.

Thus, a holistic picture collected from this play, projects highest degree of female exploitation within patriarchal frame. Though terminologically parenting is a matter of mutual sharing between father and mother, but the truth is that all credits go to father inspite of his less contribution in bringing up the children. The unpaid labour of female reproductivity is always profitable for family and the state and hence, is a nugatory matter. Domesticity including child caring never gets much attention in sociological survey. In fact, it is a trick of patriarchal pedagogy, otherwise gendering of power politics will come into existence. However, feminist intervention in parentage pays enough respect for mothering and struggle for further mutual sharing of parenting to bring gender equality.

References:

Sengupta, Poile: *Mangalam*, Calcutta: Seagull Books, 2000.

Ferguson, Ann: *Motherhood and Sexuality: Some Feminist Questions*, Source: Hypatia, Vol.1, No.2, Motherhood and Sexuality (Autumn, 1986), pp. 3-22, <http://www.jstor.org/stable/3809893>, Blackwell Publishing.

Sawicki, Jana: *Disciplining Foucault: Feminism, Power and the Body*, New York: Routledge, 1991.

Moitra, Shefali: *Feminist Thought: Androcentrism, Communication and Objectivity*, New Delhi & Kolkata: Munshiram Monoharlal Publishers Pvt. Ltd., in association with Centre of Advanced Study in Philosophy Jadavpur University, 2002.

Contributors

Anjan Dasgupta, M. Phil, Assistant Professor of English, Gour Mahavidyalaya, West Bengal (Fulbright Fellow, John Hopkins University, USA).

Arindam Ghosh, Ph. D Research Scholar, Visva-Bharati .

Arpita Dasgupta, Assistant Professor of English, Parimal Mitra Smriti Mahavidyalaya, West Bengal.

Asit Kanti Sarkar, Assistant Teacher in English, Shalbari High School, West Bengal.

Bolla Jyothsnaphanija, Ph.D Research Scholar, English and Foreign Languages University, Hyderabad.

Grishma Manikrao Khobragade, Assit. Prof. of English, Birla College, Kalyan, Maharastra.

Jaydeep Sarkar, Ph. D., Assistant Professor of English, University BT & Evening College, West Bengal.

Joy Mukherjee, Assistant Professor of English, Dinhata College, West Bengal.

Joydeep Bhattacharya, Assistant Professor of English, Kurseong College, West Bengal.

Kaustav Chakraborty, Ph.D., Assistant Professor of English, Southfield College, West Bengal.

Sk. Lutfar Rahaman, Ph.D, Associate Professor of English, Katowa College, West Bengal.

Nitai Saha, Ph.D, Assistant Professor of English, Munsi Premchand Mahavidyalaya, West Bengal.

Pathik Roy, Assistant Professor of English, St. Joseph's College, West Bengal.

Pinaki Roy, Ph.D, Assistant Professor of English, Malda College, West Bengal.

Praggnaparamita Biswas, Ph. D. Research Scholar, Benaras Hindu University.

Supriya Debnath, Assistant Teacher in English, Jarabari High School, West Bengal.

Susan Lobo, M.Phil, Associate Professor of English, St. Andrew's College, Bandra West, Mumbai.

Swati Roy Chowdhury, Assistant Professor of English, Sarsuna College, West Bengal.

Sutapa Saha, Associate Professor of English, Surya Sen College, West Bengal.

Tapashree Ghosh, M. Phil, Assistant Professor of English, South Calcutta Girls' College, West Bengal.